SERMONS

ON

LIVING SUBJECTS.

BY

HORACE BUSHNELL.

NEW YORK:
SCRIBNER, ARMSTRONG & CO.,
1872.

R. H. HOBBS, ELECTROTYPER,
HARTFORD, CONN.

ADVERTISEMENT.

In selecting this volume of sermons, I have not been swayed by any desire to give them a common character, as related to some common subject, but I have allowed them to be strictly promiscuous; that is, to be what they will be, taken each one by itself. The title I have chosen, not as giving in to that faulty kind of preaching which makes it a principal aim to be handling subjects, but because every printed sermon must have a subject, and when offered to the public, ought to have some reference to the living questions and practical wants of the times.

Quite a number of the discourses have been preached in the Chapel at Yale, and in several cases I have preferred to let the special marks remain, without taking the necessary trouble to remove them, only noting the fact by a Y. C. C. at the bottom of the page. Two of the discourses, the XVII and the XXII, have never been preached.

H. B.

CONTENTS.

XII.

SELF-EXAMINATION EXAMINED.

XIII.

HOW TO BE A CHRISTIAN IN TRADE.

XIV.

IN AND BY THINGS TEMPORAL ARE GIVEN THINGS ETERNAL.

XV.

GOD ORGANIZING IN THE CHURCH HIS ETERNAL SOCIETY.

XVI.

ROUTINE OBSERVANCE INDISPENSABLE.

I.

MARY, THE MOTHER OF JESUS.

"And the angel came in unto her and said, Hail thou that art highly favored, the Lord is with thee; blessed art thou among women."—*Luke* 1: 28.

WHAT an angel may count the most blessed and dearest lot of favor to befall a spotless and fair young woman, will not of course coincide with what her mortal well-wishers, even the best of them, might choose. Probably the being entered into such a story as the angel here opens to Mary, in a strain of high congratulation, would be regarded, at the time, by scarcely any one as a thing to be at all desired, whatever estimation might be had of the honor conferred, after ages of history have shown the stupendous significance of the event. Mary is at first confused and troubled, "casting in her mind what sort of salutation this should be," and her heavenly visitor has much to do to compose her fluttering breast. And how shall he do it more easily than by telling her that what she will receive is God's reward. "Fear not, Mary, for thou hast found favor with God." He does not say, observe, that the favor of God has found her, but that she has found favor with him. The expression, it is true, may be used in either way, to indicate what God has undertaken to do for her, or what she has obtained by the suit of her gentle, sweet-minded prayers. It is most naturally taken in this latter way; giving us to see how she has been waiting before Him, from her tender girlhood onward, asking of Him grace for a good life, and questioning His oracle as to what she is to do, or to be. She has read the prophets too, as we may judge, and her feeling, like all the religious feeling of her nation, is leavened in this manner, by indefinite yearnings for the coming of that wonderful unknown being called Messiah. And so her opening womanly nature has been stretching itself Messiahward, and configuring itself inwardly to what the unknown Great One is to be. Sighing after him thus, in the sweet longings of her prayers, she is winning such favor, and becoming inwardly akin to him in such degree, as elects her to bear the promised child of the skies, and be set in a properly divine motherhood before the worlds! Ah yes, Mary, canst thou believe it? that which the prophets of so many ages drew you into praying for, that which angels in God's highest and most ancient realms have been peering from above to look into, that for which the fulness of time has now come—that special thing of God's counsel, supereminent forever, his greatest miracle, his unmatched wonder, his one thing absolute, which lets nothing ever come to pass that can be put into class with it—even that thou hast gotten a call from God to mediate for the world, bearing it as thy

Holy Thing, the fruit of thy sweet life and maidenly prayers.

I do not undertake, of course, to say that Mary's prayers, however freighted with longings after Messiah to come, had really prevailed with God to be incarnate, but only that she drew to herself, by her singular trust and pure spotlessness of devotion, what was to be by some one, and came to her more fitly than to any other, because of the finer, more dear quality found in her life. But that she won this honor does not take her out of the class of women, or entitle her in any sense, to the honors of worship. It lifts her truly enough above all woman or even human kind, and shows her touching the zenith in the sky of God's honors, where no other mortal ever touched before, or probably ever will in the future ages. Still when we say, "other mortal," in this manner, we call her mortal too.

There has been a large recoil of unbelief, as we all know, from these first chapters of Matthew and Luke, reciting the birth-story of the incarnation. How comes it, many ask, and some of you perhaps are in the question now—how comes it, if this be any proper history of facts, that it is made up by a sifting in so largely of poetic material—legendary myths, and half-recollections in verse? These good people, having no specially poetic gift, talk poetry, all, as if it were their element. When Mary, on a visit to Elizabeth up in the hill country, enters and offers salutation, she breaks out, on a sudden, in a hymn of benediction. Whereupon Mary, in turn, responds in her famous *magnificat*, occupying ten whole verses of the story. Next Zacharias celebrates the birth of John, in a hymn of praise and prophecy. Then the angel, coming down to notify the shepherds that Christ is born at Bethlehem, can not do his errand without putting it in verse. A grand irruption of angels follows, filling the sky with song and holy gratulation, which they too put in Hebrew verse. Next comes the aged Simeon, chanting his *nunc dimittis* over the divine child in the temple. Anna the prophetess follows, giving "thanks to God," in words not given, but understood to be in verse.

What account now shall we make of this? First, there is, we must observe, so great facility of verse in the Hebrew and Syriac tongues, that minds but a very little excited almost naturally break into the couplet form of utterance. Next the incarnation itself is an event so auspicious and glorious, that every body knowing it ought to be taken by some great mental commotion, lifted by some unwonted inspiration. Any most common soul ought to kindle as in flame, and break out in poetic improvisings. Having wings in the religious outfit of our nature, it would even be a kind of celestial impropriety, if God's Spirit did not spread them here. Why the very ground ought to let forth its reverberated music, and all the choirs, and lyres, and ringing cymbals of the creation, between the two horizons and above, ought to be discoursing hymns, and pouring down their joy, even as the stars do light! It looks very strange to me now, that I once hung a long time over the scandal matter of these poetic episodes; till finally I found grace to make the discovery, that they are exactly what and where they ought to be, and that, instead of doubting, I ought even to be believing, just because of them. They are, in fact, proprieties only of the incarnation; for what have we in it but the very nearly one event of the world? This of course any one may doubt if he will, but no sane person, I think, can deny that it is either a transaction so great, or else it is nothing. It may not be a fact, but if it is, which is the exact matter here assumed, it can not be less than what these incidents and demonstrations signify. Furthermore, I will even dare to aver, that the manner of this incarnation story is natural, as it could be in no other possible way, and is cast in a form of the strongest possible self-affirmation. It comes to pass in just the only way conceivable, or credible. Thus if there were no divine election here of the mother, no annunciation to her of her office, nothing but a birth, whence coming or how she could not explain; or if it came in wedlock unhymned, bringing no evidence but the remarkable quality finally to be discovered of the child; or if it were a possession taken of some full grown man, to be divinely empowered and set on by the visibly deific forces bodied in him; who could ever become certified of an incarnation accomplished under any such conditions? Besides, the very word itself implies a visible insphering in flesh, and how can that be accomplished without a birth into it? and how that, without a divine overshadow to quicken and matriculate that birth? In short, there must be a Mary in the process, or it will not be done. And then just all the wonders of story and music of song that were staggering our faith, are seen to be only the proper all-hail, or fit salutation of the advent made.

At this point my subject, which is Mary the mother of Jesus, takes a most remarkable turn that we might not have expected. Suddenly, as it were at once, she drops out of improvising, out of song and singing joy, into a very nearly total and dumb silence; giving us to hear no spoken word again, save in a very few syllables and but twice in her whole after life. The *magnificat* she chanted in the hill country was her last, as it was her first, improvising, the swan song, as we may call it, of her life. She and her husband, "marveled," we are told, "at those things that were spoken" of the child, in the scores of hymn and music offered for him in the temple; and at that point they dropped into still life, as it were by paralysis, never once to speak of their extraordinary son, or testify any least impression of his remarkable person, or story, or gifts, or office. Things were occurring, no doubt, every day, by which he was differed more and more widely from all common children, and by which they were partly dazed or confounded. They began very soon to feel themselves overtopped by the altitude of his questions, and the superhuman affinity of his sentiments. Still they could only say the less of his demonstrations, that they had connection back with his miraculous story, of which they could not well permit themselves to speak. But to hint the feeling growing up in the house, as he best knows how, the evangelist represents that the child "grew and waxed strong in spirit, filled with wisdom, and the grace of God was upon him." His being noticed in this way before he was twelve years old, indicates a mysterious, extraordinary something growing visible in him.

Meantime Joseph and Mary, without indulging any fond talk about him as their prodigy, did what they could to give him the rudiments of an education. They at least taught him to read. And when, afterward, he rose up in the synagogue, where, as we are told, it "was his custom" to attend, and had been doubtless from his childhood, he went forward to the sacred chest for his manuscript, and turned directly to the Messianic promise of Isaiah, as being already well versed in prophecy, and began to read, saying, "this day is this scripture fulfilled in your ears." And so far had his education been carried, when he was but twelve years old, that he was already entered into the great questions of the doctors, and was so profoundly taken by their high discussions overheard in the temple, that he must needs have a part in them himself, asking questions of his own. All which he did, with so little appearance of pertness, and such wonderful beauty of manner, as well as in a tone so nearly divine, that they could only be "astonished by his understanding and answers." And there next day he was found by Joseph and Mary, when he should have been a whole day's journey on his way back with them to Galilee. They remonstrate with him only in the gentlest and most nearly reverent manner, and have nothing more to say, when he answers—"How is it that ye sought me? Wist ye not that I must be about my Father's business?" Whether he had somehow gotten hold of the fact that he had another father who was not Joseph, or had simply grown out into the mysterious feeling of some life-business, under God's spiritual Fatherhood, we do not know. But the dear dumb mother had been learning, all these years, to have her conceptions of him outrun by his own merely childish conceptions of himself, and what could she say? He probably sometimes violated her religious notions, by such liberties of sentiment that she was disturbed. And yet her very disturbance ran up into summits of reverence to his worth and beauty so high above mere childhood, that she dare not boast of him and could not do better than bow her spirit and be still. "But his mother kept all these sayings in her heart"—not the single saying just recited observe, but all the like sayings of his wonderful childhood. Observe also that she did not keep them in her memory, or her understanding, or her diary, but in her heart—that well of silence in the bosom of true motherhood, where all freshest, purest waters are kept fresh and pure. Infiltered these and stored by loving thought, they are not vaporized and shallowed by much talk, and seem to be only the sweeter the deeper fill they make. Her family story she can not carry into the street, or even speak of with her friends. And things are occurring with her Jesus every day, in which the st.mps. and signatures of his divinity are distinctly ar.d even visibly manifested, but which can not be advertised without becoming tokens of weakness in the mother and precocity in the child. She sometimes wants to even strike a song of triumph, like Miriam coming up out of the sea, but her loudest only not absurd song will be silence—a hymn that she keeps hid in her heart, as she does all the sayings and great acts of her wonderful son.

Possibly some may be harshly enough tempered, to hint the suspicion, that her silence, after all, is but the natural token of her impotence and want of character. She keeps still, at all points in the story, it may be thought, because she has nothing to say, and is in fact a person too unpositive and too drearily thin-minded to be affirmatively capable of any thing. If so it is most remarkable that in her beautiful one hymn, "My soul doth magnify the Lord," she displays the full timber of an orchestra, sailing out in exultations high and strong, boasting in God's arm that has scattered the proud and their vain imaginations, swelling in great sentiments that are possible only to some grand patriot father, some hero of God's cause and kingdom. After such high force displayed, is it by the poverty of her nature that she is silent? Besides, we have another token of her talent that is not less convincing. There was a very delicate question to be settled between her and Joseph, before the marriage could be consummated. And the wonder is that she could hold him still to confidence, by any utmost power of mortal address. A weak woman would have quite talked down her evidence, torn it even to shreds by her protestations, washed it clean away by her tears. But she stood firmly instead and composedly by her integrity, and bore her sweet innocence in a way of self-affirming truth so manifestly evened by the consciousness it gave, that neither she was flurried in her modesty, nor he by his misgiving. It is true that Joseph was instructed in the matter by a dream. But how difficult a thing, in such a case, to authenticate the dream—as we see that Mary was in fact able. For the angel of the Lord, coming to a man by a dream, is but a feeble witness, compared with the angel of innocence and truth, in a woman, who has visibly felt no shadow upon her, but the overshadow of the Highest. It may be that some other woman has existed since the world began, who, even innocent, could bear herself successfully through an ordeal like this, but of that we may very well doubt!

Besides we must not omit to notice the wise, deep gravity of this woman in the matter of her silence itself. Self-retention is the almost infallible token of a considerately deep, strong character. Weakness runs never to this, but always to unthinking clack and rattle. No great life, like the life of Jesus, begins at such a motherhood. Good sense and a closely considerate silence are its necessary conditions. Had

Christ's mother been a forward and loud woman, advertising always her miraculous child, reporting his strangely phenomenal acts, repeating his speeches and telling what great expectations she had of him, it really seems that she might have quite spoiled his Messiahship. At any rate he must have undertaken his ministry at an immense and almost fatal disadvantage. Just as any most nobly endowed son, will scarcely be great, or make any but a partly absurd figure in his endeavors to be, who is thrust on greatness by a noisy and ambitiously prognosticating mother.

Accepting these terms of wise repression, her motherly great sense and piety are kept busy by the questions of the child, requiring to be shown how the Heavenly Father feedeth men and birds alike: what the very little leaven does in going through her whole three-measure baking of bread; why her patching economy forbids putting new cloth into old garments; how the tiny mustard-seed grows large; why an old penny looks so fresh that has been found by sweeping out all the litter of the cabin; whether the lordly house over opposite, undermined and pitched headlong, by the terrible water-spout poured down the trough of the hills, had not been much better founded on a rock? So the glorious child, seizing common things by their inmost sense, is getting packed full of parable for his great teaching day.

He is now a man thirty years old, when the report arrives of John's preaching down by the Jordan. Hasting down at once to hear him, and approaching to be baptized, he is saluted by him strangely, on sight, in the crowd—"Behold the Lamb of God that taketh away the sin of the world!" The consecrating dove descends upon him, and he is sealed for his call by a word of sanction from above—"This is my beloved Son, in whom I am well pleased." He is verily come now into his Father's business. Yes, he is to be Messiah! and the discovery breaks upon his mind like a storm upon the sea. By which Spirit-storm he is hurried off into the wilderness, to consider and get his bosom throes quieted and his thoughts in train for the great strange future before him. For this and nothing else was the significance, the devil we may say, of what is called his temptation. And when this is ended, when his mind has gotten itself composed and adjusted, he goes back to Nazareth. The same that he was, he still is, yet how completely changed by his call, and the new great life he is now to begin! He is graduated forever as the Son of Mary, but nowise graduated as in love; for that he will never be. He finds her not at home, but away at the little village of Cana, back among the hills, where she is gone to attend the festivities of a wedding, at the house of a relative. Receiving an invitation that was left for him he goes up to the wedding himself. And there we are let into a new chapter, at the very hinge of his public life, and the new relation he is to have to his mother. The general impression is that he breaks off from her in a sense, at this earliest moment, reprimanding her with a good deal of severity, for what he considers to be her forwardness and officious meddling.

The wine of the feast gave out, as it would seem; whereupon the mother tells him, "they have no wine;" as if expecting of him just the miracle he is going to perform. At which Jesus turns upon her sharply, saying, "Woman, what have I to do with thee? my hour is not yet come." She pays, we notice, no attention to his rebuke, as she certainly would if she had felt the severity we do in it, but goes aside to the servants telling them to wait his orders and do whatever he bids them. She has no idea what that will be; but she evidently hopes that he will somehow make up the deficiency and permit them to go on with the distribution.

Now the first thing to be said of this supposed reprimand is that the salutation, "Woman," sounding harsh and hard in English and very nearly insolent, will be quite delivered of its harshness by just observing that no such bluffness of meaning is implied in the Greek, but that it is a form of address constantly used in salutations altogether affectionate. We have a case exactly in point, where Christ himself addresses his mother from his cross in this very salutation—"Woman, behold thy son." But the words that follow—"What have I to do with thee," have just as little of reprimand possibly; for they are words capable of all varieties and shades of temperament in the Greek idiom, the most harshly blunt and the most tenderly cordial; while in English they are nothing but a blow in the face. The Greek words, literally given, are simply—"What is there to me and to thee?" the words "to do" being stuck in to make up the English idiom. And the question, "What is there to me and to thee"—what concern that is common—may mean either "do not put this matter in my way," "do not push me with untimely suggestions;" or it may mean, harshly spoken, "let me alone;" "I will have no part with you." Taking the softer sense of the words, and adding the clause which follows, the Saviour only says, "let this matter, woman, be for me, I can not begin now—my hour is not yet come." But his hour had come nevertheless, even the hour of doing his first miracle, as we straightway see. And the remarkable thing about the speech, in which he is so commonly thought to be hard in rebuke upon his mother, is that it signifies nothing of the kind, but is only what he lets out in the recoil of his feeling, at the moment, and is passed away the next moment, as a cloud passes off the sun. "The beginning of miracles to be made even here—verily I can not begin! How can I launch myself on this Messiahship? This awful world-burden, how can I take it up?" And yet he took it up! and the dreaded break of his beginning is just here made!

The assumption that Mary has somehow come into his secret plan about the wine, and is letting it out here by a kind of untimely and officious meddling that displeases him, is unpardonably coarse and heedless. She lets out nothing, she does not bolt upon the guests in the announcement that "the wine is out!" but she simply says to Jesus, privately and apart, "they have no wine." And then his reply to her is also private of course. Neither are they low enough in their manners, to violate a wedding scene by any such indecent behavior as the open altercation here ascribed to them, by many commentators, would certainly exhibit. Besides, if Mary had any quality honorable above all others, it was in the closeness of her prudence, and the title she got to the confidence of her son, by keeping all he said and showed of his advancing story treasured in her heart. Keeping him sheltered in this beautiful confidence, she had a largely open state with him for her dear reward.

And yet we can see from the cast of this dialogue and story that something had transpired, giving it the turn it discovers in the matter of the wine. Perhaps we can not tell what, but we are at liberty to imagine any thing most convenient. Thus when Christ came up from the Jordan, after his probably two or three months absence—after the baptism, after the call, after the temptation—his mother, we will say, observed a remarkable change in his appearance. He seemed like one borne heavily down, by some unknown burden. When they were apart by themselves, she probably enough expostulated with him; whereupon he told her exactly what was come upon him; viz.: to be himself the Messiah of the prophets! Which again led them to go over, in their conversation, what the prophet Messiah is to do and to be—all the ministries he is to perform for the poor, the sick, the broken-hearted, and the oppressed, all that he is to suffer, as the Lamb of God in the taking away of transgression, according to Isaiah's recital in his fifty-third chapter, and according to John's staple idea, just now given, in his salutation at the baptism; so to set up the Kingdom of God among men and call the Gentiles into it, as the saving grace of God for all mankind. Most natural it was, in this recapitulation, to strike on that beautiful call of Messiah, when his work is done, "Ho every one that thirsteth, come ye to the waters, and he that hath no money come ye, buy and eat, yea come, buy wine and milk without money and without price." Why this, said Mary—this wine—is festivity, and you must not have your heart oppressed by a mission so glad. This free-gift wine makes a wedding-day of your Messiahship, and what are we here for, but to see the beginning of it? So they talked the night away, it may be, and why shall we not see, in the frequent recurrence of this image of the wedding, in the Saviour's parables afterwards, how deep an impression the prophet's wedding call had made upon him. And to-morrow it will come out, in the miracle of the wine, that Jesus and his mother had been somehow, or in some such way, approaching a point of expectation here. We do at least discover how little reason there may have been for the reprimand of Mary by her son, in the matter of the miracle; how innocent she was in the liberty she took, and how little thought he may have had of any reprimand at all. There is no reprimand, save under the English idiom.

Let us look a moment now at the home basis Mary has provided for Jesus, in the prosecution of his ministry. She has, besides him, four sons, and probably three daughters. It has been long debated, whether these are Mary's own children or only cousins taken by adoption, or possibly children of Joseph by a former marriage. I will not undertake the question. Let it be enough that these children ought to be Mary's, to complete the incarnation itself. For if she must needs live and die in churchly virginity, lest she bring a taint on her divine motherhood by maternity in wedlock afterward, her incarnation office even puts dishonor on both wedlock and maternity together. Or if she must save her son from being own brother to any body by his incarnation, what genuine significance is there in the fact? The debate is visibly instigated by some ascetic, over-dainty scruple, as regards the true honors of marriage and a mortal blood relation.

The ministry of Jesus shortly brings him round to Nazareth, where he is set upon, at his preaching, by the fanatical rage of his townsmen, and compelled to flee for his life. Mary can not give him up to the lot of a wanderer, but hastens after him down to Capernaum, where the whole family are soon established in housekeeping for his sake. Probably they had a very little property, else why did Mary and Joseph go up to Bethlehem for the taxing? The four brothers too appear to be now earning a support for the family. Still, having no purse when out in his ministry, Christ can only throw himself on the public hospitality. But when he comes back to Capernaum, as he is doing every few days, it is pleasant to know that some of the more frugal comforts are allowed him at his mother's house, and that there, at least, he can find where to lay his head and be a son at home.

But we ask to see the inside picture of this home. There was never on earth a family composed of material more diverse in the assortment. There are two heads in it circled with a halo, and seven that are not; one is the Sacred Child or Man, the other a Woman made sacred by his miraculous sonship. As regards the seven, there is evidence that one of them at least, "James the Lord's brother," had a large fund of power in his gifts. After the martyrdom of James the apostle, he won the apostleship by his personal merit and force of character, and presided wisely and well, in a most difficult time, over the great metropolitan church at Jerusalem. There was vigor enough doubtless in the four unsainted sons, to maintain them at cross purposes always with their elder sinless brother. But Mary was happily prepared for the molding of these ill-related elements, by the fact that her motherhood feeling to Jesus was unlike that of any mere natural mother to her child. She bent over her Holy Thing with religious awe and not in mere fondness. Her love worshiped, as it were, with the Magi, when they came with their gifts. And her silent, almost reverent respect towards Jesus, connected with no manner of partiality, put him always in their respect, and made him a kind of benignant presence among them.

Of course they had their human thoughts about him, such as were not always just or wise. Perhaps they were a little tried, or put on some hard speeches, by his dropping out of work, and throwing over the care of the family on them—as if he had found something better to do about the country than the duties of the eldest son at home! And yet he was their wonderful, strange brother, held in constant respect and, to tell the truth, in real admiration. Thus we have a scene given us and a dialogue, that, if we may judge, passes inside of the house, and shows all the brothers together. The great feast of tabernacles is about coming off, at Jerusalem, and the brothers going up—for they are all so far religious—urge it specially on Jesus to put himself forward now in his impressive demonstrations; so to let the public men of the nation see what is in him. For if he is perchance the Great King, Messiah, what may he not possibly do for their advancement! Their argument is—"For no man who has merit keeps it secret, but seeks to be known openly, and shows himself to the world." And the evangelist adds—"For neither did his brethren believe in him." He does not mean that they are spiritual rejectors, in that sense unbelievers; for that is an idea not yet born. They are willing enough plainly to believe, but he is a riddle to every body, the Messiahship itself is a riddle, and even John the prophet reels incontinently out of his faith. In their over-politic advice there is no ill nature. They even count on going up to the feast in company with him, hoping there to witness some great success, that will justify their admiration and mightily bring on the family. James, the future apostle, has been practicing in this prudentially contriving way from his childhood onward, as he will yet again show at the great council at Jerusalem; and if Jesus had been a debating character, policy and principle—the two worlds represented in the house—would have been crepitating always in their two kinds of electricity. But his way no doubt has been always, to hold the dialogue of the house a little way off, and save it thus from becoming a wrangle. So we see him contriving here—repelled and hurt as he is by their counsel—to set his clever brothers off on their religious journey, without him. How can he go up with them, thinking all the way, as reminded by their presence he must, of the high figure he is now expected to make!

In this glance at the mother's family we see them all engaged for him and with him, and if they do not believe in him, they will stick fast by him, we can see, in dearest and most faithful love. As she actually did, following him to the cross and staying unflinchingly by him in his awful hour; and as she and they together also did, still holding on upon his unknown future, after his horrible death had blasted seemingly all further hope in it; gathering in with his apostles, to wait with them the coming of his unknown promise—they alone to be specially named in the roll of the little apostolic assembly, "*Mary the mother of Jesus and his brethren*"—conspicuously honored in that record as the head family thus of the kingdom.

How absurd now is the discovery, put forward by critics who are willing to let down the personal honors of Mary by setting a stigma on her character, that about this time she joins the church party against him, and heads a kind of family conspiracy to get him under constraint. Christ has been pressed all day by multitudes in and about Capernaum, teaching them in successions of parable, and healing their plagues, and has not even found time to so much as eat bread. And now, at last, word comes to Mary, that he has been cornered and rushed into a court, where he is completely hedged in by the multitude or mob, raging madly against him. The family hasten thither, greatly concerned for him, and what is specially uncomfortable, fearing that he is finally getting quite beside himself; for his extraordinary sentiments and strangely unconventional utterances, exceeding even the eccentricities of genius, have been keeping them always in this kind of disturbance, till now they are quite unwontedly concerned lest he is becoming lunatic; a fear that is increased by the charges of foul possession, that are being debated by the multitudes inside of the house. Now the representation is, that his family are come down to the place "to lay hold of him;" but what are we to understand by that? They are certainly not absurd enough to think of seizing him by violence in that crowd, or we absurd enough to impute any such design. The natural and proper conception is that they are come to bring him off by their friendly remonstrances, or half-compelling importunities, requiring him, as it were, to go home with them and rest, and take his necessary food. They send in word accordingly, that his mother and family are without, desiring to speak with him. Perceiving at once the over-tender concern that has brought them hither, instead of going instantly forth at their call, he finds opportunity in it to say to the multitude about him, that he is here among men, as in a large and most dear family. And who is my mother, and who are my brethren, but you all here present, who can do the will of God? "for whosoever shall do the will of God, the same is my brother, and sister, and mother"—such and so great is the dear blood affinity with mankind, into which he is born. The whole significance and beauty of the appeal is, from family affection to the broader affection of God's universal family. There is nothing to be blamed in what Mary is here doing, and Christ blames nothing. To say that she is here with her family posse to seize and drag away, is a libel too absurd. Besides, it is a most sorry detraction from all dignity of sentiment in the lesson Christ is giving here, to imagine that he draws it from his displeased feeling; saying thus—"I drop these faithless relatives, and turn to you, hoping to at least make brothers of you, since these desert and betray me." The impeachment is too sharp, to allow any look of attraction, in the universal brotherhood relation thus severely commended. A family quarrel stands in winning connection with nothing so grandly fraternal.

Mary's behavior at the cross fitly ends her story. On the way out a great company of people follow, comprising many women who go to bewail him, and make up the procession of mourners. Mary, the mother, was deep enough in mourning, but she could not join that noisy company, and it does not appear that the other two Marys, Magdalene and the wife of Cleopas, were in it. At first, when the cross is set up, and the suspension made, they are with the mother at the cross. But we shortly find them in a larger circle of women, looking on from a point farther off; having floated away thither unconsciously, perhaps, in the swing of the crowd. Mary, the mother, is thus left alone, waiting there by the cross during all those dreadful hours, till Jesus dies. And observe she "stood," a word of strong composure. Her knees do not give way. She does not faint, or fall on her face. She does not toss her arms in shrieks and wild hysteric wailings; not allowing herself, when a scene so transcendent is passing, to make a scene of her own private griefs. Doubtless she remembers the word of Simeon, that went before upon her, when he said—"Yea, a sword shall pierce through thy own soul also," but there she stands, in the beloved disciple's company, holding fast the decencies of sorrow, as if the proprieties of the worlds were upon her! At length, when life is ebbing to the close, Jesus says to her, in the undertone, probably, of his failing voice, "Woman, behold thy son!" to him also, "Behold thy mother!" Under this last will and testament, she goes out silent with John, who takes her to his home. Why Jesus committed her thus to John and not to the four brothers, it is not difficult to guess; for John has a home as they certainly have not, and are not likely soon to have again. For the dreadful ignominy falling on the house in his death, he sees must utterly crush out and scatter the family. However, the expression "from that hour that disciple took her to his own home," is sufficiently justified, without understanding that she remained with him till she died, or longer than till her return back to Galilee. Besides it is to be noted too, that she and the four brothers are actually gathered family-wise, in the ante-pentecostal assembly. Where, no doubt, they all had their minds opened, under Peter's sermon, to the full discovery of what their Jesus had come into the world to do. And the scene was a kind of new birth to them all, putting them in courage again, and bringing them friends to help them by the ministration of abundant means, and a wonderful, unheard-of sympathy.

How long after this she lived we do not know. But we could most easily believe that when her mind was opened at the pentecost, to the meaning of her son's great mission, she was at once so astounded and exalted by the awful height of her relationship, that her soul took wing in the uplift of her felt affinity with the Highest, and was gone! But we have no such traditions. Possibly the suspicion that some were like to give her annoyance by the tender of divine honors, put her on ways of withdrawment and silence. The remarkable thing is that John has nothing to say of her, or to report from her—except, probably, the story of Cana ; for the conversation of that story being private between her and her son, could have been reported only by her, and is given by John alone of all the evangelists. If John had her with him even for years, speaking freely of what she knew, how many things could she have told him that we so much long to hear—the story of the nativity, at first hand, from her human point of view, in its due connection with her prayers; all the memorabilia of the wonderful childhood; all about the mind-growth and development of the child, or his advancing genius in the matter of character. And yet the apostle, beginning his gospel far back in the solemn arcana of the Eternal Word, and passing directly over Mary to speak, fourteen verses after, of "the Word made flesh," gives not so much as a trace of mention, concerning her maternal place and office in the story. Making no report of her conversations, he is equally silent as regards her death; telling never when she died, or how she died, or in what place she was buried. And it is well; for there was even a much higher necessity in her case, than in that of Moses, that her burial-place should be hidden from mortal knowledge. Otherwise it would be the center of a vaster idolatry than the world has ever known. The divine wisdom, too, as I think, somehow took her aside, with a set purpose not to let her mix her human-story products, beautiful and graceful as they were, with Christ's immortal life-word from above. About all we can say of her, therefore, under her embargo of silence, is that she appears until she disappears; which she does —most wonderful, most nearly divine of all human characters—in the stillness of a snow-flake falling into the sea.

But her disappearing from us does not bring her story to an end; it only prepares our final appearing to her, on a higher plane of life, where she will most assuredly be the center of a higher feeling than some of us may have imagined. Our pitiful mistraining here is assuredly there to be corrected, as an all but mortal impropriety. And when that correction is made, such flavors of beauty, and sweetness, and true filial reverence will be shed abroad, I can easily believe, in such loving and blessed diffusion, as will even recast for us Protestants at least, the type and temperament of the heavenly feeling itself. The true relativity of motherhood gets no place in us here, because we are in a prejudice that extirpates right perception; recoiling even from her person, as if that were somehow to blame for the dismal idolatries prostrate before it, and the mock-worship gathered in it to her shrine. Probably there was never any created being of all the created worlds, put in such honor as this woman, chosen to be the Lord's mother; all the more truly our mother, that, from her begins the new born human race.—"Hail, thou highly favored." "Blessed art thou among women!"

To her it is given, even to grow the germ-life of the Divine Man, Son of the Father, in its spring. And her behavior is beautiful enough to even meet an occasion so high. That grace of bearing, that sweet, devout modesty, such as became the motherhood of everlasting innocence; that watching of her miraculous boy, that could so easily be telling his wonders with a weak mother's fondness in the street, but which still she was treasuring in her heart; that wondrous propriety of silence at the cross, allowing her no wail of outcry in that hour, lest she might be making herself a part of the scene—O ye lilies and other white harbingers of spring, culled so often by art to be symbols of her unspotted motherhood, what can ye show of silent flowering in the white of purity, which she does not much better show herself!

We seem just now, in these modern centuries of Reformation, to be assuming that Mary is gone by, and the honors paid her ended; and if we choose to let our hearts be barbarized in the coarse, unappreciating prejudices that have been, so far, our bitter element, there certainly are finer molded ages to come. Is it too soon even now to admit some feeling of rational shame, that we have been weak enough to let our eyes be so long plastered with this clay? Doubtless it must be the first thing with us, after we have entered the great world before us, to get cleared, and assured, and at home in our relations to the Son of Man himself. After that our next thing, as I think, will be to know our mother, the mother of Jesus; for no other of the kingdom, save the King himself, has a name that signifies more. And I make no question that, when the great hierarchs and princes of other worlds and ages, who are challenged to pay their Hosannas in the Highest, throng in to meet us, they will ask, first of all, for the woman by whom, under God's quickening overshadow, Christ, the Eternal Son of God, obtained his life-connection with the race, and his birth into practical brotherhood with it. As the Sages of the east, guided by the star, brought their tribute to the child at her stall, so these ancients of God will come in with us, wanting above all to know the woman herself, at whose royal motherhood and by it, Immanuel, the King, broke into the world, and set up his kingdom. And higher still is she raised by the recognition of her son himself; for as she is yearning always fondly after him, so will he never disallow his old-time filial feeling towards her. Owning her never as in any sense the Mother of God, he has yet a mother-sense in him, that will be an Everlasting Sentiment, and apart from all idolatrous honors paid her by men, will clothe her with such honors really divine, as fitly crown the part she bore in his wonderful story.

II.

LOVING GOD IS BUT LETTING GOD LOVE US.

"And we have known and believed the love that God hath to us."—*John* 1: 4, 16.

By this it is, in other words, that we are different from what we were; and our thanksgiving is, that the love of God has found us, and begotten its like in our before unloving nature. It is not that we have volunteered loving towards God, bringing on the love ourselves, but that he is beforehand with us, and that, simply knowing and believing the love God hath to us, we so let in, or give welcome to it, that we have it reproduced in ourselves. Discoursing in a similar strain, in the previous verses of the chapter, the apostle declares our part in this change more negatively, but to the same effect. "Not that we loved God, but that he loved us." Also, "God is love—fountain, flood, and sea—and he that dwelleth in love dwelleth in God, and God in him." So that being immersed in God's love, we are saturated with it, even as our garments would be with water. We do not exactly take it by absorption, it is true, we give it space. We let God love us into love, which itself suffices, and carries all grace with it.

I propose then, for the present occasion, a truth which ought to be received most hopefully and tenderly by you all, and will be received with a specially eager delight, by any one who is struggling heavily with the burden of his sins, and does not find the way to cast them off. It is this—*That loving God is but letting God love us—giving welcome, that is to God's love, knowing and believing the love God hath to us.*

A very different impression prevails with many—sometimes with disciples themselves, but more generally with such as have come into no Christian experience. They suppose that something very great, and difficult, and almost impossible, is required to be done. Perhaps they have in mind the Scripture call, commanding them to strive as if they had a narrow gate to pass, to cut off right hands, to pluck out right eyes, to sell all, to forsake houses, and lands, and even to give up life itself. How then can it be they will ask, with such representations before us, that we have nothing more to do for the new love's sake—that which brings salvation—than to just let God love us? But they will have their answer by only observing how these throes, these seeming violences of self-renunciation are all in the way of giving room and welcome to God's love; because they are needed to clear away the barricades and obstructions by which we are always and habitually, though, perhaps, not consciously, fencing the love of God away. In one view this simply letting God love us appears to be a very slight and facile matter, as indeed it should be, but we have a way of making it fearfully difficult when it is not in itself and should not be. The difficulty is artificial, created wholly by the recoil of our own guiltiness. It is the lie we are in, which can not bear the truth. This will appear more fully as we go on to unfold the proposition stated.

1. I make it a point distinctly asserted that all men living in sin repel or draw back from the love of God, and will not let it come in upon them. It seems impossible that a truth so glorious for man, so grandly luminous, one that raises him so high as that God, the infinite Father loves him, loves the world that is made for him, flames all round the sky as a circle of day by his love—it seems impossible, I say, that such and so great a creature will not be so great, and will not let God love him. Yet so it is. I do not mean by this that we undertake to stop God's love, or actually command it away, but only that we ignore it, let it come on our back and not into our face or heart. We do not say "Go thy way," but we go our own way, and that means just the same thing. When we are required to love God, we consciously enough reject the requirement; but if it were given us as the really true version of it, that we are simply required to let God love us, we probably should not be conscious of any withstanding, or unletting hindrance, and yet we do withstand by a resistance so subtle that we scarcely know it, so intractable as to be fatally sure.

And the solution of the matter is, that we instinctively recoil and can not give the true God-welcome to God's love, not being at all in affinity with it. We see the same thing in our relations to one another. We never really consent to be loved by another whose ways, manners, character, are any way distasteful. Every affection we can not reciprocate creates a degree of revulsion in our feeling. If we are averted from another by our own fault, to know that he loves us, makes us for the time still more averse. And thus it is, how often, that God is only too good and pure and high, to be any but a visitor—unwelcome; because he wakens guilt and self-disgust, and is felt as a disturber even in his love, more than as a friend. As to letting in his love upon us, we do not want it, we desire not the knowledge of his ways.

Conceive the instance of a son who has fallen into ways of vice and profligacy. The sad thing of his condition is, that he does not like so much of the parental love, engaged in ways so many, and tender, and deep in sacrifice, to win him back to virtue. All such love comes to him as in qualms, and the very words, and promises, and tears, that should be eloquent, only raise a stifling smoke in his feeling, even as if they were but fumes of sulphur falling on hot plates of iron. Doubtless there is much goodness in the good father and mother, but the goodness offends him, and he will not let it be the appeal it should, because he is so possessed by his vices, as to have no affinity for it. And yet he can, or probably will have such affinity when his spells are broken. When the bitter woes of his vices, his lot of shame, his want, his all devouring appetite, bring his infatuations to a full end, as they may, and turn him back in sad relentings on the love he could not accept, you shall hear him bless himself in it, saying, "O it is all that is left me, I can not deserve it, I can never be worthy of it, or fitly return it. All that I can do is just to let it bathe me in my shame and hopelessness." His recoils are ended now, because the spells that were on him are all broken. Able now to say "I am no more worthy to be called thy son," the tendernesses that before seemed over-fond or foolish, melt a way through his memory, and the letting in of the old, once rejected love becomes a new, profoundly filial love in his bosom. Just so it is with all bad minds in their relation to the love of God. They recoil and close up against it. Doubtless it is good in God to be tendering himself in such love, and a certain sensibility is moved by it, still there is a revulsion felt, and no fit answer of returning love is made; where, as we can see, the true account of the matter is, that the love is unwelcome, because there is no want of it, or consentingness of mind towards it; which is the same as to say, that the man does not let God love him. That love would be photographed in him by an answering love, but he offers only his back to it. As if the artist at his camera were to put in nothing but a plate of glass, prepared by no chemical susceptibility, saying to the light, "shine on if you will, and make what picture you can." He really does not let the light make any picture at all, but even disallows the opportunity.

2. We shall be farther advanced in our understanding of this matter, if we observe how constantly the scripture word looks to the love of God, for the ingeneration of love in men, and so for their salvation. The radical, every where present, idea is, that the new love wanting in them is to be itself only a revealment of the love of God to them, or upon them. Thus the new born life is to be "the love of God, shed abroad in the heart by the Holy Ghost;" where we can not understand by the love of God, the disciples' love to God—that would be a salvation quite one side of the gospel plan, which proposes the unbosoming of God's love to man, that it may be shed abroad in him by the Holy Ghost, and become a salvation, as it begets, by the Spirit, an answering love. So again when it is declared that "Love is of God, for every one that loveth is born of God;" the meaning is not that God's love is of God, but that ours is of God—the love, that is, of every one that loveth. It is not a love created in us by some fiat of power, but a love begotten or born in us. So that when it is born, we are to say, "our love is of God," or more exactly still, "our love is of the love of God, a ray of the divine, kindling its warmth in us." So again, yet more expressly, the new spirit of love to our fellow man is ascribed to the love of God in us—"If we love one another, God dwelleth in us, and his love is perfected in us." To the same

effect again is the word of our apostle—"We love him because he first loved us." Our love is nothing, it is God who appears in his Son, declaring—"For God so loved the world;" and what we call our love is nothing but the warmth of that. Hence, too, the incarnation itself. It incarnates the love of God to melt a way into our love. "Hereby perceive we the love of God—" "In this was manifested the love of God toward us." The plan is to beget love by love, and nothing is left us to do in the matter, but simply to allow the love, and offer ourselves to it. There is no conception any where, that we are to make a new love ourselves; we have only to let the love of God be upon us, and have its immortal working in us. That will transform, that will new-create, in that we shall live. Consider again—

3. What tremendous powers of motion and commotion, what dissolving, recomposing forces come upon, or into a soul, when it suffers the love of God. For it is such kind of love as ought to create, and must, a deep, all revolutionizing ferment, in the moral nature. It is no mere natural love, such as the love of kind, or parentage; no friendship love, no love of merit, no merely approving love; but it is a thing how different, a disapproving, condemning, sorrowing, often a suffering, and in all the great Christ-story, a much abhorring, morally offended love. And here is the reason why we can not let it be upon us, or have its dear great way in us. It rakes up our bad convictions, it stirs our bosom disorders, it chokes our

remorse. And O what moral majesty is there in it, overtopping all we know of God beside, and casting its not baleful, but awfully oppressive and ominous shadow upon us. It melts in pity, it is tender as fresh rain, and yet, being so abhorrent, so deep in displeasure and moral offense, what will the letting of it in upon us, and the knowing and believing what it hath for us, and the true accepting of it—what will it do but scald, and shake, and decompose, and recompose every thing in us? The letting God love us in this manner—out of Pilate's court, under the crown of thorns, out of the cross—is not assuredly the making up of a merely smooth salvation. Love though it be, it is the silent artillery of God, a salvation that wins by a dreadful pungency; raising up conviction of sin, to look on him whom it hath pierced, moving agitations deep, stirring up all mires. So that when the love gets welcome, it has dissolved every thing, and the new-born peace is the man new composed in God's living order. Letting God love us with such love, is adequate remedy therefore and complete, and is no mere nerveless quietism, as some might hastily judge. Or if any doubt on this point may remain, I proceed—

4. To ask what more a sinner of mankind, doing the utmost possible, can be expected or required to do. Can he tear himself away from sin by pulling at his own shoulder? Can he pluck himself out of selfishness, or eject selfishness out of himself, by an act of his will? Can he clarify the currents of his

soul by willing that his thoughts shall flow angelically? Can he, by a mere self-weeding culture, clean out all the tares of the mind, and make it a garden of beauty, when it has no germ of God's planting to spring up and grow in it? Can he starve out his sins by fasting, or wear them out by a pilgrimage, or whip them out by penances, or give them away in alms? No! no! none of these. All that he can do to beget a new spirit in his fallen nature, we now come back to say, is to offer up himself to the love of God, and let God love him. He can be changed only as the ice of winter is, by letting the great warm sun shine from above into its crystal body, not by willing in itself to assume the liquid state. Or, to use a different comparison, as he can see only by allowing the daylight to stream into his eyes, so he can expel the internal disorder and darkness of his soul, only by letting the light of God's love fall into it. Furthermore, as he can not see a whit more clearly than the light enables him, by straining his will into his eyes, so he can do no more in the way of clearing his bad mind than to open it, as perfectly as possible, to the love of God.

Need I say again, to make this point more sure, that letting God love us, as we now speak, implies a great deal more than a mere negative surrender to it. There is no resistance to God that is more absolute, or in fact more effective, than that which we sometimes offer in the mere *vis inertiæ* of a self-indulgent, negatively resigned quietism. No, to let God love us means a great deal more, which I need not specify and could not if I would. You must be transparent to God, that he may shine through. All unrighteous practice, all ungodly habit, all self-worship and self-pleasing, all perverse lustings and envies opposite to God's love, must be cast out, else the love can not have room; and, to comprehend every thing, your prayers must fan your desires, waiting as porters at all the gates and windows of your feeling, to hold them open to God's day.

And then, again, it is vain to imagine that you can let God's love flow in, if you can not let it flow out. We must let the love we are to receive have free course, flowing through us, in such kind of works and lovings as it will naturally instigate. It must be allowed not only to beget itself in us, but to make us to others what God is to us. Hence the soul that is actuated or impelled by any kind of hatred or revenge, or that holds a grudge against another and can not, will not forgive him, can not really be said to let God love him; for God's love to him is a forgiving love, that bends in blessing and even bleeds over all enemies. If you have it, you must have it in its own divine properties, admitted, in them, to reign. And now it remains to say—

5. That when we come to accurately understand what is meant by faith, which is the universally accepted condition of salvation, we only give, in fact, another version of it, when we say that the just letting God love us, amounts to precisely the same

thing. For if a man but offers himself up trustfully and clear of all hindrance to the love of God in Jesus Christ, saying, though it be in silence, "be it upon me; let it come and do its sweet will in me; O there is nothing I can so much desire as to be loved by God, however abhorrently and disgustfully; this I will trustfully take and tenderly rest in, for it is all the salvation I want,"—plainly that is but letting God love him, and yet what is it but faith? In proposing it then as a saving condition, that we let God love us, we do not dispense with faith. We only say "believe," with a different pronunciation. Indeed there is no so good way of describing faith, as to make it convertible at every point, into the mere suffering trustfully of God's love upon us. Yes, O guilty one, let God love thee; yes, believe the love God hath to thee, and rest thy all eternally in it. Go thou to Bethlehem, and catch that hymn of worship that rolls along mid air, and down the face of the mountains—"Peace on earth, Good will to men." Rise ere the day breaks, and climb the solitary peak, where Jesus kneels apart and look upon the burdened love of his prayer. Overhear his words of gentle sympathy at the grave of Mary's dead brother, and note the gentler tears he drops at that grave, as being himself a divine brother mourning with her. Steal up the hillside, in the deep silence of the night, and watching there under the olives of the garden, behold the heavier night of agony that rests upon the loving heart of Jesus. Struggle up the street with him, as he goes out bearing his cross, and there behold the only beautiful unmarred spirit of the world, exhale itself in prayer and apology to God for its enemies—then say, "This is God—God so loved the world;" adding also something yet more personal, dearer and closer to feeling,—"who loved me, and gave himself for me." Strange then will it be, if you do not also love him, and are not quickened by him as by some new life loved into you; even as he himself was raised from the dead by the glory of the Father. This is your faith, neither more nor less; or we may call it simply your letting God love you, in the life and cross of his son. Be it one or the other, it is still the same. Enough that under this description or that, the love has gotten its just power in you, and settled its eternal indwelling in your hitherto unloving nature.

I conclude, then, after so many illustrations given, that loving God is no change beginning at us, but a coming rather of God's love upon us; where the utmost we can do is to simply let him love us, and give him unobstructed, everlasting welcome. How then is it—for this, in fact, is one of the chief wonders of our trial in the matter of religion—that we encounter in it so many insurmountables and impossibles?

Even they who have sometime seemed to take Christ's yoke and find it easy, forget how shortly after the sweet ease they enjoyed, and only have the yoke by itself. We find them sighing again for some more complete deliverance, asking by what throes and agonies, or by what mighty works, they may push away their condemnations, and come into liberty. They even wrench themselves in fierce endeavors often, with no result attained to, but a final despairing of deliverance till they are delivered of life itself. It is even as if they were lifting in mires that give way and let them deeper down. Who could imagine, looking in upon these desperations and faintings of mortal courage, that after all nothing more difficult is required of them, than to just be in the love God pours upon them, and about them. This indeed is difficult, but only because it is so simple and easy, that it can not be believed. Know and believe the love God hath to you, and you shall have all that you are willing to receive, more than you can ask or even think. You have nothing to do but to let God's love possess and fill you, which it assuredly will, even as it fills the great and wide sea of his infinite bosom.

The reason why your sanctification, brethren, goes on so slowly, probably is, that you believe so little, endeavoring so much, it may be, in yourself. If you believe that God loves you little, then, of course, you will love little. If you believe that he loves you much, then you will love much, and you will be changed or sanctified just according to the measures of God's love you receive. If you let Him flow in as a river, then your peace will flow as a river.

The only hard thing you have to do is to let him do what he will—to pour his love into you according to the exceeding abundance of his love.

At the same time it is here permitted us to say, that such as truly seek after God have no right to find any one of the difficulties they so often complain of. They are utterly baffled, somehow, in finding the gate, and can not enter in; and they even quote the words of the Saviour when he calls it "the strait gate," not observing that it is strait to them, only because they are so narrowed down in themselves, that they can not believe it to be wide as it is—wide even as the love of God. Nothing after all is required of them more difficult, than to just accept and welcome the love of God, as set forth in his Son. There is no penance prescribed, there are no deficiencies to be made up, no mountains of righteousness to be piled—nothing is required but to give free course to the love of God, and let it have its own renewing, divinely sufficient power.

Is there any tenderly doubting one present, groaning under the burden of his sins and the bondage of his evil life—what has he to do for deliverance? What but to simply know and believe the love God hath to him? This do, and he is free. O thou sorrowing, dejected, fainting bondman of sin, believe, believe, and thy chains are broken, thy burdens gone forever. The moment thou canst let God love thee, a new answering love kindles in thee, shed abroad there by the Holy Ghost.

And it is, accordingly, a very strange part of my duty here, to warn you, that a great many, who begin to seek after God, defeat and fatally obstruct their endeavor, by overdoing, unable to simply believe and let God's love be upon them; because that certainly can not be enough. Ought they not to be much afflicted, and suffer long, and heavily under their convictions? Must they not put themselves forth in immense self-endeavor?—must they not break in or out, by huge throes of will?—must they not repent hard and doubtfully, and take up against their repentances a long time, so as to be fitly commended to God by their thoroughness? Passing thus into their own will, to assume the charge and do the work of their own regeneration, they take themselves quite off and away from the revelation of God's love, as the Spirit waits and works to reveal it, and so they are defeated by their excess of doing. Thousands are beaten off from God in just this way. Overdoing, if I should not rather say over-undertaking, is even one of the most common hindrances to salvation. No! the most that you can do is to let God do everything; that is to offer yourself up to him in a perfectly, open, unobstructed state. Love is of God, and every one that loveth is born of God.

And yet, exactly on the side opposite, there are some who begin to seek after God, and defeat their own effort by a certain expectation of what would be overdoing on the part of God. They expect the Holy

Spirit to put omnipotence on them, and do the change they need, by an act of supreme efficiency. They forget that while God, in the department of mere things can do all that he pleases by his creative will and fiat, he still can do nothing in that way in the matter of character. He can pile the seas on the mountains, and lift the mountains into the stars, or hurl seas, mountains, stars, all together through space, as he does the light of the morning. But no such force-work can change the mold of a character. In the last degree every moral change must be wrought in us, through consideration, feeling, choice; that is by the sense and belief of what God is in his love. He can do nothing over and above what he does by his excellence, save as by his Spirit and Providence he prepares us to behold and be transformed by his excellence. To expect more of him, therefore, is fatal. And is not this enough? Should he over-do, in the way just described, he would only do less. If his love can not reach you, then you can not be reached. And if his love can not save you, then you can not be saved; for salvation is character, and love is the power by which only it is, or ever can be, wrought. O the perversity, blindness, hardness—apart from all thought of retribution we say it—that can not be gained by all that God has done, or does, or shows, or suffers, in his Son!

There is yet one thought standing off alone, as it were, that demands a right to be itself the conclusion of this subject. We are always thinking, or trying to think, that we have reasons, or half justifications, for not accepting God and religion. God we say is absolute, and we have insuperable difficulties in accepting any kind of absolutism. God again commands, and authority is not pleasant. He maintains a Providence over the world, and while we like to have the world well taken care of, there is a good deal in the method, which is satisfactory to nobody. God maintains a way of rigid and exact truth, and truth which admits no variation, tolerates no accommodation, is not agreeable. He is said to be everlastingly just, and justice is only appalling. His character they say, is infinitely, spotlessly pure, and the thought of such purity is not altogether welcome. He requires repentance for all wrong, and we can not humble ourselves to it easily. He is patient and we do not like to be endured by mere patience. He is commended to us as a long suffering God, which is no commendation to our feeling, for how can we like to be merely suffered by long suffering? So by these many considerations, one or all, we are averted from God. And we half convince ourselves that we are justified in them, at any rate they are reasons to us, and we indulgently consent to let them be. But here, as now we see, you add another and last reason, that God is moving on you by his love, and you do not like to be loved in the style of the cross. You turn yourself away from this, you are offended or put in revulsion by it, as by all the other so called reasons that are more severe. It may be good enough for God to love you, but you can not let him find you inwardly by it. Ah, that in this so perversely excusing mind you are going in shortly, to make answer before him. And there bringing forth your reasons—all the long catalogue just named, and especially the last—what face will you put upon it? Verily I can think of nothing so dreadful as that this bad mind, going in thither, is to carry in with it just what it is—able never hitherto to heartily welcome even the love of God.

III.

FEET AND WINGS.

"When they stood they let down their wings."—*Ezekiel* 1: 24.

It is the distinction of all flying creatures that they have a double apparatus, wings for the air, and feet for the ground. Accordingly they draw their feet up under them when they fly, and when they settle on their feet drop their wings at their side. Thus our prophet, in the words here cited, puts a touch of nature on God's cherubim, as if they, too, when they settle in their flight, must do it of course in a manner correspondent—"When they stood they let down their wings."

He intends, of course, no specially religious lesson here, but the fact he cites may be used, I conceive, with some advantage, to illustrate a very important subject of Christian experience, otherwise difficult to be effectively presented; also the related fact, that so many make up what they call a religious life, that has no really Christian experience in it.

I. The subject of Christian experience, what it is, and how to be maintained.

This nether element of ours, called Nature and the

world, is a kind of base-level on which we trudge, and drudge ourselves in our works, and take what grime of it we must, having faculties of locomotion, feeding, sensation, natural sentiment, and sense-perception, coupled with discursive understanding—by all which we act our parts on foot, as it were, and have our opportunity in the uses given us. Meantime, we have a higher range permitted us into which it is our privilege to ascend; with attributes of faith-perception, love-appropriation, spiritual imagination added, for the sensing of God and the taking of his revelation to live in it; in all which we become aerial creatures, so to speak, resting suspensively on things above the world, and ranging freely in them. And it is this glorious uplifting that produces the transcendent mystery of experience in Christian conversion. For the major, infinitely nobler, part of our faculty is here opened out for the first time into worlds above the world ; even as a worm bursting its chrysalis begins to fly, or as a balloon, when the cords are cut, leaps with a bound into the sky. O, what buoyancies of faculty now take us, all struggling upward after God! So that now, becoming spirit, and no more flesh only, the new inspirations lift us into quite another range of experience.

And the Word of Life represents this uplifting of souls in a great many different ways that are yet all concurrent. "Conversation in Heaven"—"Raised up together to sit together in heavenly places in Christ Jesus"—"Risen with Christ to seek those things that are above"—"Ye are come unto the Heavenly Jerusalem"—"They shall mount up on wings as eagles." The conception is that souls new-born "from above," as Christ speaks, are in this manner lifted above, and go clear of the foot-levels of the world and the mere natural understanding. The smother of flesh and sense is taken off, and they rise.

They were creatures of understanding and creatures in the higher capabilities of faith; but living in the understanding, in that always looking down, they saw the coarse, nether element only; so that when they come to open their windows on God by their trust in him—admitting the full revelation of his truth and friendship—they are taken up off their feet into a higher range of life. They sail abroad in a kind of upper-world liberty. Duty now is inclination; truth an infinitely serene element; perception broad as Heaven and full as the sea; and all the detentions of world-worship and lust are fallen away. They, as it were, only see the world, when they look far down where it lies.

All this by faith; because when we rest ourselves, our life and life-character on God, we prove him and have the sense of him revealed to our immediate knowledge. But this faith, it must be observed, is not, as appears to be very often understood, any belief in something about God which is not God; no belief in a proposition, or truth, or doctrine, or fact, even though it be an atonement made, or legal justification provided—these things are things round about, having, it may be, a certain relationship and preparative concern, but the faith is a wholly transactional matter toward God himself, and no mere creditive assent or conviction regarding something notional or notionally affirmed. It is the man's new, self-committing, trusting act, by which he puts himself out on trust, and begins to live suspensively on God, as every created spirit, whether under sin or clear of it, is made to live. It is a trusting of person to person, substantive being to substantive being, sinner to Saviour; in this manner it is in effect a sublime act of migration upward into the range of spirit, where it lives inspirationally, and has all things new.

Accordingly, just here begins the great struggle of Christian experience I am wishing to illustrate. Can the soul thus lifted stay above in that serene element into which is is ascended? Plainly enough, it is possible only as we keep good the faith, or, when it ebbs, renew it. It must be faith too still in the person of God or of Christ; not any faith in something about God and secondary only to what is personal in him. It must be such faith as lives derivatively from him, and bathes itself in the revelation or inner sense of his friendship. And precisely here—here and never any where else—is the difficulty; that the disciple has gravitations in him still, that pull him all the while downward, and settle him on his feet before he knows it. And then, as soon as he begins to stand, his wings are folded, of course. Even as the flying creatures fold their wings instinctively when they settle on their feet, having, for the time, no use for them. The moment he begins to rest on mortal supports, and find his hope in mortal good, he ceases in the same degree to live by faith. And it comes to pass so naturally or insensibly that he forgets himself. Let us trace some of the instances and ways in which it comes to pass.

He is a man of enterprise, and begins to think of independence; and the independent state that draws him on becomes, how easily, how insensibly, the non-depending state. His successes are honest successes. His economies are only rational and right. But he does not hang on Providence as he did, in a perpetually sweet, bright confidence. His prayers lose out their fervors, and his peace flows only as a turbid river. Even God is far less dear and less consciously present than he was. How long is there going to be faith enough left to have the consciousness of his presence at all?

Sometimes the disciple drops out of faith unwittingly, in overdoing the search after evidences of it. What should be that evidence but the faith itself, even as the day bring its own evidence; or, better still, as we get evidence of warmth by the immediate feeling of it, when we can not find the heat by any hunt of inspection or search beside. Suppose he finally gets the evidence of his divine calling made up. It is made up in his understanding, of course, and it might as well be made up by computations in arithmetic. He has, in fact, descended out of faith to get evidences that dispense with faith. He wants no inspirations longer, for he has made good his proofs. Henceforth he burns, if at all, without flame. He is down upon his feet, and has really undertaken to be a foot-passenger all through.

By a very common mistake, the disciple who is losing ground, instead of going back to his faith, puts his will into the struggle, and thinks to recover himself by his will. Fighting out his battle now by self-endeavor, he makes it a losing battle, of course. Defeated and discouraged, he knows not how, he answers, with a sigh, Am I not doing everything for success? Yes, every thing but the only thing, viz., to believe in God; that is forgotten. And what can he do by his mere will-force and resolvedness, when the heavenly trust is wanting? He might as well think to leap out of the Gulf Stream by the spring of his feet. The harder throes he makes, the deeper he sinks, of course.

Another class of disciples, of a naturally faithful habit, when their fervors abate, and their enjoyment of God ceases to buoy them up, seeing no help for it, subside, as it were dutifully, into a mere routine practice, or observance of times. They gravitate downward on regularity; consenting thus to a regulation service on foot, since it can no longer be a service in impulse and liberty. Unblest and dry, they are none the less punctual and exact. They mean at least, to be faithful; and they hope there may be some good in it, only of a duller sort than it should be. Perhaps there may; only how much better if they could be sure of some little faith in their faithfulness; which, if they had it but as a grain of mustard seed, would kindle, at least, an observable fire. Had their faith but a one-wing power, it ought, in the flapping, to lift them visibly a few feet upward now and then.

Sometimes again it happens, that a disciple who is losing ground, is taken advantage of by the plea of worldly conformity, and tempted to make his losing more complete than he knows. He thinks he can do more by a more winning address, that more readily propitiates favor. So he shortens the distance between himself and the world, that he may shorten the distance between the world and himself. He undertakes to be more human, expecting to be as much more Christian, and becomes, in fact, as much less Christian as he is more human. I grant the possibility of an over-austere practice, that may fitly be softened; but this study of conformities is a wonderfully delicate matter, which none but a man of inflexible tenacity should ever dare to indulge; nor even he, save as he is high enough lifted by his faith in God to suffer no bent downward, but in social recognitions, or Christian pity and tears. Cultivating the conformities is only a plausible way of being mired in them. Buying off the world by taking its manners, shows, fashions, and pleasures, turns out, almost certainly, to be a selling off to the world and joining it. A conversation above is the same thing as living above, and whoever undertakes to grade, and guage a smoothly fascinating, ground-surface road will, of course, be moving on the ground, and not ascending into faith at all.

To give one illustration more: it often happens, that a disciple thinks to steady and fortify his faith, by a more practiced investigation and deeper studies in matters of opinion. And it is not to be denied, that certain benefits may thus be gained. But the difficulty is that when he gets occupied in questions of the understanding, he is likely to be engrossed by them, and seek his light in them, having it no more by faith at all. Then, of course, he is down upon the levels of mere Nature. Hence the fact so often remarked, that young men going into theologic studies are apt to lose ground visibly, to the grief of many friends, in their piety. They pass into a sphere where scheme and system are building, and get stalled in the industry of the head. They forget that opinion builds from below, and undertakes to be a pillar by its own firm standing. We think, it may be, that we touch bottom, and get sure footing in it; but the fatal thing is that it is a footing more literal than it should be—a standing that is on the feet. We are going, as we think, to be kited or aerially floated no more, and will now have things in the solid. But our solidity turns out to be a living on the dry nuggets of articulated deductions, and not on the uplifting grace of God's inspirations. We settle thus out of grace into formulations of grace, when, of course, our wings are down. Would that a great many thousands of the more gifted souls could not find the meaning of this.

Our conclusion, then, is that all unsteadiness, wavering, collapse in Christian living, is caused somehow, in one way or another—for the ways are numberless—by dropping out of the simple first faith, and beginning to rest on supports from below. The moment any disciple touches ground with but the tip of his foot, and begins to rest himself but in part on earthly props, a mortal weakness takes him and he goes down. And there is no need of it. Nothing is more simple than this law of trust. God, too, is a being faithful enough to be trusted in at all times; and if the disciple is faithful enough to abide in his trust, he will abide in God, and have God's inspirations in him, move in God's liberty. If at any time he begins to subside, a calm and loving return to his trust will assuredly recover him. And he is not obliged, living in this key, to remit or let go any of his studies, or toils, or engagements. He will only carry himself the more steadily in them, and with less friction of disturbance, that his soul is rested in God by his faith. Sometimes it may be that his faith is shut in by morbid vapors, obscurations from disease; but then he has only to believe the more strongly, waiting for his obscurations to be cleared. He need not ever be troubled or put in concern by them. Even the sun has obscurations; but above them it abides in the tranquillities, and waits till it has burned a way through.

II. It will be seen by help of the same illustration, how it is that a great many persons who mean to be, and really think they are, disciples, miss ever going above a service on foot, by not conceiving at all the more ethereal range of experience, into which true faith would lift them.

They undertake, for example, to become reformers and philanthropists, and really believe that they are more superlatively, genuinely, Christian in it, than others who have more to say of experiences. They, at least, mean business in their religion; caring little, as they think they ought, for the fervors that are not fervors of work. Their argument, or operative power is commonly human opinion, and the combining and rolling up of great masses of opinion is the means by which they expect to carry their projected reforms. In such a mode of action, censure and storm and fiery denunciation are naturally close at hand; and are not much further off when they assume to be wielding most especially the motive principles of religion. They would be very much hurt by any reluctance to own them as disciples; and yet they do not even conceive themselves, many times, that they are disciples because of their repentances, or prayers, or the sensing of God by their faith, or by meekness, patience, or any other grace that separates them from the world. Their element is agitation, seldom any way of appeal that bears a look of Christian peace or repose. They have much to say of love; but they visibly hate more strongly than they love. Their very philanthropy is pugnant and oppugnant, and works altogether by that method. Sometimes the reform they are after is a good one, and is sorely wanted; which makes it the more sad that they must drive it by mere human force, going never above, to descend upon it by inspirations there kindled, but keeping their feet and warring with the evils to be removed hand to hand, on the same level with them.

Sometimes, again, there is a way of self-culture attempted in the name of religion, which is not in any proper sense religious, having no element of faith in it, and expecting no uplifting help from gracious inspirations. The self-culture is what a man may do upon himself; mending his defects, correcting his mistakes, chastening his faults, tempering his passions, putting himself into the charities he has learned, from Christ perhaps, to admire, finishing himself in the graces that have won his approval or commanded his respect. But the work is a far more hopeless one than he imagines, and is almost sure to result even visibly, in more affectations of character than are likely to be much approved. Besides, it holds him to a continual self-contemplation which is selfish, and keeps him all the while filing and polishing on his nature by his will; which is, in fact, the most wearisome possible, or rather impossible, kind of self-attention. The old faults conquered, too, will be coming back on him just when he is conquering another set. And, turning round to fight them off, he will find the whole swarm loose upon him again; till, finally, getting worried and vexed and soured and discouraged, he virtually, though perhaps not consciously, gives over his whole undertaking. O, if he could have gone up to Christ, or to God, in a true faith-culture, and let his faults fall off, as blasted flowers fall off the trees, dislodged by the life-principle in them, his beautiful thought of finishing a character would have been how easily put forward—without a care, too, and in the sweetest liberty. No man finishes a character who does not go above himself, and take the culture of God's own Spirit; by that growing out a character from within which can not be manipulated inwardly from without. If there be any good gift that cometh from above, and can not be made below, it is character.

Ritualism is another foot-passenger that having no sufficient conception of faith, has, of course, no better conception of the higher ranges of life prospected by it. There is, in fact, a gravitating principle in us all, that settles us down upon the ritual way when it can. Bound to have a religion of some kind, because we have a religious nature, we begin, almost unwittingly, to have one that is manipulated by our senses and sensuous tastes. We are caught thus by the forms. They are beautiful, and a fine-looking, comely religion they make. All the better that they are so nearly level with our natural faculties, and just as easy to be used without faith as with! These reverential rounds and airs, these priestly ceremonials—what a charm of worship is in them! How convenient, also, to have a religion that works *secundum artem*, and lets the faiths and fervors take care of themselves! Saying prayers, too—how much better and easier than to pray, and find how to be heard. Having gotten thus a good sufficiency of religion below, and settled their feet down squarely on it, they really think it a considerable improvement. But the sad thing is, that, instead of raising the disciple up in glorious inspirations, and giving him free wing, they humble him and keep him down; so that, if at any time his native longings set him on being more earnest in them, they become, in fact, a superstition.

Again, there is a class of men outside of the church, or sometimes in it, who undertake to be religious or Christian, and really suppose they are because of a certain patronage they give to the church and the word. What they do not bring in fellowship they propose to add by counsel and management. Consciously not being in the gift of spiritual discernment, their tastes will be the better, and they will the better know what excesses are to be restrained, and what aberrations avoided. And, as there are always a great many reasons why a thing should not be done, to any single reason why it should, they assume, as they are rich in the negatives, to be specially qualified critics. These critical powers, too, they propose to contribute for the benefit of the cause; while others less gifted in such matters may contribute their prayers! Of course, these negatives belong not to the range of the Spirit and the glorious proprieties of

God; but to the nether world of fashion, or opinion, or custom, and are only rude, blind prejudices at that. The sermon has too much faultfinding. The deacons are too ready to appear on all occasions. It would be much better if the brethren would be more silent. The women are a great deal more forward and strenuous than belongs to their sex.

O, these unilluminated wisdoms, that have only feet and no wings at all—it is as if eagles had fallen out of their element and descended to be cranes, pleased that the legs they stand upon have grown so tall and trim, and are able to wade in such deep water! But, alas! for these infantry birds; if they could but drop their uncomely stilts, to soar as eagles do and burn their wings in the sun, they would be as much higher in their range as they pretend high standing less. Giving themselves over in trust to the Saviour, instead of giving their opinions and tastes, their patronage of his cause might cease, and their contributions to it have a worthier significance.

Once more, there is a class who distrust all the supposed experiences in religion, doing it thoughtfully, as they suppose, on grounds of sufficient reason. All visions and revelations of the Lord they disrespect. It offends them to hear any thing said of spiritual discernment, or the discerning of spirits, or of special gifts, or of divine monitions, or of answers to prayer, or of calls to particular duties and works. They like to see things keep the level of Nature more nearly, and observe a more prudent and judiciously moderated way. Inspirations are nothing; judgments every thing. And they have it as a maxim, that soaring experiences of every kind, all supernatural upliftings and fervors, are only fantastics that had best be avoided. Now Moses was a great lawgiver, and has always been considered a very solid man; but he was most certainly in a different way. Or, taking a later and more strictly Christian example, the Apostle Paul, what shall we say of that story he tells the Corinthians of his very strange experience "fourteen years ago?" Perhaps he was a little bewildered by it himself, and has kept the thing under advisement all this time, to be sure of it. But he is able now, as we see, to glory somewhat. Was he not caught up to the third heaven? Was he not even doubtful whether he was in the body or out of the body? Why, it is a first point, is it not, to know that we are in the body. And some of us would be as good as nowhere if not in the body. True, the great man talks in his overmodesty here of glorying in his "infirmities;" but he dares, we see, to glory a little, nevertheless. And it was his way to be going up always into these high regions, so that he was not sure at times whether he had a thing by revelation or not, and even had a considerable notion that angels were getting high impressions out of him, and God's work in him and by him. Yes, he was just the kind of high-flying saint that the wise, blind folk of this world most surely disrespect. Not knowing what faith is, how could they know to what third heaven it may lift? So they called him "mad," as we know. They could not call him a mystic, or a quietist, or a pietist, or a Methodist, or a Calvinist, or a Low Churchman; for these terms of stigma were not yet ready. So they called him "mad," because he did not stay on foot in their level of sanity. Was he then a flighty person? Does not the world even bow down to him, nevertheless, as the grand, intellectual, theologic chief of Christianity? And was there ever, in fact, a soul more massive and sublimely steady in its equilibrium than his?

What, now, having all these expositions before us, is the conclusion of the whole matter? What but this, that true religion, according to the Christian idea, makes an immensely wide chasm by the faith at which it begins, or in which it is born? It is not any mere playing out of Nature on its own level; but it is the lifting up of the man above himself in a transformation that makes him new to himself. No more flesh, but spirit, ranging above the world in all the liberties of spirit. In so far as he is a Christian, he occupies another sphere, and becomes the citizen of another kingdom. This he will believe, and will not only dare to be thus lifted, but will scarcely dare not to be. For, whatever disrespect he may encounter, in what so many will consider his fantastic way, he will have evidences in himself that ask no certification. Besides, he will have learned, shortly, that the only safe way of living for him is the highest, and that no other is entirely safe. For in this highest range he will be conscious that his disorders are quelled, his internal jars and discords laid, his irruptions and tumults brought under, and a glorious serenity and clearness, pervasive as the day, established in him. All which, if he settles away from his trust, or sinks below his calling, gives way correspondently before the refluent forces of night and nature in him, and leaves him sweltering in the old misrule. The ancients had a fabled giant who could not be subdued, because, whenever he fell, his mother, the earth, let such power into him that he forthwith sprung up, at the moment of contact, and slew his antagonist; till, finally, Hercules, discovering the secret, held him up in his grapple, not allowing him to touch the ground, and so crushed him. Exactly contrary it is with the Christian. The earth is not his mother, he is a child of the sun; and, if he descends to settle on the ground, his strength vanishes.

If, then, we are to make our ascent into this higher plane of true Christian experience, it will be seen that all the ties which bind us down, or hold us to our feet, must be effectually cut by our habitual self-renunciations. Not even right hands and right eyes can be kept back from the sacrifice. Selfishness and self-indulgence are no more for us. Coming down no more upon the world, we must lift up every thing we do in it, and hope from it, into that pure life of sacrifice and trust in which we abide with our Master. It must be with us here as it was with Noah when he made the ark. He did not expect partly to wade and partly to float; but he went in, he and his, taking all the freight of his world-stock with him, when the Lord shut him in. The waters now became his element, and he had no other. So, when we go up into faith, we need to be shut in by severance from every natural trust. Our expectation must be rested on God, not on pillars of any kind below—pillars are not wanted under wings.

IV.

THE GOSPEL OF THE FACE.

"For God who commanded the light to shine out of darkness hath shined in our hearts, to give the light of the knowledge of the glory of God in the face of Jesus Christ."—2 *Cor.* 4: 6.

The light of the knowledge of the glory of God—a mighty and glorious gospeling certainly! and where is it shown or testified? In the face of Jesus Christ. Faces are the natural images or exponents of persons, windows in bodies at which we see the souls looking out. Every face accurately represents the man behind it; so that when we get once thoroughly acquainted with him, we can not imagine the possibility that he should have a face at all different. I am not sure, however, that the apostle meant to make so fine a point of the mere face taken simply as the forefront of the head. The word he uses is a larger word than our English word face, denoting the whole aspect, or personal embodiment, that which reveals the true presence and character-type of the man. And this revelation regarding it as made by the Saviour's whole person—he conceives to be the fact-form gospel, blazoned in his life, and brought forth into living expression by his personal demonstrations. And he even conceives that there is a kind of absolute force in it, though he probably means to say it only in a figure; declaring that God hath shined in our hearts, even as when he commanded the light to shine out of darkness in the creation of the world. It is a kind of personal power, he would say, that is next thing to omnipotence.

What I propose therefore, now, is to speak of *The Gospel of the Face,* or more accurately and scripturally stated, *The Gospel in the Face of Jesus Christ.*

My conviction is that we put the gospel too generally out of its proper divine form, into our own human form, serving it, as it were, in our own color, as we have shaped and colored it for ourselves. We conceive what it ought to be to answer the conditions we appoint for it, and then, by a huge milling process of construction—by much theologizing, propositionizing, schematizing, and abstractionizing, we show it builded together, for the very ends and uses we have reasoned for it. It becomes in this manner our gospel; if not the expression of our face, the abstractional form and framework we have gotten up to do the work that required, as we think, to be done. How far we go in this abstractive, theoretic way may be seen from the terms we bring in to serve our speculative, scheme-building uses. Thus in our theology we have these for the staple of our doctrine, not one of which is found in the Scripture at all—justice, satisfaction, merit, substitution, compensation, expiation. When I say this I am not objecting wholly to abstractional and theoretic efforts in religion. Some I know are strong in the conviction that formulations of the Christian truth are necessary to save us from being floated away into all kinds of laxity and confusion. Perhaps it may be so, as regards the parts of Christianity more easily reducible to propositions and terms of abstract statement. But I seriously doubt whether the more strictly proper matter of our gospel is capable of any such thing. For it lies in sentiment wholly, in what goes to make impression by expression—in love, in purity, in divine beauty, in sorrow, in suffering well and wisely. Conceive what a person may impress, and do, and be, in the phases of a tragically great life, and how far off are we from so much as imagining the possibility of propositionizing the man. Besides, what is Christ in his person, but God's own formulization of himself, *i. e.* not the statement, but the image of himself. What less than a very bold irreverence then can it be to substitute the revelation-form or face of God, by any so prosy thing as a formula in words. And the more evidently is this true that all that Christ was and did, is summed up in character and feeling. Perhaps we make up an account of Christ, or of what he has done, which is like this—God is just and must be; therefore he could not forgive sin, without first satisfying his justice by some expiation, or making amends to his government by some exhibition equivalent to the execution of penalty; he therefore takes from his Son and his suffering cross, what was justly due from us, and we are released, or rather justified. Is it then possible, I would ask, for any human creature, to read over this mortally dry record, this mere pile of bricks —and not miss something most dear, every thing most dear, in hearing him talk, and looking in his face, and going with him out into Gethsemane and up to Pilate's hall of judgment?

Let us see now if there is not a gospel of the face, an all transcending fact-form, life-form gospel made out for us, which it behooves us always to live in, and have also living in us; for the most living form of the doctrine is that, of course, which as our human nature works will have the most immediate and divinest power.

1. Let us look into the New Testament and distinguish, if we can, what is called preaching there. And we find our apostle testifying,—"*Whom* we preach, * * that we may present every man perfect in Christ Jesus." He does not say *about* whom, or the just account and formula of whom, but *whom;* the fact-form man, the life, and life-history, and feeling, and sorrow, and death, and resurrection of the man. "Whom we *preach*," that is, cry, proclaim, publish as good tidings, set forth as a fact-matter news or story—the word is not theologize, resolve, reduce, but *preach*. The souls to be gained are also to be presented "perfect *in Christ Jesus;*" that is, in the new possibilities and powers of grace embodied for them in the face and person, or personal life, of their incarnate Redeemer.

Again the same apostle declares, more stringently and by exclusion, what and what only he could suffer himself to preach,—"For I determined not to know any thing among you save Jesus Christ, and Him crucified." We often cite the words as authority for preaching nothing but a certain ruggedly articulated, formulated doctrine of the cross, or justification by the cross. This is our meaning, not his. The very thing he means to say, with sharpest emphasis, is that, when preaching among them, he had felt bound to make Christ himself every thing, and his own speculations or humanly contrived opinions, nothing.

Great varieties of word and symbol come up on all sides in the New Testament, centering in the same general impression. Thus Christ is *bread*, calls himself "the bread that came down from heaven." But no preaching about bread ever fed any body. Nothing answers but a fit dispensing of the bread, that is of Christ himself. "He that eateth *me* shall live by *me*."

Again he declares that, when he is *lifted up*, he is going to become a healer of souls in being simply looked upon, as the serpent lifted up was a healer in the wilderness. He does not imagine that some notional view, or opinion, or doctrine of the being lifted up, is going to heal, but that he himself lifted up will do it. Medicines cure by what they are, not by what is said of them or reasoned about them.

Again, calling himself the *truth*,—"I am the truth,"—he does not think of his gospel as a propositional matter, but as being worded in his person, and receivable only from his person—just the point where Christianity differs from all the theorizing doctrines of the philosophers. It is no Christian idea that we are going to be converted and sanctified through the truth, in the sense that we are going to manipulate and manage, convert and sanctify ourselves by good abstractions installed in our heads. Our Christ is to be the truth beheld in living expression. No matter what notions we have gotten booked for a gospel, he is all the gospel there is himself.

He is called again and calls himself *the life*. How the life? Because, the abstractional believer will commonly answer, he clears our liability to punishment which is death, and prepares a salvable condition for us. A salvable condition, life! Any condition, life! Soil, sun, dew—are these vegetable life, any or all of them? No, the soul lives only when life itself comes, that is, when Christ has entered the soul as life. "And you hath *he* quickened who were dead in trespasses and sins." It is he within that is life, and not any thing he is conceived to have done, to prepare a new condition, or work out a governmental exigency for us.

It is very important, also, to notice what directions are given concerning the use of the incarnate person —and especially that all questions of psychological analysis are put by. The word is, "This is my beloved son, hear ye *him*." It does not say, fall to work upon the problem of his person, resolve the psychology of his parts, as if he were no miracle, but let him be the miracle he is and hear; hear ye him, the one single being *him*. Distinguishing the parts of his composition in a manner that is quite too common, the part that suffers and the part that does not, the part that increases in knowledge and the part that does not, the part that prays, and the part that does not, the part that works in a miracle, and the part that does not, makes him two persons, and not one, a Son of God who is not Son of man, and a Son of man who is not Son of God; and then what is he to us but a kind of double personation, dodging all apprehension? Exactly contrary to this he is to be two poles in unity, a solidly concrete, impenetrable, unsolvable person—God's full beauty and love in the human type or face, "the Word made flesh." Look ye hither, mortals, the Eternal is here, a Friend—perfect, sinless, bringing good-will, and emptying God's bosom into yours—hear ye him. God is the meaning, man is the face—so much we know, for it is given; more we do not care to know.

But there is a common belief that Paul, who had the very best and deepest understanding of the gospel, made up carefully and steadily preached a theorizing gospel, dealing with all ruggedest and deepest problems of abstraction, even as our Christian schools do now. The fact is very different. He did present and publish Christ in terms out of which we are accustomed to draw, by inference, many articles, but he never drew them himself. We have done it so long that his words appear to signify, themselves, the very things we get by construction out of them. But in this we greatly mistake, as may be seen by the one single fact, universally conceded by the Christian scholars and writers of dogmatic history, that no theoretic or abstractive doctrine of Christ's work was ever stated or taught during the first ten centuries of the Christian Church—none, of course, by Paul; for in that case, being formally set forth in his epistles, it took the church ten whole centuries to find it! Far more likely it is that we draw him into such constructions by our own inferences. The inferences may be just, but, since he did not make them himself, they are no part certainly of the gospel he preached. The remarkable thing about his preaching, on the contrary, is that he adheres so closely to the fact-view of the gospel. Using many terms that we have carried on to a point of meaning more theoretic and abstractive, he stops short himself, in the purely practical power of the story. Other men have gone farther since his day, and seen, perhaps, just as much less. His *justification* is practical, based in no speculated scheme of satisfaction, being simply "the righteousness of God," in Christ's most righteous life, "unto all and upon all them that believe"—a "declaring [in-showing] of the righteousness of God," to make us righteous before him. Neither does he quit the fact-form view of the Gospel, or go at all beyond it in the figures of *offering* and *sacrifice*, and *blood*, and *cleansing*, so profusely applied and with so great unction, to set forth its meaning. It has taken long ages of drill and observance to prepare these figures, and he sees God's evangelic purpose working in them from the first. He finds them made ready as chariots for his Master's life and passion, and putting them, in harness, drives them, burdened with atoning love and grace, directly into men's hearts. How else but by these images from the altar could he tell a guilt-stricken world what the incarnate Son of Man, obedient unto death, has done for them. Meantime he is always recurring to the gospel of the face, the manifested and expressed glory, as to the pole-star of his Christed life and ministry; testifying that "God was in Christ;" that "we all, with open face, beholding as in a glass [*i. e.*, in Christ] the glory of the Lord, are changed into the same image from glory to glory;" that "God hath, in these last days, spoken to us by his Son, who also is the brightness of his glory, the express image of his person."

Consider now,—

2. What importance there may be in some revelation, or presentation of God, which enters him into the world as he can be entered in no form of abstraction. The very purpose of the incarnation is to get by or away from abstractions, and give the world a concrete personation. Thus in Christ's living person, we are to have God, who is above all history, entered into history, and by such human ways of life as history takes note of, becoming incorporate in it. And to make the fact historic, and no mere theophany, he

stays thirty whole years among us, descending to our human level, as being under all but the sin of it, weaving all God's charities and healing mercies into it, teaching how divinely, as no mortal teacher could, suffering with us and for us, and strangest of all by us, and so unbosoming all God's beauty as a God who can pity and seek after his enemies. And he has, withal—expressing in it, we may almost think, more than by all beside—a face. Who of us has not sighed many times for a look upon that face, and the light of the knowledge of the glory of God therein revealed! O what depth of meaning, and height of meaning, and purity of meaning, what tender composure, what restful strength, what majesty of good, and grace of sorrow, and close-drawn human sympathy was there in it—all saying "look unto me," "come unto me." And such is the concrete, staple matter brought in for us in the gospel. It is all person, what a person is and feels and does and suffers in the out-door forms of human life and action. It hangs for the matter of it, not on abstract teachings, but on the personal pronouns, the *I*, the *me*, the *he*, the *him*, of his divine manifestation.

He is to be the concrete of all government and perfection, let into the world in such visible deific force and super-earthly quality, that, having once gotten the sense of it, and the transcendent miracle embodied in it, we are satisfied—we know God; the light of the knowledge of the glory of God hath shined in our hearts.

There is also another most cogent reason for this concrete or incarnate presentation; viz., to beget a more benign, more thoroughly felt, impression of the just severities of God. They must come as out of feeling, else they are feeble and cold and without evidence beside. Terrors and reproofs, let fall thumping on the world out of abstract deity, do not come in power. They sufficiently impress only when they speak out of a mind that feels, or is visibly bathed in sympathy and sorrow. Who but Christ then ever gave us any vital impression of God's hatred to sin? Authority had been asserted before, condemnations pronounced, judgments uttered, but who ever heard them, as when spoken by the loving, suffering Son of Man? Hell was never so deep, justice never so dreadful, or so close at hand, as when they lowered in his divine face. Woe to the hypocrites! Woe to the oppressors! Woe to the learned thieves of God's kingdom! Woe to all ungodly now! No such appalling sense of God's justice was ever bolted into human bosoms by the severities of unseen, abstract deity, as when that justice spoke in the voice, or glittered in the wrath of the Lamb. Here is justice in feeling, and this concrete man who feels, is the judge of the world. Many persons who are much concerned lest Christ should not make due compensation to the justice of God for the release of sin, appear to be concerned without reason. Half his power consists in the fact that justice comes out as in concrete embodiment with him.

Advancing now to a point still deeper we perceive—

3. That if there is to be any remedy for the precise disability and woe of sin, it must be such as may, in some way, restore God to his place in the soul. What is our misery in the state under evil, but that we are separated from God's occupancy or indwelling by it—"alienated from the life of God?" Therefore no mere body of opinional truths or doctrines meets our case—nothing meets it but to give us back, in some way, the personal inhabitation we have lost. Our gospel has no relativity, save when it embodies or envisages the divine love and friendship powerfully enough to enter them into our life. Reinspiration is our first want; for not even the Holy Spirit reinspires save as he shows the things of Christ objectively within. "I in them, and Thou in me, that they may be made perfect in one," is, in fact, the very gospel, and the whole of it. Finding us emptied of God, it undertakes to bring us God, and recommunicate God; not some notional truth or truths about God, but God's indwelling life itself—"I in them." God is to look himself in again from the face of Jesus. Or, what is nowise different, Jesus dying into our dead sympathies, is to enter back the Divine, and quicken us to life. Opinions, formulated notions, or abstractive articles can do nothing plainly as regards the rehabilitation of God. Nothing is at all apposite but incarnation, or what is the same, a living gospel worded to our feeling, in the face of Jesus and the concrete matter of his life.

4. It is a consideration having great weight, that no other kind of doctrine but that which adheres to the concrete, matter-of-fact gospel makes a true, or any but a false point for faith. Salvation we say is by faith, and what is faith? A great first question at which many stumble. Faith they assume to be a belief in something true propositionally. They even assume that we put men in a way to be saved, only when we give them just the propositions they must believe. Now the propositions may be true or not—I make no question here about them—I only protest that such a notion of faith totally mistakes the nature and meaning of faith. Gospel faith has nothing to do with any propositional truth whatever. There is no proposition, or hundred propositions, that can not be believed, and have not been, times without number, having yet no gracious effect whatever.

No, the faith that brings salvation is the act of a being towards a being, sinner to Saviour, man to God. "He that believeth in *me*," says Christ, not he that believeth some things, or many things, about me. It is the act of an undone, lost man, giving himself over in trust to Jesus Christ, person to person; a total consenting to Christ, to be of him, and with him, and for him, to let him heal and renovate, and govern, and be made unto him wisdom, and righteousness, and sanctification, and redemption, in one word, every thing. The simple first point of it is Christ, a Saviour, manifested in such love and divinity that, taken for salvation as a being, he can be trusted. And when he is thus trusted, that is faith. Propositions are needed of course, facts about him are needed, to prepare the conception of him, so that he may be trusted—the very gospel story is made of such. These too must be believed, but the believing of them is not faith at all, and never did or can save any body. Saving faith is person trusted to person—that and nothing else.

5. It is a fact to be carefully noted, that all the best saints and most impressive teachers of Christ are those who have found how to present him best in the dramatic forms of his personal history. Such were Chrysostom, Augustine, Luther, Tauler, Wesley. These great souls could not be shut up under the opinional way of doctrine, or even under their own opinions. Their gospel was not dry, and thin, and small in quantity, as being in man's quantity, and therefore soon exhausted; it was no part of their idea to be always hammering in, or hammering on, some formulated article, but they had a wonderful outspreading of life and volume, because they breathed so freely the supernatural inspirations of Christ, and let their inspirations forth in such grand liberties of utterance. They were men thoroughly Christed by their inspirations and deep beholdings in the gospel facts. They had gotten such insight into the ways and times and occasions of their Master's life, that subjects enough, and truths always fresh, were springing into form, in all points of the story. And they were not mere surface subjects, but they were cogent, mass-

ive, piercing, pricking in conviction, melting ice-bound states away, battering down every citadel of prejudice, and flowing out in senses of God that make a wonderfully divine atmosphere about the circles they live in, and the audiences before which they appear.

Such now I conceive is the true gospel of Christ and our question is answered. But the answer itself will be questioned in two or three points which also require to be noticed.

Thus it may be questioned, whether certain persons of a sharply inquisitive mold will not do best in con-conducting their processes more analytically and abstractively, that being the form in which all subjects have most reality to them, and take the deepest hold of their convictions. But if what is simply beheld or presented takes no hold of their convictions, if only what they reason or think, or logically sift, has meaning to them, it may be questioned with quite as good reason whether they are living in God's light at all. There certainly are many such, just as there are many children who can never be satisfied when a flower is given them, till they have picked it in pieces—when of course it is no flower at all. Fire is the greatest analyzer in the world, and the product, ashes. Analysis requires dead subjects, but the gospel is not dead, and ought not to be killed. Any character analyzed, Hamlet for example, and put in terms of abstraction, is therefore dead. The only Hamlet is

Hamlet himself, alive in his own mystery, and not the particular salts of tragedy into which he has been resolved. So when the disciple, instead of knowing Christ himself, a person abnormal, in some sense infinite, more than we can think, deeper in his mystery than human soul can fathom, thinks of nothing but analytic powders sifted through his mill of logical opinion, the powders may be very abundant and very fine, but the Christ is nowhere.

But there is a duller kind of objection that may possibly arise, asking what shall we find to feed us in this manner? Shall we not soon have used up all the fact of our story, and then what shall we do? As if nothing could be inexhaustible but some mere syllabus or propositional wisdom; or as if we were likely to find that we have used up the gospel! No, rather judge there is a poverty of soul in the objection itself, that very nearly disqualifies the man. Why, my friends, the miners of Nevada will sooner have bored out all the silver of the globe and made an empty honeycomb of it. Such words spoken by such a character, seconded by such miracles, representing visibly two worlds, opening vistas into God's deep nature and feeling and counsel, and declaring in self-evidencing majesty, the kingdom of God in the world—such a gospel vaster than the sea, will not soon be exhausted. If the objection were, that one's soul must be oppressed and stifled rather by the overwhelmingly grand subjects it will be raising, it might be more difficult to answer.

I was thinking, a few days ago, of the large blank chapter, so to speak, of the Master's life, between his dispute with the doctors in the temple and his public ministry—"those eighteen silent years, would that we knew something of them." Whereupon it came up, that Jesus was all this time, "subject to his parents," training his great presentiments in a key of filial duty both domestic and lowly; that able to dispute with doctors, he does not hasten to the schools to be occupied with books and questions, but is meditating his "Father's business"—O what meditation that!—in the trade of a carpenter; that his custom was "to be always at the synagogue in the Sabbath worship, feeding his great thoughts in what of grace and fellowship he could find, among the rustic elders of his people; that he must have been reading the scriptures largely, or at least hearing them read, to know exactly where the scripture was, relating most to himself, as he plainly did, when he stood up, on his last synagogue day, to read; having, all the while, O what emotions rolling through his soul in the discovery of what the prophets were thinking beforehand, of what is now dawning in his personal consciousness; till finally his patience, in the waiting of these eighteen silent unhistoric years, occupied with so many thrilling foregleams of his future, lift him—rustic boy and man that he is—to a pitch of dignity almost inconceivable. And so I was sketching a volume, without knowing it, and the matter was coming faster than I could seize it. Facts that are divine will open wonderfully fast. Propositions are poor and fruitless, in comparison. Thus it is for example with every most silent, most scantily expressed thing in the life of Jesus; his forty days in the wilderness, his "Go and sin no more," his turning to the lepers afar off, the box of ointment, the hem that was touched, the tear that stood on his face at the grave of Lazarus, his sleep in the boat, his look at the penny, his look up at Zaccheus in the tree, his look down upon the city. He can not turn his eyes, without turning ours into some wondrous discovery of his meaning and glory.

It is as if he were the index hand of the creation and of all God's works and meanings in it beside, and yet there is a misgiving felt in some lest this glorious, mysterious, ocean-deep life of Jesus will shortly give out; when one or two dull formulas, perhaps, drawn out in a few short lines, which a man may learn, as an ancient poet said, "standing on one leg," are a quite sufficient gospel stock, ready to be preached and kept in preaching, ready to be pivoted and kept in seesaw, year by year. No, it is sheer indolence and sterility that can be stocked in this manner, and ask to be excused from the real gospel, lest it should not yield enough; as to them it certainly will not to keep them in supply. The secret of the imposture is evident. If the preacher wants a syllabus, and then to call it bread, he scarcely knows, I think, his Master's face, and the light of the knowledge of the glory of God has scarcely flickered in his listless mind. O, it ought not, whether we make much or little of formula, to be a very irksome thing to study the Lord Jesus Christ himself; and whoever does it will have subjects rise upon him faster, and vaster, and deeper in riches than he can ever even name, without some painful sense of only brushing surfaces and saying adequately nothing.

At this point be it also understood as a fact that must not be disguised, that it requires a very deep and grandly vitalized experience to know Christ well enough to preach him. One may preach a formula and know almost nothing of him—nothing but what is verbally stuck in his head, or pigeon-holed in his memory. But the real Christ is what a Christ may be; what he shall signify in a man's heart; what he is to feeling, and faith, and guilt, and bondage, and everlasting hope, and liberty that makes a sinner free. It wants a Christed man to know who Christ really is, and show him forth with a meaning. He must be had by inspiration; manifested within; opening his gates outward, and upward, and abroad, into all height, and depth, and length, and breadth.

And yet no mere way of study and inward experience will suffice. Christ is no deep meditationist, no recluse working out his problems and living in his frames, but a wonderfully out-door character. He never had a study. He lives on foot, mingles with men in the market-places, touching and touched by every thing human, chambered not seldom in his sleep under the open sky. Common life is the element of his sanctities, and his very intuitions have an out-door way; hitting every human creature, low or high, at his exact point of merit. He moves about among all grades of people, the humble, the weak, the guilt-stricken, the proud, the learned, the great ecclesiastics, and high public magistrates, superior alike to all, gentle as he should be, dreadfully severe as he ought to be, doing always what a perfect insight, tempered by divinest benefaction, requires. He can not be a leveler, will not be a moral or political reformer, steadily refuses on principle to be a revolutionist, and yet there is no problem of society, as we are discovering more and more distinctly, that is not somehow illuminated by his teachings and conduct. No man really knows him, therefore, who can not take the open air of society with him. If his disciple was never out-doors in his life, as many disciples never were; or if he never saw any thing, or felt any thing, or had any thing touch him when he was, he can not have the right sort of experience, and will rather conceive him as the God-recluse, than as the gloriously real and true God-man.

I will not turn this great subject wholly on the faults of preaching; for it is a fact most remarkable that Christ has notwithstanding, at this very time, the attention, so to speak, of the world as never before? He is not only the chief problem of theology and theologic learning, but the literature of the day recognizes him, and society has a kind of hope in him, and the unbelievers, in all grades and conditions, think of him with respect and a certain half-developed expectation. This dim feeling after him, is everywhere. The report that was brought him by his disciples, "all men seek for thee," was never, I think, so widely true. I do not mean, of course, that it is the Christ of the church articles, or the Christ of the saints, that is thought of so desiringly; it is only some wonderful first-fair, it may be, bursting up out of humanity and kindling hope in man's possibilities; who he is to be, and whether he is to be any Saviour of sinners at all, is the question perhaps to be decided. What is wanted, therefore, now, and silently called for, is the preaching of the fact-form Christ,—just such a Christ as the charities, and miracles, and fellow tendernesses, and death, and resurrection of Jesus put in outline before us: God in Christ reconciling the world; he that could suffer, the just for the unjust, to bring us unto God; he that could endure enemies and came down from heaven to bear the curse of their bad lot to gain them; he that loved the poor and feared not the great; he that flavored the world by living in it; he that went through society and made his quickening, medicating power felt everywhere; he that has gone up to prepare mansions and to set his judgment seat for the world. O, if he could now be preached, as he might be and sometime will, what a cleaving to him would there be. And the supernatural glory of his life and works, instead of being an objection, would only kindle the greater fire. Men want the supernatural, after all, and even hunger for it, if only they can have it in its own self-evidence and concrete self-assertion.

One thing more yet remains which must not be omitted. The very same reason that required the gospel to come in by the face of Jesus Christ, or to be impersonated by him, and get expression through his gentle emotions and the sanctities of his divine sorrow, holds good still, as before he went up to the Father. We are always imagining that we want some better qualified advocacy—high preaching, sturdier argument on points of theology, better command of logical resources, more science, more fine rhetoric, more I know not what. No, the thing that we most want is what we miss or lose out, in toiling after these expected vanities, namely, a divine light in souls, the light of the knowledge of the glory of God in such power as to light up faces. Come what will of preaching, or come not what will not, the grand law of Christian power goes with faces. The gospel is nothing now, any more than it was at the first, unless it is reincarnated, and kept incarnate. It must get expression not through tongues and propositional wisdom, and the clatter of much argument, but through living persons, seen in all the phases of the better life they live. The real sermons are the great pure feelings, the generosities of holy sacrifice, the patience, the abiding with Christ in his sorrows, the worship of humility. By these every best preacher will preach his best; by these every humblest, most downtrodden believer will be the best preacher. Into this field then, one and all, God bids us come, and receive the power from on high which came on the first disciples, and which comes on all, when the light of the knowledge of the glory of God shines in their faces and irradiates their persons. More briefly, genuine good living is the gospel, and that not because the man lives well as for himself but because he LIVES—born into Life from above.

V.

THE COMPLETING OF THE SOUL.

"And ye are complete in him which is the head of all principality and power."—*Col.* 2: 10.

If then we are only to be complete in Christ, the inference must be that we are incomplete without him. It follows in this view, or is rather a part of it, that a soul, after being made or created, is still to be completed. It may be a germ to be developed, or a blasted germ to be restored, or it may be both. In either view, it is not the full completed integer it was made to be. Here accordingly is the true work of Christ and his gospel. We may say, that he is here for the salvation, or, with equal truth, for the completion of the soul. And this latter is now to be my subject, viz., *The completing of the soul.*

We do not commonly speak in this way. Our manner is to regard the soul as God's highest, noblest work, and we love to think of it as being even more complete than any thing else. But we do not observe, that it is only the greater, or is seen to be, in the fact that so much is necessary to its completion. If it were some lower form of being, a rock, or a sea, or a sun, it could be struck out by a fiat of God, and be complete at the first; but being a moral nature to be unfolded by its own action into thought and character and deific inspirations, and so into an eternal, self-affirming greatness and beauty, it must needs pass through great changes and lofty trainings after it is made, and in them be completed, as otherwise, or as being merely created, it was not and could not be.

What then, following in this train, do we mean by the completing of the soul? how does it appear to need any such completion? and how is the fact accomplished?

Without putting the subject in this form, it is remarkable that we so readily and constantly assume the necessity of a great after-work to be done upon the soul of our child, to make it the complete man or woman we desire it to be. Taken as being merely born, we look upon it as a barely embryonic life, the possibility or rudimental germ of a man, and not a man. What we call our child's training, or education, is only our attempt to advance or bring him on towards completeness. He is to be instructed, we assume, corrected, governed, formed to self-government, unfolded in his intelligence, fashioned in his tastes, configured to principles of honor and truth. The result is a being in higher quantity, dignity, and power, in a finer quality, and in a capacity, both of action and enjoyment, immensely enlarged. Could we look in upon the inner scenery of thought and working in two human creatures, one a wild, the other an educated man, how different should we perceive them to be in their apprehensions, currents of feeling, prejudices, superstitions, resentments, satisfactions, pleasures, causes of trouble, views of life, and thoughts of what is beyond. Neither will be really complete, but how different one from the other—he perhaps that was originally most gifted, how far inferior to the less gifted.

At the same time, it is not to be assumed that we are right in all our conceptions of what takes place in the education or training of minds. They will not be complete because they are full educated in the intellectual sense. Sometimes they will in fact be hampered and stunted by their education, or even by what is considered to be their wonderful attainments in scholarship; crippled in their inventiveness, drugged by the wisdoms of their great authorities, in that manner incapacitated by the overload they have taken. Perhaps one hour with God would have done more for the widening out of their consciousness, and the kindling of all divinest fires in their powers of thought and feeling, than many such whole years of drill in the schools.

Sometimes we allow ourselves to think, that our child is going to be complete only when he is educated above and away from certain ranges of employment. We measure his completeness, perhaps, by the range for which we prepare him. If he can only be a blacksmith, or a tanner, or even a school-teacher, we perhaps think he is too little complete, and that we have not made enough of him. Were he a qualified commander, banker, physician, lawyer, we should be better satisfied, and think him more nearly up to the measure of his possibilities. But God does not grade our completeness by any such law. He may have rated Bezaleel the brazier, far above Aaron the priest, and considered him to be a man far more nearly complete—I really suppose that he was. He has no such thought as that a blacksmith, or a tailor, or a shepherd, or even a fisherman at his net, is of course a man incomplete, or at all less complete than if he were the light of a college. Who ever came nearer to being mated with Shakspeare than the tinker Bunyan? A great, growing, grandly unfolding soul, can be fashioned any where, if only God is with him, and his faculty, it may be, will be completing itself, as truly in one employment as in another. His heart will grow as big, his imagination kindle itself in fires to him of as great beauty, he will be as original, as deep, as free, and will swing his nature into as high force every way, in using a hammer as in using a pen. He may not pass the scholarly conventionalities as well, but may pass the eternal dignities better. God nowhere allows, what we so constantly assume, that souls are kept back from their completeness, by their trades, and grades, and employments. He is going to complete them all, if they will suffer it, in the highest and most perfect form of being possible. In what manner, and by what means, will be shown hereafter. I only go thus far before my subject, in a way of enlarging and correcting our too insufficient, merely earthly conceptions of what the soul's completion implies. No mere schooling, or human training, to whatever grade of life or social estimation it may raise, is any but the faintest approximation to a true completion of the soul.

This now will appear more fully and determinately, as we go on to consider the supposed incompleteness, and show wherein it lies. If it were a question relating to the first man, Adam, in his lot of innocence, the answer would be more simple but far less evident. We should say, at once, that with all his perfect harmonies and beautiful instincts, he is yet unexercised, unformed, a full grown, beautiful child, but yet a child. That his perceptions are all to be gotten, his will to be trained, his habits formed, his memory stored, his love unfolded by its objects, his acquaintance with God practically matured, and all that constitutes a great and true wisdom learned. Until then he is an essentially incomplete creature; so incomplete that he will not stand fast in good, but plunge himself into wrong, and all the unspeakable disasters of wrong. Indeed we shall begin to see that our first man, commonly thought to be so great and grandly perfect, is put on probation only that he may get his nature completed in knowledge and right habit, and so matured in good that he will come out able to stand.

Our question, after this, relates to him partly under

the conditions of moral disaster, into which he is fallen. We take the soul as it is, in our present moral state, and the moment we fasten our thought down squarely upon it, we see, by every sort of evidence crowding upon us, how very incomplete it is.

In the first place it is universally conceded that it *scarcely at all answers its* true end. There might be some disagreement as to what that true end is. No matter; whatever it be, there is a feeling everywhere, in every body, that there is something out of joint, and that souls are going wide of their mark in a thousand ways. Some call it sin, some call it circumstance, some mistake, some misdirection. Be that as it may, while the heavenly bodies keep their track to the thousandth part of a hair, and every great power of nature exactly performs its office, for some reason or other, souls go amiss, jerked out of their places and turned away from all conceivable ends. And the fact is proof beyond a question of their incompleteness. A watch is complete when it keeps time, not when it quarrels with all the notations of suns, and dials, and almanacs. A vintage process is complete when it makes wine, not when it makes vinegar. Souls in like manner are complete when they make the good they were made for, whatever it be, fulfilling exactly their glorious ends and uses. And as long as they fail of that, even in the least degree, they are of course incomplete.

They are seen again to be incomplete, in the fact that their enjoyment is not full, but confessedly a great ways short of it. Their instincts are unfulfilled, their wants are unsupplied, their objects are not found. They seem to themselves to be living in confined quarters. They are hungry. They are tormented by a general unrest. It would not be so if they were complete. They would be exactly, absolutely full of enjoyment, just as by their sublime, inborn necessity they crave to be. When every thing is complete, all outreaching instincts are filled. No bee misses the shape of his cells, no bird of passage misses the direction of his flight, no plant aspiring towards the light misses the color and kind of its flower. No more will a soul, as being a creature set for joy, miss the state of absolutely full enjoyment, unless it is somehow incomplete, sweltering in some torment of negation, or inbred disorder.

Souls again do not, as we know them, meet, or at all fulfill the standards of beauty, truth, and right. These are standards we all admit for souls, just as all fruits and flowers of nature have the standard figures and colors of their kind. An apple is not complete when it comes out a gourd. A rose is not complete when it comes forth blue or in a sandstone grey. An orange is not complete when it turns out a melon or a potato. What then does it signify, when a soul forgets and misses its kind, when it puts forth itself in deformity, falsity, and wrong? Requiring itself all exactest and most perfect beauty, all divinest truth and right, and having these for the standard of its kind, how comes it thus to be turned off, into all abortions of kind—evidently, confessedly, nay even universally falling away from itself and its own high nature? Just so far is it incomplete, and there is no other answer to be given.

Take another and more entirely surface view of mankind, and let the question settle itself, as it will inevitably, under mere first impressions. Why then is it, and how, that so much meanness, trickishness, oppression, unregulated and wild passion, self-corrosion, painfulness, bitterness, distraction, are found in the world? How is it that no soul is able to assert the power of self-government, steadily and stiffly enough to keep itself in harmony? Or if we look away at society and the outward relations of persons, how is it that they are in so many quarrels, and complaints of wrong, and suits of redress, so continually plagued by acts of injustice and robbery and fraud, tormented by so many resentments, scorched by so many hatreds, weeping so much, bleeding so often, dying on so vast a scale, by a really criminal carelessness in the use of their machineries, or by the skillful, scientific use of machineries and armies gotten up to kill? What can we think, looking on such facts, but that human souls are under some terrible dispossession that crazes their action? Who can even imagine them to be creatures complete in their order. To put the whole matter under the eye, in a very comprehensible example, suppose all the grains in a bushel of wheat were to commence acting in themselves, and towards and upon one another, in just the same manner as souls are seen to be doing in the specifications just made, what a bushel of tumult would it be! how wild, and hot, and fierce the little stir so many malcontents would make, whirling one another out of the measure, and finally burning up the measure itself. The only reason why such kernels of wheat do not behave in this way, is that they are every one complete creatures, resting in their own perfect mold, and in quiet harmony with each other—they that are at the top lying just as heavily, and they that are at the bottom supporting the weight just as bravely as they must. Souls completed in their order would do the same, just as all God's finished worlds and societies in glory are able to do, without one rasping of bad thought, or pang of mutual accusation.

Take another kind of illustration still. We have a way of saying, how often, concerning this or that man, that he is a ruined man, or we take a different figure and say, that he is a man blasted by his vices or his moral distempers; in which we refer mentally to the incomplete state of the flower, or the germ setting in the flower, which we say is blasted when it does not come to fruit. And the figure is rightly chosen. These men so blasted are incomplete men, men in the process of being completed, which they never in fact are or can be. And so in the awful desolations of talent, power, liberty, and hope, we see about us—strewing the world under the heavens, as the blasted germs the ground under a tree—we have just so many proofs that man who can not fully and completely be, perishes so miserably, because he can not bear the experiment.

I must name yet one other evidence of the incompleteness of souls, which, though apprehended by few, will be to such as it reaches most convincing of all. It is a very curious and remarkable distinction of souls that, being finite, they have yet infinite wants and aspirations; their very longing is to be somehow cleared of all bounds or completed in the outspreading of some infinite possession. And this, I think, however extravagant it may seem, is the exact and sober import of their problem in life. They are creatures to be somehow infinited, to be eternized in their continuance of good, to have all truth, to possess all things and wield all power, as completely as if it were theirs, and reign with a supreme will, having every thing done just as if it were, or as in fact being, from their own will and counsel. To this end their instinct runs, and stops not any where short of it. They are so made as to be possibly completed, only as they take possession of the infinite—just as in God they may, and as it is the sublime purpose of our gospel that they shall. What a falling short, therefore, is it, when they fall short of God. In their love they were to possess him; in their self-centered, bitterly stringent littleness, they tear themselves away; and the result is that their soul, which wants to fly all boundaries, shrivels to a point and only aches, where it should joyfully spread itself on boundless good, and in that element begin to reign.

But if souls are so far incomplete, as by manifold tokens we see, we have it as a matter next in point to find, how in Christ they can be made complete. And here we shall discover three great powers and agencies provided for this purpose.

1. Inspirations. Separated from God, man dwindles to a mere speck, he is nothing. He was made to have magnitude and be in flood, by having great inspirations roll under him and through him. Existing therefore in mere self-hood, he can not push himself out any way to be complete as from himself. A sponge might as well complete itself out of the sea, in dry mid air. It must have the sea, it must let in and possess the sea—all the currents, and tides, and even the salt of it—drinking and swaying, and feeding in its element, and then, as being sea-like in its habit, it fulfills its kind and is complete. Just so a soul must have all God's properties and perfections flowing in and through—liberty and life in his life, power in his power, counsel in his counsel. It must be true in his truth, righteous in his righteousness, secure in his security. That is, it must have the Infinite Life, which it was originally made for, flowing through it, and wafting in upon it, all the divine properties that feed and freshen, empower and impel, a really great and complete nature. It only gasps till the infinite touches it, and then it lives.

Now it is this everlasting inspiration-force that Christ arranges for, and promises in the gift of the Spirit. He enters the soul to fill out every lack, and every secret fault, knowing it all through, with a most subtle and perfect knowledge. He communicates, imbreathes, sheds abroad himself, configuring it inwardly to all that is most perfect in himself. He does it by a working in the nature of inspiration, not putting the will on forming this or that particular trait for itself, but by flooding and floating it on towards this or that, by his own divine motion, turning its very liberty towards all it wants and needs to receive. These inspirations are to be currents running exactly where it requires to be carried, and it is just as if every ship in the sea were to have a Gulf Stream given specially to it, running the exact course of its voyage, and drifting it on to its port. The inspirations are all perfect, they are adequate, exact, and steady, so that no completest issue may be missed. Then again—

2. We have ideas and ideals in Christ, who lives God in the human figure and relation, so that when we think him as a person, or take hold of him in belief, we have the exact figure in our feeling of what requires to be fashioned and completed in us. We not only have inspirations thus from behind, as we just now saw, but we have ideals before us to kindle inspirations in our eyes; so that while we could not even conceive any such perfect form of character, item by item, we can yet be fashioned by it, as a whole displayed to our love, in the living, loving person of our Master. We have nothing to do but to be in the Spirit, and keep ourselves in Christ's dear walk and company,

and we shall be set on surely and constantly, towards the completeness required. Christ is the mirror that glasses God's image before us, and the Spirit is the plastic force within, that transfers and photographs that image; and so, beholding as in a glass the glory of the Lord, we are changed into the same image from glory to glory, even as by the Spirit of the Lord.

Then once more—

3. To make the provision perfect, we are set in a wonderfully various scheme of relations, that we may have a training in duties, qualities, virtues, equally various, and be perfected in them and by means of them. Nothing could be done by setting us to the fashioning and finishing of a character, conceived by ourselves to be complete. We are too coarse and clumsy and half-seeing to even form the notion of a nobly complete excellence; the only way is to put us milling in rounds of duty, and drill, and sacrifice, wherein we shall be trained to completeness without conceiving it. And we have it as our remarkable advantage in Christ and the faith that seals our unity with him, that we have him as the perfect divine man with us in all these manifold human conditions. And we go into relation with our fellows, having him in company. We admire him, and by our love he is copied into us, when it is not our particular intent to copy him. We see how he lives for mankind, and we make common cause with him, in the practice of a like self-sacrifice. All our human rela-

tions in this way become a drill of occasions. And we are to get an experience in these relations, that is both corrective and creative. In our relations to the church and the ministry of the word; in our relations to the state and to public law; in our relations to the schools; in our relations to the family, where age, and sex, and fatherhood, and motherhood, and wifehood, and husbandhood, and childhood, and family property, and family want, and ten thousand other things are concerned; in our relations of business, and debt, and credit, and hire, and employment; in our relations of neighborhood and society; in our relations with unbelievers, neglectors, irreligious, unreligious, them that go to public worship, and them that do not; in our relations to the poor and the rich, to superiors and to inferiors, to friends, and flatterers, and enemies, and such as do us wrong—in all these multiformities, which no inventory can exhaust, we are put on just as many multiformities of duty and experience, so that trying to do the exact Christly thing in them all, we are to get benefit in so many forms and degrees, and be brought on thus at last, when all is done and suffered, to a real and full completeness in the will of God. In this wondrous mill, this laboratory of training, every blemish is to be removed, and the soul cut into form, after the similitude of a palace, polished as it were sapphire, sharpened as the point of a diamond. There will at last be no spot or wrinkle left, or any such thing. It will be washed, whitened, made clean, all glorious without, all beautiful within, a divinely gifted creature, complete and perfect in God's own image forever—ready for the enjoyment of God in all his sacrifices, beatitudes, benedictions, and judgments; ready for all God's future, and to have that future as its own.

This now as I conceive is the real completeness of man. And the impression into which we are inevitably brought, is that religion, the gospel and graces of the Lord Jesus Christ, are the only power that is able to bring man forward into the principal intents and highest summits of his nature.

As already intimated, we try education, getting much from it, but never any thing which even approaches the standard of completeness.* Meantime, we perfectly know that we only run the risk in it of making a small misery more miserable, and a small incapacity a greater, fearfully damaged incapacity. Nothing is completed by it, rounded out, and put at rest in good. In what we call self-improvement, a great deal more is attempted, because the endeavor is to cover the whole ground of the moral and religious nature. But if there is no cultivation of God or of Christ within, no inspirations moving, the work is a poor, desultory affair, polishing one thing, while another more important goes rough by neglect; and the result is, finally, that the great self-improvement issues in a great self-consciousness, painful to behold; a self-pleased finish of patch-work painfully made up,

* Y. C. C.

and destitute of all great liberty. Also, to itself, how dry!

We try self-government and self-regulation under the standards of morality, but the most we obtain or accomplish is to pile up what we think good acts on one another, as some day's man might the cents of his wages, but they will even be as dry as cents, with as little continuity in the pile. There is no life either in the acts or in ourselves. O if there be any thing tedious beyond measure, it is the legality method, going after a total of merit to be gotten up in ourselves, by good acts singly and persistently done. It would even choke a saint, much more a sinning man.

There is also another more superlative way which is greatly praised and magnified, and is therefore much aspired to by some, I mean philosophy. But the ideals raised in this discipline, will be forever outrunning the possible attainments, and the fine philosophic consciousness will be only a kind of equilibrium under dryness and felt limitation; a bitter kind of wisdom whose quiet is the assumed quiet only of a mind withholden from all highest truth, and bending itself down upon its own low thoughts and opinions. The wars of the mind, its disorders and dissatisfactions, are kenneled perhaps under what is called the philosophy, but not composed.

There is nothing in short but religion, or the life in God, that can be looked to for the completion of a soul. And it has three great advantages that differ it from every thing else. (1.) That it takes hold of the soul's eternity and its sin, to raise up, harmonize, inwardly purify, glorify and settle it, in a rest of everlasting equilibrium in God. (2.) That it takes hold of all possible conditions and callings, completing as truly the menial as the employer, the bondman as the master, the unlettered as the scholar, the man that is grimed by labor as the man of leisure or the monk in his cell. (3.) That it completes one degree of capacity as certainly as another, preparing even the feeblest to fill out its measure as roundly and blissfully as the highest.

Such is religion, the great all-formative grace for man. Nothing but this can even dare to promise any fit completion of humanity. All the harmonies, all the great inspirations, all the immovable and immortal confidences, all the contacts of infinity and seals of infinite possessorship are here. And yet, after all, how impossible is it, when we show all this, to get by the feeling of men not religious, that there is something humiliating in religion? What absurdity! what pitiable unreason! Religion humiliating to men! Religion a humiliation not to be endured! O my friends, if it be so with you, if you have so far lost the proportions of reason, that you can see nothing to respect and draw, in the becoming a really complete soul, there is nothing I am sure that can ever beget a right mind in you, but to go apart and listen for the secret monitions of God. Who but he can ever set in truth, over a barrier of false pride so irrational and so unaccountably blind.

Some of you, I know, have better thoughts, and yet have many great struggles with your own remaining disorders. You are mortified often, you sometimes half despair of yourselves. Be it so, you had best despair of yourselves; for you can not complete yourselves, and can only fail when you undertake it. But the more incompetent you seem to be, the more fatally mixed up with disorder and sin, the more glorious it is that Christ, the complete man, the only complete man that ever trod the earth, is with you. Him therefore you are to follow, in his brotherhood to walk. Being complete in himself, all that you are apprehended for he knows, and will help you to attain. Enough! enough! blessed is the assurance. But ye are washed, but ye are sanctified, but ye are glorified in the name of the Lord Jesus, and by the Spirit of our God—complete in him who is the head of all principality and power. O the grand conception of that world we have before us, that it is to be made up of men everlastingly complete! God grant that we may every one be there.

VI.

THE IMMEDIATE KNOWLEDGE OF GOD.

"For some have not the knowledge of God."—1 *Cor.* 15: 34.

WHO then are these Corinthian disciples, that they have not so much as the knowledge of God? Plainly enough our apostle is not charging them here with ignorance, but with some lack of the divine illumination which ought, if they are true disciples, to be in them. They certainly know God in the traditional and merely cognitive way. Indeed the apostle is discoursing to them here of the resurrection of the dead, which is itself a matter based in Christian ideas. Besides, he adds, "I speak this to your shame;" having it in view that they are not Pagans, but so far informed, as disciples, that they ought to know God in a way more interior.

We shall best understand the point assumed in this impeachment, I think, if we raise the distinction between knowing God, and knowing about God. Doubtless, it is much to know about God, about his operations, his works, his plans, his laws, his truth, his perfect attributes, his saving mercies. This kind of knowledge is presupposed in all faith, and constitutes the rational ground of faith, and so far is necessary even to salvation. But true faith itself discovers another and more absolute kind of knowledge, a knowledge of God himself; immediate, personal knowledge, coming out of no report, or statement, or any thing called truth, as being taught in language. It is knowing God within, even as we know ourselves. The other is only a knowing about God, as from a distance. To put this matter of the immediate knowledge of God in its true doctrinal position, it may be well to say, that we have two denials set against it, both as nearly fatal as need be to any such possibility.* One is the denial of the philosophers outside of Christianity, speculating there about the cognitive functions, and making what they conceive to be their specially profound discovery, that knowledges are possible only of things relative. Therefore, God being infinite, can not be known — God is unknowable. They say nothing of faith, they have no conception of any such super-eminent, almost divine talent in our humanity, shut up or drawn away from God by our sin—an immediate sensing power, to which God may be as truly known, as we know the distinct existence of objects perceived by the eyes. Could they simply trust themselves over to God, to live by his tender guidance and true inward revelation, they would never again call him the unknowable. Meantime, there will be many children of sorrow, unlearned and simple, who will easily know the God they have it as their point of philosophy to show can not any way be known! This

* Y. C. C.

most false and feeble doctrine of negation, I do not feel called upon to discuss—it will die of inanity sooner than it can by argument.

The other and second form of denial as regards the immediate knowledge of God, sets up its flag inside of the Christian church and among the muniments of doctrine. Here the possibility of faith is admitted, and the necessity of it abundantly magnified. But the faith power is used up, it is conceived, on propositions; that is propositions which affirm something about God. It does not go through, and over, and beyond, such propositions, to meet the inward revelation or discovery of God himself. The accepted doctrine is that we know, or can know God, only so far as we know something about Him, no immediate knowledge of Him being at all possible, or even conceivable. The continually reiterated assumption is that never, in our most sacred, dearest, deepest moments of holy experience, do we get beyond being simply acted on by certain truths we know about God. And when men are called to God, saying, "Come unto me," they understand the meaning to be, that they are called only to believe something about him put in words, and work their feeling or their faith by what the words supply. They do not even conceive it as a possibility, that we should know God himself as a presence operative in us; even as we know the summer heat by its pervasive action in our bodies. We do not know the heat by report, or debate, or inference, or scientific truth interpreting medially between us and it; we do not see it, or hear it, or handle it, and yet we have it and know that we have, by the inward sense it creates. So in what is called the Christian regeneration, our being born of God implies the immediate revelation of God within—all which these teachers can not so understand, but imagine that we are born of something about God rather; that is of truths, affirmations, notions, working medially or instrumentally between us and God.

What then is the truth in this matter? Why it is that human souls, or minds are just as truly made to be filled with God's internal actuating presence, as human bodies are to be tempered internally by heat, or as matter is made to be swayed by gravity, or the sky-space to be irradiated by the day. God is to them heat, gravity, day, immediately felt as such, and known by the self-revelation of his person. So at least it was originally to be, and so it would be now, had not this presence of God internally and personally to souls, this quickening, life-giving God-sense, been shut off by sin. For by this they tear themselves away from God, and become self-centered, separated creatures, even as growths in a cavern, or as fishes on the land, having no longer that immediate knowledge of God which is their normal state of subsistence. Henceforth they know or may know, much about God, but they do not know God. They are shut up as to God, dark to God, except, as by the head, they may think, discover, learn, or reason something about him. Never do they know him till he becomes centered in their soul again as its life, and the crowning good and blessing of its eternity. And this is fitly called being born of God, because it is the entering of God again into his place—to be the beginning there of a new movement and life derivative from him, and fed by the springs of his fullness in the heart. Which entering in of God supposes, in fact, a new discovery of God. Not that the subject is put back now into a new cognitive relation; his cognitive function is nowise altered, and if there were no other, would still be as blind to God as before. The new discovery made is made by faith, opening the heart to receive, and in receiving feel or inwardly sense, what should have been the original and always normal revelation.

Is it then to be said or imagined that, in this new-birth, or new-begun life of faith, the subject really knows God by an immediate knowledge? He may not so conceive it, I answer, but it is none the less true. He will speak, it may be, only of his peace, but it will seem to him to be a kind of divine peace. He will testify that God is wondrously near to him, and he will put into that word *near* something like a sense of Him. He will be conscious and will say that he is, of a strangely luminous condition, as if his whole body, in the words of Christ, were full of light; and all the scripture terms that set forth God as a light, and a sun, and a power opposite to darkness, will come in, as it were, to answer, and to interpret the force of his experience. Still he will not conceive, it may be, of any such thing as that the peace, the nearness, the luminousness of his soul, supposes an immediate knowledge of God now discovered to Him. He may even disown such a conception, as implying a kind of irreverence. Nevertheless that is the exact verdict of his experience, and nothing else can at all give the meaning of it. Indeed, if we can believe it, he was made originally to be even conscious of God and live eternally in that kind of immediate knowledge; which design is now beginning, for the first time, to be fulfilled.

Thus you have every one two kinds of knowledge relating to yourself. One is what you know mediately about yourself, through language, and one that which you have immediately as being conscious of yourself. Under the first you learn who your parents were, what others think of you, what effects the world has on you, what power you have over it, and what is thought to be the science it may be of your nature, as an intelligent being. Under the second you have a knowledge of yourself so immediate, that there is no language in it, no thought, no act of judgment or opinion, you simply have a *self-feeling* that is intuitive and direct. Now you were made to have just such an immediate knowledge of God as of yourself; to be conscious of God; only this consciousness of God has been closed up by your sin and is now set open by your faith; and this exactly is what distinguishes every soul enlightened by the Spirit, and born of God. Whether he says it or not, this is the real account of his experience, that God is now revealed in him, and that he begins to be conscious of God; for it is a fact, as every soul thus enlightened will testify, that he is now conscious, not of himself only, but of a certain *otherness* moving in him; some mysterious power of good that is to him what he is not to himself, a spring of new-born impulse, a living of new life. It is not that he sees God without by the eye, any more than that he sees himself without by the eye, when he is conscious of himself; it is not that he has any mind-view of God awakened in him any more than that he has in consciousness a mind-view of himself. It is only that he has the sense of a sublime *other* not himself; a power, a life, a transcendently great felt Other—who is really and truly God. Hence the rest, and strength, and peace, and luminous glory into which he is born—it is nothing but the revelation of God and the immediate knowledge of God. Probably enough he will not say this, not having been trained or accustomed to this mode of conceiving the change, but he will say that God is *near*, wonderfully, gloriously near, and will press into the word all nearness possible, even such as to include in fact the felt consciousness of God, and the immediate knowledge of his presence.

Observe now in what manner the Scriptures speak on this subject. And the time would fail me to merely recount the ways in which it is given as the distinction of faith or holy experience, that it carries, in some way, the knowledge of God, and differs the subject in that manner from all that are under the blindness of mere nature.

Discoursing thus, for example, of the state of love, it distinguishes that state as being one, in which God and God's love are actually revealed in the soul—"For love is of God, and every one that loveth is born of God, and knoweth God. He that loveth not knoweth not God, for God is love." And accordingly there was never a soul on earth that being born into the great principle and impulse of self-sacrificing love, did not have the sense of God in it, and consciously live, in some mysterious participation of him.

The Holy Spirit, in like manner, is spoken of in a great many ways, as the intercoursing life and immediate inward manifestation of God. Thus he is said to "witness with our spirit," which means that there is to be a consciousness raised of his presence in the soul, and a sense of reciprocity established by what is called his witnessing with us; as if he carried himself into our feeling in a way of internal dialogue. So there is a discerning of the Spirit spoken of, which does not mean a reasoning out, but an immediate knowing of the mind of the Spirit. Christ also declares when promising the Spirit, that the world seeth him not, neither knoweth him, but ye *know* him, for he dwelleth with you and shall be in you." And in immediate connection—"the world seeth me no more, but ye see me—[know me, that is, in him.] At that day ye shall know that I am in the Father, and ye in me and I in you." And then again—"He that loveth me shall be loved of my father, and I will love him, and will manifest myself unto him." And what is manifestation but immediate knowledge?

This new consciousness of God is plainly declared by the apostle when he says—"That Christ may dwell in your hearts by faith, that ye, being rooted and grounded in love, may be able to comprehend with all saints what is the breadth, and length, and depth, and height, and to know the love of Christ which passeth knowledge; that ye might be filled with all the fullness of God." What language but this, "to know the love that passeth knowledge," to have revealed in conscious participation what can not be known or measured by the notions of the cognitive understanding—what but this can fitly express the sacred visitation of a Christian soul, when through Christ and the Spirit it is wakened again to the eternal consciousness of God.

O this wonder of discovery, the knowledge of God—who can find words for it, or the change it must needs make! It even makes the soul another creature to itself. Now it is no more blank to God, tortures itself no more in guesses dim, sighs no more—"O that I knew where I might find him." It has recovered, as it were, the major part of existence that before was lost; it knows not only itself, but it has the knowledge of God; and in that fact it is raised out of its mere finite speck of magnitude, into the conscious participation of being infinite. Every thing is now become luminous. Old things are passed away, behold all things are become new—great as new, and holy as great, and blessed as holy.

But there is an objection to this mode of conceiving holy experience, as implying an immediate discovery of God, which I am properly required to notice. What is the use, in this view, some will ask, of a Bible, or external revelation? what use of the incarnation itself? Are not these advances on our outward knowledge superseded and made useless, when we conceive that God is offered to immediate knowledge or experience? In one view they are, and in another they are not. Does it follow that because we have an immediate knowledge of heat, we have therefore no use at all for the scientific doctrine of heat, or the laws by which it is expounded? Suppose it is a part of our interest in this article of heat, that we be able to generate more of it, or use it differently and with better economy. So far we have a use in knowing about heat, as well as knowing heat. In the same way it is of immense consequence to know every thing possible about God, that we may find how the more perfectly to know God. We want, in this manner, the whole Scripture, and not least the incarnation and the cross, and the story of the pentecost. These things are matters given to us about God, for the very purpose of showing us how to find God. The inherent use of all medial knowledges, all truths, cognitions, books, appearings, and teachings, is that they bring us in, to know God by an immediate knowledge. So far I would give most ready assent to the Quaker doctrine. We are never to put the book between us and God, to give us second-hand knowledges of him, and there accept our limit. The book is given us to carry us beyond the book, and put us in the way of finding God as others have found him; then and there to be in the Spirit as they were, and know Him by such private interpretation as he will give us. The mine is given, not that we may have the gold already dug, but that we may go a mining for ourselves. And as these great saints of holy scripture were men of like passions with us, it is to be our glorious privilege that they pilot us on, by telling us how to know and grow as they did.

There is also another objection to be noticed here, which moves in the exactly opposite direction, where those who know not God complain that revelation, as they look upon it, does not reveal him, and that God is dark to them still, as they could not expect him to be. If there be a God, they ask, why does he not stand forth and be known as a Father to his children? Why allow us to grope, and stumble after him, or finally miss him altogether? They are not satisfied with the Bible, and if we call it a revelation of God, they do not see it. Why should he be so difficult of discovery, hid in recesses so deep, and only doubtfully and dimly known? If there be a God, is he not of such consequence, that being hid is even a wrong? Is it not also the right most plainly of every human creature, to have an easy and free knowledge of him?

I certainly think it is; only we must not make him responsible for the blear and self-blinding of our sin. And if it were not for this, I think we should all see him plainly enough, and always, and every where. For it is the whole endeavor of his management to be known. He not only meets our understanding processes in the facts of his Bible, but he offers himself to be known without any process at all, just as the light is; nay, if we will have it so, to be a kind of second consciousness in us, and be known to us even as we know ourselves. He is even pressing himself into knowledge when our eyes are shut—in our self-will, our hate, our denial, our desolation. O that for one hour you could have the ingenuous mind that is needed to really give him welcome! No more, after that, would you complain of him that he withdraws from your knowledge.

Now this exposition of God's truth, here brought to a close, converges practically, as I conceive, on a single point of broadest consequence; correcting a mistake almost universally prevalent in some greater or less degree; the mistake I mean of being over much occupied in religion with matters of the head. The true evidence of discipleship is knowing God. Other men know something about him. The Christian knows him, has him as a friend. And there is no substitute for this. Observances, beliefs, opinions, self-testing severities—all these are idle and prove nothing. If a man knows God, it is a fact so grand, so full of meaning, that he wants no evidence beside. All curious explorations and deep searches in this matter are very much as if a man were trying himself carefully, to find whether he sees the day. If a man knows God in the revelation of his Son, he is *ipso facto* full, and wants no more. Therefore he should not even begin to be elaborate in his self-testings, or his questions about himself; the sign is a bad one. When the true day hath dawned, and the day-star hath risen in the heart, the man himself ought to know it without much trouble. Let thine eye be single, serve God, seek God, know God only, and thy whole body shall be full of light.

Now as these keep off the light of their day, by the ever-busy meddling of their understanding, there is another class who have never found the day by reason of their over-busy, over-curious endeavors to make ready for it. They are waiting, and reading, and reasoning, as they think, to get light *for* conversion. They are going to be converted rationally, nursing all the while a subtle pride of this, which only makes them darker, and puts them farther off. They quite misconceive the relation of our previous opinions, knowledges, and wisdoms, to the state of faith or conversion; and putting themselves down upon these, they are all the while at work, as they think, grading a road into the kingdom of God, so that when the road is done, they expect to be steered straight in, guided by, and rested on, the rails they have now finally laid down. But there is, alas! a great gulf of transition here to be passed, that forbids eternally any such conceit as that. There is no such relation between the knowing about God and knowing God, as they think there is. All the speculative preparations made, and roads of knowledge graded, stop inevitably short of the kingdom, and whoever imagines that he is going to be trundled logically along the plane of his notional wisdoms and arguments, into God's bosom, will assuredly find that he is not there, but has fallen infinitely short of it. What then, must you drop out your very intelligence in order to become a Christian? Far from that as possible; you are only required to use your intelligence intelligently. That is, perceiving that all you know, debate and think *about* God is, at best, only introductory to the knowledge of God himself, and some way off, take care rather to let go your speculations and open your heart in faith to the true manifestation of God. After all you have reasoned, faith is still to come. The roads of the natural understanding are in a lower plane, you must rise, you must go up into trust and *know God—God himself*—by the inward discovery of his infinite spirit and person.

What is wanted, therefore, for us all, is summed up in this Christian word faith—faith in Christ, or faith in God; for it makes no difference. Thinking and questioning stir the mind about God, faith discerns him, and by it, as the soul's open window, he enters to be discerned. Would that all of you could know how much this means. Cease then from your questions, all ye that are afar off, not knowing God, and asking sometimes, with a sigh, where shall we find him? Know that he is here in thy mouth and in thy heart; only believe in him, and you shall know the greatest bliss a soul can know, the Father of all glory, manifest within.

VII.

RELIGIOUS NATURE, AND RELIGIOUS CHARACTER.

"That they should seek the Lord, if haply they might feel after him, and find him, though he be not far from every one of us."—*Acts* 17: 27.

SOMETIMES a truth or distinction of the greatest consequence will come into expression in a writer's language, when he does not notice it, or is not particularly aware of it himself. Thus Paul, in his notable speech here to the men of Athens, drops out, unawares to himself, in the form of his language, a most accurately drawn distinction that is of the highest possible consequence. In passing through their city, and beholding their devotions, he had been strangely affected by finding, among others, an altar to the *Unknown God.* That was the type, in a sense, of all their idolatries. In them all, impelled by a natural instinct for religion, they were ignorantly worshiping; wanting a God, and feeling after him, but not able to find him. And yet he is not hidden, wants to be found, orders every thing to bring them to himself.

This expression, "feel after," has a mental reference plainly enough to what they, as God's blind offspring, were doing; and the expression, "find him," to what God, never afar off, wants to have them do. In one, the deep longings of a nature made for God and religion is recognized; in the other, a satisfied state of holy discovery and rest in God.

What I propose, accordingly, at the present time, is to unfold, if I can, the profoundly real and practically wide distinction here suggested, *between having a religious nature, and being in a religious life;* or, what in fact is the same, *between feeling after God, and finding him.*

In proposing this distinction, it may be important to say, that I do it with deliberate reference to what appears to be a great religious danger of our time. It used to be the common doctrine of sermons, as many of you will remember, that mankind, under sin, have really no affinity for God left. Total depravity was made total, in such a sense as to leave in the soul no receptivity for God whatever. Human nature itself, it was declared, is opposition to God; able, therefore, only to be the more exasperated in its opposition, the nearer God is brought. Instead of having still a religious nature, it seemed to be supposed that we have rather an anti-religious nature, and that nothing can be done for us or by us till a new nature is given.

All which now is virtually gone by. We familiarly recognize now the fact of a religious nature still left, hungering and heaving in us, and beginning oft to be in want; longings after the divine, however suppressed by the overmastering tides of evil and vain desire. The soul, we believe and acknowledge, has a sensibility to good and to God, able to be drawn by Christ lifted up, capable thus of being recovered to holiness without being literally new-created in it. And the result is what might well enough be expected. Where before, the soul, heaving and hungering and often much disturbed, was battered and beaten down by the huge impossibility of religion,—dumbed even to prayer, and kept in stern dead-lock, waiting for the arrival of God's omnipotence to remove the opposition of nature, and give the new heart of grace—we are passing out rather now into a kind of holiday freedom, talking piety as a natural taste, enjoying our fine sentiments of reverence to God, and protesting our great admiration of Christ and his beautiful lessons,—all in the plane of nature itself. Multitudes of us, and especially of the young, congratulate ourselves that we are about as good Christians, on the ground of mere natural sentiment, as need be. Nay, we are somewhat better Christians than there used to be, because we are more philanthropic, better reformers, and in that are so easily up to the level of Christianity, in a fashion of piety so much more intelligent. Our doctrine of the gospel grows flashy, to a large extent, in the same manner. High sentiments, beautiful aspirations, are taken, sometimes wittingly and sometimes unwittingly, as amounting to at least so much of religious character. Where we shall be landed, or stranded rather, in this shallowing process, is too evident. Christianity will be coming to be more and more nearly a lost fact. A vapid and soulless naturalism will be all that is left, and we shall keep the gospel only as a something in divine figure and form, on which to play our natural sentiments. In this view it is that I propose the distinction stated, between having a religious nature, and being in a religious life. That we may unfold and verify this distinction, consider,—

1. What it is, accurately understood, to have a religious nature.

It is neither more nor less than to be a man, a being made for God and religion; so far, and in such sense, a religious being. It implies, in other words, that we are so made as to want God, just as a child's nature wants a mother and a father. It does not follow, that the child ever knew, or, practically speaking, ever had either one or the other. And yet the want is none the less real on that account; for when it feels itself an orphan, out on the broad world alone, it only sighs the more bitterly, it may be, for the solitary lot it is in: and, when it notes the tender love and faithful sympathy in which other children are sheltered in their homes, how sadly does it grieve and weep many times for that unknown, unremembered parentage it can never look to or behold! So it is with our religious nature. It may not consciously pine after God, as an orphan for his lost parents; and yet God is the necessary complement of all its feelings, hopes, satisfactions, and endeavors. Without God, all it is becomes abortion. It wants God as its completest, almost only want; feeling instinctively after him even in its voluntary neglect of him, and consciously or unconsciously, willingly or unwillingly, longing and hungering for the bread of his fatherly relationship. And it hungers none the less truly that it stays aloof from him, refuses to seek him in prayer, tries to forget him and be hidden from him, or even fights against all terms of duty towards him; even as the starving madman is none the less hungry, or fevered by hunger, that he refuses to eat.

Now this natural something in the soul, which makes God its principal and first want, includes very nearly its natural every thing. It has not a faculty that is not somehow related to God. It feels the beauty of God, even his moral beauty. All its bosom sentiments would play around him, and bask in his goodness. Considering who God is, it has the feeling of admiration towards him, rising sometimes even up to the pitch of sublimity. God's creating strength and all-dominating sovereignty in good, are just that in the soul, without which he would not be sufficiently great. His omnipresence, thought of it may be with dread, is yet thought of also as the needed qualification of a complete world-care and government. Reason gets at no limit of rest and satisfaction till it culminates in God. The imagination flies through solitary worlds of vacancy and cold, till it feels the brightness of God's light on its wings, and meets him shining everywhere. Even fear wants to come and hide in his bosom; and guilt, withering under his frown, would only frown upon him if he were not exactly just, or less just than he is.

There is a kind of incipient feeling after the state of piety thus, in what we call the religious nature. It has great sentiments swelling in its depths, honors

12

waiting there for truth, glad emotions waiting to spring up and meet the face of God's beauty, aspirations climbing after his recognition, dependencies of feeling running out their tendrils to lay hold of him in trust.

Nor let any one imagine that these things are at all the less true, under the perverse and perverting effects of human depravity. Human nature as created is upright, as born or propagated, a corrupted and damaged nature. But however corrupted and damaged, however fallen, it has the original divine impress on it, everywhere discernible. It has the same feelings, sentiments, powers of thought and affection, the same longings and aspirations, only choked in their volume, and crazed by the stormy battle of internal discord and passion in which they have their element. The most sad fact—fact and also evidence—of human depravity is, that the religious nature stands a temple still for God, only scarred and blackened by the brimstone fires of evil; more majestic possibly as a ruin, than it would be if it did not prove its grandeur by the desolations it withstands.

Denying therefore, as we must, that human nature is less really religious because it is depraved, or damaged by sin,—as on mere physiological principles it must be—denying also that it is made incapable of approving or admiring God, or being drawn by his beauty, it is not to be denied that there are times or moods, when it will even be exasperated by his very perfections; that is, when it is tormented by its own guiltiness, and resolved on courses of life which God is known, with all his might of sovereignty, to oppose. At such times, there will flame up a horrible fire of malignity; and the better he is, the more dislike of him will be felt. But these are only moods. The same persons, in a different mood, when they are not thinking of themselves, and not pressed by the sense of conflict with him, will think of him admiringly, and almost lovingly; as it were, feel after him, to know him more perfectly. The religious nature in them is more constant than their moods of perversity, and is reaching after God in a certain way of natural desire all the while. Holding fast now these conceptions of the religious nature, let us pass on,—

2. To inquire what it is to be in the practically religious life; or, what is the same, to be in religious character. There is nothing practical in having a merely religious nature. A very bad man has it as truly as a good: the most confirmed atheist has it. Mere natural desire, want, sentiment God-ward, do not make a religious character. They are even compatible and consistent often with a character most profoundly irreligious. What does it signify that the nature is feeling after God, when the life is utterly against him? If a man has a natural sense of honor, does it make him an honorable man, when he betrays every trust and violates every bond of friendship? If a man has a fine natural sensibility to truth, does it make him a true man, when he is a sophist or a liar in all the practice of his life? Where there is naturally a fine sense of

moral beauty, and a capacity to draw the picture of it even with admirable justice and artistic skill, does it make the man a morally beautiful character, when his life, as will not seldom happen, is a life in utter disorder and deformity? Even a thief may have a good sentiment of justice, and be only the more consciously guilty because of it. There may even be a wondrously tender sensibility in the heart of a robber or assassin; such, that in his family, or among his clan, he will be abundant in the most gentle and kindest offices. And in just the same way a man may have the finest feeling of natural reverence to God, the highest sentiments of admiration for God's character, the grandest rational convictions of his value to the world, as its moral Governor and providential Keeper, and yet not have so much as a trace of genuine piety in the life. He may even go so far as to enjoy the greatness and beauty of God, and have the finest things to say of him, and have no trace of a genuinely religious character, any more than if he were enjoying or praising a landscape. He will do the two things, in fact, in exactly the same manner; and one will have just as much to do for his piety as the other.

What, then, is it to be a practically religious man? When is it and how, that a man begins to be religious in the sense of religious character? To conceive this matter distinctly, two things need to be understood beforehand. First, that religious character is more than mere natural character, and different from it, as what we are by constitution is different from what we do, and practically seek, and freely become. It is that which lies in choice, and for which we are thus responsible. It is made by what the soul's liberty goes after, with a reigning devotion,—what it chooses and lives for as its end. If the man, therefore, lives for himself, or for the world, as all men do in the way of sin, he is without God, without religious character, and is all the more guilty in it, that his nature is feeling after God in throes of disappointed longing. Then again, secondly, it must be understood that souls are made for God, to have him always present in them, and working in their liberty itself, even as gravity is in matter, impelling its motions. They are to know God and be conscious of him, even as they know and are conscious of themselves. They are to live and move and have their being in him,—not as omnipresence only, but as inward revelation. Inspiration is to be their life, and their freedom is to be complete in the freedom and sovereignty of God. As they are God's offspring, they are to live in his Fatherhood, and have their finite being complemented in the sense of his infinite greatness and perfection inwardly discovered.

Assuming these two points, it follows that a man is never in religious character till he has found God; and that he will never find him, till his whole voluntary nature goes after him, and chimes with him in his principles and ends. Whatever ends he has had of his own must be given up, as being his own, and God's must be enthroned in him by a supreme devotion. "Ye shall seek for me and find me, if ye search for me with all your heart." God can not have room to spread himself in the soul, and fill it with his inspirations, when it is hugging itself, and is habitually set on having its own ways. A great revolution is so far needed, therefore, if it is to find God; for God can not be revealed in it, or born into it, save when it comes away from all its lower ends to be in God's. No movings of mere natural sentiment reach this point. Nothing but a voluntary surrender of the whole life to his will prepares it to be set in this open relation to God. And just here it is, accordingly, that religious character begins. The soul, as a nature, feeling instinctively after him, baffled still and kept back by self-devotion, has in fact no trace of piety. It is only when God is moving into it, and living in it, that the true piety begins: this is the root and life of the religious character. Now it communes knowingly with God, receives of God, walks with God, and lives by a hidden life from him. Now, for the first time, the religious nature is fulfilled, and all its longings rest in the divine fullness. It has found God. Observe now,—

3. How easily, and in how many ways, the workings of the mere religious nature may be confounded with the workings of religious character, and, as successful counterfeits, take their place. The admiration of God's beauty—what is it, some will say, but love? Do we not, then, all of us, love God? The sentimental pleasure felt in God's qualities,—what is it but the real joy of religion? and how satisfactory it is to think so! Even the soul's deep throbs of want,—what are they

but its hungerings after righteousness? and that void of hunger must be filled, even though it refuses to be. So they think. In short, there is a vast religious poetry in the soul's nature; and what is it all but a religious character begun? Is any thing more certain, as we look on man, than that he is a religious being; and what is this, by a straight inference, but to say that he has a naturally religious character? And so it comes to pass, that religion is the same thing as mere natural sentiment; and the feeling after God—poor, flashy delusion!—substitutes the finding God altogether. And this it is thought, by alas how many, is the more intelligent kind of religion! They love to hear of it, because it plays on their natural sentiment so finely. It is almost a modern discovery, and they love to be religious in this way. It will not organize a church, or raise a mission, or instigate a prayer, or help any one to bear an enemy, and even quite dispenses with finding God; the Spirit of God bearing witness with our spirit is not in it; but, for all this, it seems to be a more superlative kind of religion!

We can hardly think it possible that a feeble imposture like this should beguile the most common understanding; and yet we have had a most eloquent teacher of this religion vaunting himself in it, here in our New England, as if it were the true Christianity! He finds a natural reverence for God in souls, sentiments of adoration towards him, longings that feel after him; and that he calls religion. All men have it; no man, even the worst, wants it. And the true doctrine is, that, living in the plane of nature, we are to cultivate ourselves in it, and grow better always—certain always of being religious because of it. And this kind of mock gospel is infusing itself, by a subtle contagion, into the general mind of our times; appearing and reappearing in our literature, sometimes in our sermons, and turning our youth quite away from every thing most vital and solid in the supernatural, soul-renewing doctrine of Christ.

It is exactly the religion of Herod, who did many things under John's preaching, and heard him gladly, and then took off his head to please a dancing woman. He had all the sentiments of religion, and loved to have them brought into play; but the graceful trip of dancing feet pleased him a great deal more! Pilate, the Roman, had the same religious nature, felt the greatness, quivered in sublimest awe of Jesus, and devoutly washed his hands to be clear of the blood, and ended by giving up the glorious and majestic victim to his murderers. Felix had the same religion; so had Agrippa; so had Balaam; and the world is full of it, —sensibility to God, truth, right, coupled with a practical non-reception of all.

It results, accordingly, just as we should expect, that there are always two kinds or classes of religion in the world; those which are the product of a religious sentiment more or less blind, and those which look to the regeneration of character; religions that are feeling after God, and a true religion that finds him, and discovers him inwardly to the soul. The religion of the

Athenians was of the former class, and all the idolatrous religions of the world are of the same kind. What a sublime and almost appalling proof of the religious nature of man, feeling dimly, groping blindly after God, imagining that he is somewhere and everywhere; in the sun, in the moon, in the snakes of the ground, the beetles of the air, the poor tame vegetables of the garden, the many-headed monsters carved in wood or stone, that never were any where but in the crazy fancy of superstition! Look on these, and see how man feels after God: does he therefore find him? And if we speak of character, truth, love, mercy, purity, in what do those blind struggles of our almost divine nature issue, but in a defect of every thing heavenly, and even comely? What but hells of character are these idolatrous religions?

Under the guise of Christianity, too, we may distinguish at least two kinds of religion, that are corrupted in a greater or less degree by infusions of the same error. One is the religion of forms, where the soul is taken by them as a matter of taste; loves to play reverence under them; has a great delight in their beauty, antiquity, order; and takes the mere sentimental pleasure it has in them, and the hope of being buried in them, for the certain reality of religious character. The other is a religion of sentiment throughout, and fed by reason; feeling after God in the beautiful and grand objects of nature; pleased to have such high sentiments towards him; taking hold of these sentiments to cultivate them more and more; delighted with Christ's beautiful lessons of natural virtue; and praising him even as the finest of all the great men of the world! It is not intended, under either of these mistaken forms of worship, to renounce Christianity; and the mischiefs they propagate in their adherents are in all degrees. Sometimes the infusion of sentimentality is slight, sometimes it quite takes the place of piety, and there is no room left for so much as a vestige to grow. Now, the true gospel is that which brings a regenerative power, and creates the soul anew in God's image. Any religion that has not this is so far a mock religion. The true test question, therefore, by which every man is to try his religion is this,—have I found God in it? Has it more than pleased me? has it pierced me, brought me to the light, given me to know God? If it has not done this for you, too little can not be made of it. And the sooner it is cast behind you, with all its fine sentiments, in a total turning of your heart to God himself, the better. *The life of God in the soul of man*,—that is religious character, and beside that there is none. And that is salvation, without which there is no salvation. For this it is that makes salvation; that the soul, before without God alienated from the life of God, is won back to a real God-welcome, and has him revealed inwardly in holy Fatherhood, as the life of its life. Hungry as the prodigal, it has come back from its wanderings in shameful penitence, to be greeted with a kiss, and clothed again, and feasted, and hear its Father say, "O dead, thou art alive again!"

Having endeavored, in this manner, to impress the wide distinction between a religious nature and a religious character, between feeling after God and finding him, I must bring my illustrations to a close.

The sum of the whole matter is this,—understand, have it never to be disguised from you, that your salvation lies in finding God, and that you may know your salvation only as you know that you have found him,—know that you have found him as the graciously felt preserver, the conductor, guide, peace, joy of your heart. You will not know him outwardly, but within by the secret flood of his movement in your life. You will be consciously configured to his character as once you were not; raised, exalted, married to his ends, one with him. Count yourself no Christian, because you like thoughts and discourses about God. Be jealous of any gospel that merely pleases you, and puts your natural sentiments aglow. See God in the flowers, if you will; but ask no gospel made up of flowers. Look after a sinner's gospel, one that brings you God himself. Doubtless you are hungry; therefore you want bread, and not any mere feeling after it. Understand the tragic perils of your sin, and think nothing strong enough for you but a tragic salvation. Require a transforming religion, not a pleasing. Be enticed by no flattering sentimentalities, which the children of nature are everywhere taking for a religion. Refuse to sail in the shallows of the sea; strike out into the deep waters where the surges roll heavily, as in God's majesty, and the gales of the

Spirit blow. Man your piety as a great expedition against God's enemies and yours, and hope for no delicate salvation, not to be won by great sacrifices and perils.

Let me add in this connection, also, a word of necessary caution respecting a particular form of unbelief that is now common. How many are beginning to say, and have it for a fine discovery, that there is no such thing as a distinction of kind among men; nothing to hang a distinction of worlds upon; nothing to make that distinction better than a superstitious moonshine of the past ages! Saints, and not saints; born of God, and not born; sons of God, and aliens, —these are all a kind of fiction that has come to an end. Are we not all religious, all good?—some a little, some more, and some very good? Even where there is no pretense of piety, where there is great wrong, corruption, brutality of life, is there not still a little sense of God that only wants to be increased; some tender yearnings after God, however suppressed? What have we, then, but distinctions of degrees, and no distinction of kind? Where, then, is the footing for heaven and hell? Let this fiction go: it is time now to be clear of it. I have shown you here, I think, where the true distinction lies, and the profound reality of it. No great gulf fixed was ever thought of that is wider or deeper, or more absolute. It is the distinction between a religious nature and a religious character. We all have such a nature, feeling after God; but we have not all found him. We all have religious sentiments, desires, yearnings; but how many never choose a religious end! how many, in fact, never did any thing in the practical life, but trample the sentiments, desires, yearnings of their nature, in lives of disobedience, and a fight of rejection against God and every holy thing! No, my friends, the gospel distinctions are not gone by; the heaven and hell of the Scripture are not yet antiquated. Here they stand, based in the everlasting distinction of kind: darkness and light, chaos and order, falsehood and truth, are not more opposite, more impossible to be reconciled. A religious nature signifies nothing where there is no religious character; nothing, I mean, but the greater wrong and wrath the more deserved.

Once more, it must strike you all alike, the most unreligious as truly as the others, that it is a very great thing, in such a view as that now presented, to have a religious nature. Oh, if you had any true sense of it, you would even begin to tremble at the thought of yourselves! See, the whole world over, in all ages and times, men shaping their strange religions: they are groping all and feeling after God, to them the unknown God. And you, it may be, are doing the same. Your great nature, made in his image, answers to him, reaches after him in suppressed longings. A sublime uneasiness keeps you astir, and you know not what it means. You think of it often, perhaps, or even speak of it complainingly, that God has made your life so strangely barren. The secret of it is, that you are empty, hungry, shivering in the cold, for want of God;

and that because you seek him not. Always feeling after what you always have not, and even refuse to have: how can it be otherwise? And what is to become of this great, almost divine nature, that is heaving thus in your bosom? This will become of it, and nothing else. It will grope and writhe and sigh, only tasting now and then little admirations of God, till finally its lofty affinities will all go out and die. All faculties that can not have their use grow stunted and thin and withered, as inevitably even as an arm or a leg. How much more the godlike powers and affinities of the religious nature, when for years and years they can not have their God,—receptivities all, yet never allowed to receive.

So God understands himself; and therefore keeps himself near, wanting to be found. Even as the apostle told those groping, blind men of Athens, "Though he be not far from any one of us." They were all feeling after him instinctively, even in their vices and grim idolatries; and still he was nigh, ready, behind their thinnest veils of thought, to break through into the discovery of their heart. God was pronounced, in fact, upon their whole nature, in every faculty and fibre. And yet they could not find him. Therefore, also, he became at last incarnate in his Son, and put himself before their senses, and took society with them, and showed them what they might have thought impossible, that the unseen, infinite Being has a suffering concern for just those hungry natures that in sin are groping after him. And this Christ is for us all,—

"the light of the knowledge of the glory of God." The veil is taken away. To come unto Jesus now, and believe in him as one come out from God is really to find him. No one can earnestly seek him now, and miss of him. Mere feeling after him by dim instinct will not find him, but earnest, honest, prayerful seeking will. And therefore he declared himself, in his first sermon, when he took up his ministry,—would that all ye hungering and groping souls could hear the promise!—"Ask, and ye shall receive; seek and ye shall find; knock, and it shall be opened unto you. For every one that asketh receiveth, and he that seeketh findeth, and to him that knocketh it shall be opened." What an opening is that which opens the discovery of God! and what a finding is that which finds him!

VIII.

THE PROPERTY RIGHT WE ARE TO GET IN SOULS.

"For I seek not yours but you."—2 *Cor.* 12: 14.

It is our common way as well as delusion, to be desiring what men have, and not the men themselves; to get a property if possible out of their property, and not to create the same by our own industry. The manner of our great Apostle is exactly contrary. He has sought these wayward Corinthians in two voyages and two campaigns of gospel service, and is writing now his second long epistle to them, promising to come a third time and restore them, if possible, from their aberrations and scandals. They have heretofore not even borne his expenses, it would seem, or so much as taken him to their hospitality, and now they are most ungratefully decrying and depreciating his ministry. But he can not let them go, though the more abundantly he loves them the less he be loved. Is he not their father? and it is not the common way, he reminds them, for children to lay up for the parents, but the parents for the children. Uninvited, therefore, expecting neither welcome nor reward, he says he will come to them again for their sakes only—"for I seek not yours but you." He had come into his master's way so perfectly, in short, that other men, or souls, were valuable to him, even as children to parents—the best, the only substance that he cared to seek. Here, then, is the subject I propose for your consideration, viz :

The value one man has to another ; or, what is the same, the real interest of property which a true disciple has, or may have, in the souls of other men.

It is common to speak of the immense value of the soul, that is, the value it has to itself; it is common to speak of the love which one soul ought to have to other souls ; neither of these is the subject I propose ; but it is to show the real value of one soul, or man to another, as being in some very true sense a possessory value.

I suppose there may be some who had never such a thought occur to them in their lives. And the reason, if we care to understand it, is that in the great life-struggle we maintain with each other, under the dominion of selfishness, we take up the impression that we all stand in the way of each other, and are really nothing but a hindrance to the comfort and happiness one of another. We have so many public wars and private quarrels, so many rivalries, the problem of obtaining wealth is so often nothing but a finding how to get what belongs to others ; we have so many frauds, hatreds, oppressions, envies, jealousies, and are brewing so constantly in these selfish turbulences, that it becomes a great part of our life to keep off, or if possible to keep under, one another. Hence it can not even occur to many, as their grandest right and privilege, to get a property in one another, and have it for a permanent and dear possession.

Furthermore, we get accustomed to the idea that there is no property but legal property; no property right, therefore, in a man to be thought of, save the ownership that makes him a slave. Whereas the dearest, broadest properties we have are not legal. The wife does not legally own her husband, though she says, with how much meaning, "he is mine." No man legally owns his friend. So, also, we all have a most real, but not legal, property in all beautiful landscapes, in the air and the light, in the stars and the ranges of the sea. In a still different view, whatever and whomsoever we love, in the sense of religion, becomes a positive value to us, though it be no legal value; for it is the nature of this love that it gets a property in its objects; so that if we love a man's successes, or his grounds, or his gains, we possess the usufruct, in a more complete enjoyment, possibly, than he does himself. Putting aside then all such insufficient or false impressions, I now undertake to show that one man has to another a value more real than gold, or lands, or any legal property of the world can have.

And I open the argument here by calling your attention to the fact that God so evidently means to make every community valuable to every other, and so far, at least, every man to every other. We see this on a magnificent scale in the article of commerce. Here we find the nations all at work for each other, in so many different climes and localities, preparing one for another articles of comfort, sustenance, and ornament; and then commerce intervening, makes the exchanges; so that every people is receiving back to itself supplies that the whole human race, we may almost say, have been at work as producers to contribute. Even if they owned the industry one of another, they could not turn it to better account. Thus if you raise the question at your breakfast-table, on almost any morning of the year, whence come these simple comforts of food, and condiment, and furniture, you will find that almost every people and clime under heaven is represented as a contributor—the coffee is from one, the tea from another, the urns, and cups, and plates, and spoons, it may be, from as many others; and so on down to the sugar, and salt, and pepper, and all the outfit of the table. Your breakfast is gotten up for you, as it were, by the whole world; and so far you possess the world.

The same, again, is true of all the arts, professions, trades and grades of employment, in a given community. They are at work for each other in ways of concurrent service. All injustice, wrong, and fraud excluded, they so far own each other. Their industries and gifts are all so many complementary contributions. The capital, the science, the contriving heads, the operative hands, the powers of every sort, are mutually concurrent, mutually own each other, and taken together, constitute a complete whole of endowment—called a community because the unity is for all, and a commonwealth because the weal or wealth is common to all.

And again, what we discover in these mere economic relations is the type of a mutual interest and ownership, in qualities that are personal. The very idea of society and the social nature is that we shall be a want, and a gift of enjoyment, one to another; necessary in such a sense to each other, that existence itself can be only worthless, save as we lay hold of each other in some fellow feeling, and fulfill answering conditions of social benefit. We possess, in short, society, and society is universal ownership.

To see what reality there is in this, you have only to imagine how desolate, and how truly insupportable, your life would be in a state of complete solitude, or absolutely sole existence. Not that you want merely to receive outward conveniences, such as no one person can produce, or prepare for himself—the privation is not a merely economic privation—you want society of soul, though by the supposition you have never known what it is; to speak and be spoken to, to play out feeling and have it played back by some answering nature; to see, in the faces of men like yourself, the beaming intelligence of kindred beings, who are struggling with the same thoughts, and suffering the same dread mystery of experience with yourself. For this hitherto unknown something you ache, though you can not imagine where it is, or whence it may come. So pressing is this want, that even life itself becomes a silent agony. You wade the rivers, and creep through the forests, and climb the hills, looking for you know not what, resting nowhere, sighing and groaning everywhere. You gaze into the sky and try to get a look of recognition from the stars; you listen to the wind as if it were trying to vent itself in sighs like your own; you peer into the faces of the animals and, though they are faces plainly enough, the fellow something is not there. The world, in short, even up to the sun and the stars, is nothing but a prison about you of absolute solitary confinement; a vast grand prison, indeed, but yet a prison; nay, a horrible dungeon, dark at noonday to your heart; and it will not be strange if, for the simple want of society, you crumble down at last into idiocy, as malefactors are so often known to do, under the heavy years of unnatural torture to which they are subjected, in what is called their discipline of solitary confinement.

What we call society, in this manner, is the usufruct we have of each other, and has a property value as truly as the food that supplies our bodies. We may not commonly think of it in this way, and yet we are making constant experiment of the fact, even when we do not. Almost every full aged man, for example, has, at some time, been a weary traveler, picking his way through some wide forest, or roaming across some solitary prairie. From early morn till noon, and toward evening, he has seen no human being, heard no voice. Consciously his tone of feeling has been sinking, and a kind of oppression has been coming upon him. The long solitude of so many hours has damped his spirits, and he begins to imagine how good it would be to meet and speak to some person. At last he sees a man approaching in the distance. They stop, of course—the two strangers—and change salutations, multiplying inquiries that have no object but simply to protract the interchange or feeding time of their social nature; talking about the weather, and the way, which both of them knew well enough before; giving volunteer suggestions about the place whence they are from, and the object, very likely, of their journey; till finally, when they start again, which they will do with a lighter heart and a freer motion, the humanity they have given out, and the humanity they have taken in, will be a bath of refreshment to them for whole hours after. The same thing may be seen, under another form, in the case of those monks and eremites, who, like St. Anthony, withdrew voluntarily from the society of man, to live in deserts and solitary places alone; violating, in the name of religion, all God's appointments for their life. The remarkable thing is that, in so many cases, they began to be assaulted—as they thought, and even seemed with their eyes to see—by many and fierce devils of temptation. It was only the necessary wail of their own disordered, fevered soul, shaping into visible demons the crazy woes of its inward life, exasperated and frenzied by the unnatural torment of their solitude. What should they see but devils, when they refuse to see their fellow men for whom Christ died?

Again, what interest every soul may have, or what property get, in other souls, will be seen still more affectingly, in the fact that, bittered as we are by selfishness, almost every thing we do looks, in some way, to the approbation, or favoring opinion, or inspiration of others. We dress, we build, we cultivate our bestowments generally, with a view to the impressions or opinions of others. See, for example, how the great soul of a Newton bows itself to study for years and years, in the intensest self-application, that he may discover and give to the world's mind his grand expositions of light, and of the laws of the astronomic worlds. He values that mind, and even lives for what he may put in it, or dispense to it, or be in its thought. So of the great poets, painters, sculptors, antiquarians, writers of history, travelers, magistrates, heroes—no matter how selfish they may be, they are looking still to other souls, or minds, and resting their great expectations there.

I have lingered thus in the domain of the natural life, because the illustrations here furnished are so impressive. Let us enter now the field of Christian love and duty, and carry our argument up into the higher relations here existing. If selfishness even finds so great value in the sentiments, opinions, homages of other men, how shall it be with goodness and benefaction? Here it is that we come out into the great Apostle's field where he says—"not yours but you." "It is not," he would say, "what you can give me, or withhold from me, but it is what I can do to you, and be in you, and make you to be—to raise you up out of sin into purity and liberty and truth, to fill you with the light of God and his peace, to make you like God, and transform your disordered nature so that your inmost currents of thought, and feeling, and life shall be changed by me forever—this is my reward, which, if I may get, I want no other. For this I journey, and preach, and write, and pray, and will do so, till I have made you my joy and crown of rejoicing." He does not conceive that he is saving souls simply as being valuable to themselves, but as being valuable also to him, just according to the benefits he enters into them. He makes them in this manner a property to himself.

Let us look a little into this matter of property. How does it come? How does a man, for example, come to be acknowledged as the owner of a piece of land and to say to himself, "it is mine?" The general answer given to this question, for I can not stay to settle it by discussion, is that we get a property in things, by putting our industry into them, in ways of use, culture and improvement. This makes our title, and then the ownership is bought or sold as by title. Just so when a Christian benefactor enters good into a soul; when he takes it away from the wildness and disorder of nature, by the prayers and faithful labors he expends upon it, the necessary result is that he gets a property in it, feels it to be his, values it as being his. Neither is it any thing to say that he gets, in this manner, no exclusive title to it, therefore no property at all. No kind of property is exclusive. God is still concurrent owner of all the lands we hold in fee. The State is so far owner, also, that we hold them as of the State, and so far subject to State ownership or eminent domain, that they may be rightfully taken for public uses, when it is necessary. So a man may get ownership in his neighbor, and his poor brother, and the State may have ownership in both, and God a higher ownership in all. And the ownership in all such cases is only the more real because it is not exclusive. So then, it comes to pass that improvement in a soul gets ownership in it, even as it does in land; and the Christian disciple makes any soul that he saves valuable to himself and a property, just according to what it is made to be to itself, by the good he has entered into it. And how great and blessed a property it is to him, we can only see by a careful computation of the values by which he measures it.

First, as he has come to look himself on the eternal in every thing, he has a clear perception of souls as being the most real of all existences—more real than lands and gold, and a vastly higher property—because they are eternal, and the title once gained is only consummated by death, not taken away.

Next, finding this or that human spirit or soul, in a

condition of darkness and disease and fatal damage, he begins forthwith to find an object in it, and an inspiring hope to be realized in its necessity. He takes it thus upon himself, draws near to it, hovers round it in love, and prayer, and gracious words, and more gracious example, to regain it to truth and to God. For if it be a matter so inspiring to a Newton that he may put into other minds the right scientific conception of light, or of the stars, how much greater and higher the interest a good soul has in imparting to another goodness; the element of its own divine peace and well being.

Then, again, as we get a property in other men by the power we exert in them, how much greater the property obtained by that kind of power which is supernaturally, transformingly beneficent; that which subdues enmity, illuminates darkness, fructifies sterility, changes discord to harmony, war to peace, and raises a spirit in ruin up to be a temple of God's indwelling life. If it be something great to make ourselves felt, acknowledged, respected in a diseased soul, how much more to change that disease itself into health; if it be something to fill a place in bad souls, how much more to make them beautiful in truth and love and purity. What a thought, indeed, is this for a Christian disciple to entertain, that he may exalt the consciousness of a human soul, or spirit, forever, and live in it forever as a causality of joy and beauty. And this it was that so fervently kindled the disinterested zeal of our Apostle—"For ye are our glory and joy."

Furthermore, when one has gained another to God and a holy life, there is a most dear, everlasting relationship established between them—one leading, so to speak, the other's good eternity, and the other beholding in him the benefactor by whose work and example he is consciously exalted forever—and this gracious relationship will give them an eternally mutual property in each other. And so all Christian friends will have gotten a property in each other, as they have done each other good, being entered thus into one another, and so into the sense of relationships answering to their mutual benefactions and the good offices by which they have bought an everlasting interest in the feeling, history, personal well being and inmost life, one of another. In this manner it is given us for our beautiful divine privilege to have a property in every one we meet, if only we can find how to bless him. Owning society, we have a field where mines richer than those of gold are open to us on every side. Going after what men have, we get nothing; after men themselves, a property that is everlasting.

Hence, also, it is, that the Scriptures of God's truth are so much in the commendation of this heavenly property. If we go after fame, they tell us that the name of the wicked shall rot. If we go after riches and cover ourselves with the outward splendors of fortune, they tell us that we must go out of life as poor as any; for, that having brought nothing material into the world, we can carry nothing material out. And then they add, do the works of love and truth, and these shall go with you. He that winneth souls is wise. They that turn many to righteousness shall shine as the stars forever and ever. Be fishers of men. Watch for souls. If thy brother sin against thee, gain, if possible, thy brother. Be all things to all men, if by any means you may gain some. And then, when you have worn out all your powers in benefactions put upon souls, and believe that you have many who will be your crown of rejoicing in the day of the Lord Jesus—then, I say, when the last hour is come, and the scenes of your mortal labor are retiring from your sight, have it for your song of triumph, and leave it to be chanted over your rest—"Blessed are the dead that die in the Lord; for they rest from their labors, and their works do follow them." All material properties are left behind; these can not follow: but all the properties of duty and love must follow, and be gathered in after you to bless your fidelity, and crown your peace, and be your sacred wealth forever. Then it shall be seen what is meant by the value of one soul to another.

Just here, in fact, will be opened to your now purified love the discovery of this great truth; viz., that there is indeed no real property at all but spirit-property, or property in spirit; a possession, that is, by each soul of what he has added to the moral universe of the good. All values here become social, values of truth, and feeling, and worship, and conscious affinity with God. And this is heaven; the state of mutual ownership and everlasting usufruct, prepared in all God's righteous populations, by what they have righteously done.

Accepting now the solid and sublimely practical truth thus carefully expounded, the salvation of men is seen to be a work that ought to engage every Christian, and a work that to be fitly done, must be heartily and energetically done. If we talk of it simply as a duty, and push ourselves into it by that kind of compulsion, we shall do nothing but simply to make a feint of it. We may tell how great value the souls we are after have to themselves; but, if they have no value to us, they might as well have none at all. It is unfortunate, in this matter, that we speak of souls and not of men; for *soul* is a ghostly word, and we are doubting, half the time, whether a creature so far out of body is any thing. If we speak of souls, let them be men, everlasting men, whom we everlastingly want, and have it for our privilege to gain, our right to enjoy; and then what practical energy and holy stress will there be in our endeavor. Our difficulty, in this matter, is that we are too delicate, too tenderly conventional, too mindful of the respectabilities. We are so careful to avoid excess that we can not be earnest enough to show any due valuation of our object. See what stress of exertion we display in the pursuit of gain—what sharpness of attention we practice, what watching of opportunities, what indefatigable contriving, what persistency. See, again, how we put ourselves to the work in a political campaign. What mean these great assemblages, these nightly harangues, these processions, these thousand and one consultations at the corners of the streets—all this heavy strain of action, what does it mean? Simply that a great cause is earnestly pressed according to its supposed value. The object is to gain voices or votes, and the words are, "yours but not you." What, then shall be the stress of any single man, or church of God, when the point is to gain everlastingly the men themselves? If there is so little fear of excess when we are after votes, how much less should there be when we are after the men. The intensest energy in a work so nearly divine, the most earnest endeavor, the wisest adjustment of means in the possible compass of invention, labor in season and out of season, supplications that are groanings with Christ in his Gethsemane—these are the way of all true Christian men and assemblies.

To this end, my brethren, consider well that you are set to gain a property in every man you save. In some dearest, truest sense, he is to be yours forever, to own you as his benefactor, and to be your crown of rejoicing, having your life entered into and working through his forever. Taking it as the law of his ministry—"not yours but you," what a glorious company did our great Apostle gather in to be with him, to pack, as it were, the heavenly mansions, and be in the everlasting unfolding of their life and blessedness, his ever increasing property! What a world of riches, too, is that great commonwealth of blessing to be, where so many ties of mutual ownership and benefaction are to exist forever. There are mothers that have brought in their children, pastors that have brought in their flocks, teachers that have won their classes, employers that have gained their employed, young friends that have led in their comrades, sick and solitary, whose prayers have brought salvation to strangers, or the great in high places, who never knew till now their nameless benefactors. These all have taken possession, so to speak, of one another. As they learned to say "not yours but you," so they are allowed henceforth, in loving thought, to say, "these are mine." And this adjective *mine,* how steadily are we educated into it; as if it were God's purpose, first of all, to waken the sense of property in us, that we may be set every one upon the endeavor to win a possession for eternity. This property notion that puts us delving, striving, going to the death for gain, is only to be converted, not to be disappointed. A bubble in itself, it foreshadows an everlasting reality. For when it is fulfilled in the grand, eternal future to which we are going, we shall find that heaven itself is but a glorious, enduring ownership.

Consider, also, how this double-acting property relation holds good, even between Christ and his people. "Not yours but you" is the principle that brings him into the world. Understand how a perfectly good, great, unselfish, loving and true mind will value a populous world of mind in ruins, and the seeming disproportion of the cross vanishes. And when we hear him say and repeat, in words of visible endearment, "those whom thou hast given me," we can see that he is counting over his property beforehand. For this he travels in the greatness of his strength, for this he is red in his apparel, and treads the wine-press alone. All the amazing stress of his sacrifice is crowded on by the immense valuation he has of the prize to be gained. And then when he has made that gain, and his everlasting property in those that were given him is established by the purchase of his sacrifice, what stronger tap-root of confidence could we have than to hear him add—"and no man shall pluck them out of my hand." We can even see that he would sooner die again than give us up. O, thou timid, misgiving soul, distrust thyself as thou wilt, only do not distrust the unalterable ownership of thy Master! As thou art Christ's sure property, given him before the foundation of the world, that foundation will sooner break down than his strong title of possession. Did he not also say—"I will that those whom thou hast given me be with me where I am?" What, then, shall we answer, each one for himself, but this—"I will, O Master and Lord, that I be with thee where thou art—have me thus for thy possession, and I ask no more."

And yet there is more; for as there is no exclusive right in the benevolent properties—all brothers, in all circles of brotherhood, owning each other—so it is given us to own even Jesus himself; to say, "O Christ thou art mine,"—"My Lord and my God,"—"Whom have I in heaven but thee." Having thee, I can easily renounce, or lose, all things beside. I would not care to possess, even if I could, thy stars. Enough that I shall possess the internal contents and the bosom furniture of thy divine excellence; the sea-full of thy love wherein the leviathans of thy purposes play; the splendors of thy intelligence, which make my day eternal without any sun; thy great will which makes me sufficient in power; all thy goodness and beauty, all thy plans and dispositions; and shall I not be so established forever—let me humbly dare to speak it—in the dear blessed ownership of Christ and his kingdom?

IX.

THE DISSOLVING OF DOUBTS.

"And I have heard of thee, that thou canst make interpretations and dissolve doubts."—*Dan.* 5: 16.

DOUBTS and questions are not peculiar to Nebuchadnezzar, but they are the common lot and heritage of humanity. They vary in their subjects and times, but we have them always on hand. We live just now in a specially doubting age, where almost every matter of feeling is openly doubted, or, it may be, openly denied. Science puts every thing in question, and literature distils the questions, making an atmosphere of them. We doubt both creation and Creator; whether there be second causes or only primal causes running *ab æterno in æternum;* whether God is any thing more than the sum of such causes; whether he works by will back of such causes; whether he is spirit working supernaturally through them; whether we have any personal relation to him, or he to us. And then, when we come to the matter of revelation, we question the fact of miracles and of the incarnation. We doubt free agency and responsibility, immortality and salvation, the utility of prayer and worship, and even of repentance for sin. And these sweeping, desolating doubts run through all grades of mind, all modes and spheres of life, as it were telegraphically, present as powers of the air to unchristen the new born thoughts of religion as fast as they arrive. The cultivated and mature have the doubts ingrown they know not how, and the younger minds encounter their subtle visitations when they do not seek them. And the more active minded they are, and the more thoughts they have on the subject of religion, the more likely they are, (unless anchored by true faith in God,) to be drifted away from all the most solid and serious convictions, even before they are aware of it. Their mind is ingenuous, it may be, and their habit is not over speculative, certainly not perversely speculative; they only have a great many thoughts raising a great many questions that fly, as it were, loosely across their mental landscape, and leave no trace of their passage—that is, none which they themselves perceive,—and yet they wake up by and by, startled by the discovery that they believe nothing. They can not any where put down their foot and say, "here is truth." And it is the greatest mystery to them that they consciously have not meant to escape from the truth, but have, in a certain sense, been feeling after it. They have not been ingenious in their questions and arguments. They have despised all tricks of sophistry, they have only been thinking and questioning as it seemed to be quite right they should. And yet, somehow, it is now become as if all truth were gone out, and night and nowhere had the world. The vacuity is painful, and they are turned to a wrestling with their doubts, which is only the more painful that they wrestle, as it were, in mid-air, unable to so much as touch ground any where.

The point I am sketching here is certainly in the extreme, and yet it is an extreme often reached quite early, and one toward which all young minds gravitate, as certainly as they consent to live without God and carry on their experience, steadied by no help from the practical trust of religion. Probably some of you, my friends here before me, are at one point of doubt or unbelieving, and some at another; I sincerely hope that none of you have reached the dark extreme just described. But whatever point you have reached, I propose for my object this morning to bring in what I can of countervailing help. I shall speak of the dissolving of your doubts, showing how you may have them dissolved in all their degrees and combinations. If they do not press you, or at all trouble you; if you like to have them, and amuse yourself in what you count the brilliancy of their play, if you love to be inventive and propagate as many and plausible as you may, I have nothing for you. But if you want to know the truth—all truth—and be in it, and have all the fogs of the mind cleared away, I think I can tell you in what manner it may, without a peradventure, be done. Shall I go on? Give me then your attention, nothing more. I shall not ask you to surrender up your will or suppress your intelligence, would not even consent to have you force your convictions or opinions. All that I ask is a real desire to find the truth and be in it.

Before proceeding, however, in the principal matter of the subject, it may be well to just note the three principal sources and causes whence our doubts arise, and from which they get force to make their assault. They never come of truth or high discovery, but always of the want of it.

In the first place, all the truths of religion are inherently dubitable. They are only what are called probable, never necessary truths like the truths of geometry or of numbers. In these we have the premises in our very minds themselves. In all other matters we have the premise to find. And there is almost no premise out of us that we do not some time or other doubt. We even doubt our senses, nay, it takes a very dull, loose-minded soul, never to have, or to have had a doubt of the senses. Now this field of probable truth is the whole field of religion, and of course it is competent for doubt to cover it in every part and item.

In the second place, we begin life as unknowing creatures that have every thing to learn. We grope, and groping is doubt; we handle, we question, we guess, we experiment, beginning in darkness and stumbling on towards intelligence. We are in a doom of activity, and can not stop thinking—thinking every thing, knocking against the walls on every side; trying thus to master the problems, and about as often getting mastered by them. Yeast works in bread scarcely more blindly. When I draw out this whole conception of our life as it is, the principal wonder, I confess, is that we doubt so little and accept so much.

And, again, thirdly, it is a fact, disguise it as we can, or deny it as we may, that our faculty is itself in disorder. A broken or bent telescope will not see any thing rightly. A filthy window will not bring in even the day as it is. So a mind wrenched from its true lines of action or straight perception, discolored and smirched by evil, will not see truly, but will put a blurred, misshapen look on every thing. Truths will only be as good as errors, and doubts as natural as they.

Now it will be seen that as long as these three sources or originating causes of doubt continue, doubts will continue, and will, in one form or another, be multiplied. Therefore, I did not propose to show how they may be stopped, for that is impossible, but only how they may be dissolved, or cleared away. I may add, however, that the method by which they are to be dissolved, will work as well preventively as remedially; for though it will not stop their coming, it will stop their coming with damage and trouble to the mind, and keep it clear for all steadiest repose and highest faith in religion.

And the first thing here to be said, and it may be most important, is negative; viz., that the doubters never can dissolve or extirpate their doubts by inquiry, search, investigation, or any kind of speculative endeavor. They must never go after the truth to merely find it, but to practice it and live by it. It is not enough to rally their inventiveness, doing nothing to polarize their aim. To be simply curious, thinking of this and thinking of that, is only a way to multiply doubts; for in doing it they are, in fact, postponing all the practical rights of truth. They imagine, it may be, that they are going first, to settle their questions, and then, at their leisure, to act. As if they were going to get the perfect system and complete knowledge of truth before they move an inch in doing what they know! The result is that the chamber of their brain is filled with an immense clatter of opinions, questions, arguments, that even confound their reason itself. And they come out wondering at the discovery, that the more they investigate the less they believe! Their very endeavor mocks them,—just as it really ought. For truth is something to be lived, else it might as well not be. And how shall a mind get on finding more truth, save as it takes direction from what it gets; how make farther advances when it tramples what it has by neglect? You come upon the hither side of a vast intricate forest region, and your problem is to find your way through it. Will you stand there inquiring and speculating forty years, expecting first to make out the way? or, seeing a few rods into it, will you go on as far as you see, and so get ability to see a few rods farther? proceeding in that manner to find out the unknown, by advancing practically in the known.

No, there is no fit search after truth which does not, first of all, begin to live the truth it knows. Alas!

to honor a little truth is not in the doubters, or they do not think of it, and so they dishonor beforehand all the truth they seek, and swamp it, by inevitable consequence, in doubts without end.

Dropping now this negative matter, we come to the positive. There is a way for dissolving any and all doubts,—a way that opens at a very small gate, but widens wonderfully after you pass. Every human soul, at a certain first point of its religious outfit, has a key given it which is to be the *open sesame* of all right discovery. Using this key as it may be used, any lock is opened, any doubt dissolved. Thus every man acknowledges the distinction of right and wrong, feels the reality of that distinction, knows it by immediate consciousness even as he knows himself. He would not be a man without that distinction. It is even this which distinguishes him from the mere animals. Having it taken away, he would, at the same instant, drop into an animal. I do not say, observe, that every man is clear as to what particular things may be fitly called right and what wrong. There is a great disagreement here in men's notions; what is right to some, or in some ages and some parts of the world, being wrong to others, in other times and countries. I only say that the distinction of *idea* or *general principle* is the same in all ages and peoples, without a shade of difference. Their ideas of space and time are not more perfectly identical. So far they are all in the same great law; constituted, in that fact, men, moral beings, subjects of religion. Their whole nature quivers responsively to this law. To be in the right, and of it, to mean the right, and swear allegiance to it forever, regardless of cost, even though it be the cost of life itself,—they can as well disown their existence as disown this law. There may be now and then a man who contrives to raise a doubt of it, and yet, driven out with rods, it will come back, a hundred times a day, and force its recognition; especially if any one does him a wrong.

Here, then, is the key that opens every thing. And the only reason why we fall into so many doubts, and get unsettled by our inquiries, instead of being settled by them as we undertake to be, is that we do not begin at the beginning. Of what use can it be for a man to push on his inquiries after truth, when he throws away, or does not practically honor, the most fundamental and most determinating of all truths? He goes after truth as if it were coming in to be with him in wrong! even as a thief might be going after honest company in stolen garments. How can a soul, unpolarized by wrong, as a needle by heat, settle itself in the poles of truth? or who will expect a needle, hung in a box of iron, turning every way and doubting at every point of compass, to find the true North? But a right mind has a right polarity, and discovers right things by feeling after them. Not all right things in a moment, though, potentially, all in a moment; for its very oscillations are true, feeling after only that which is, to know it as it is.

The true way, therefore, of dissolving doubts, as I

just now said, is to begin at the beginning, and do the first thing first. Say nothing of investigation, till you have made sure of being grounded everlastingly, and with a completely whole intent, in the principle of right doing as a principle. And here it is, let me say, that all unreligious men are at fault, and often without knowing, or even suspecting it. They do right things enough in the out-door, market sense of the term, and count that being right. But let them ask the question, "Have I ever consented to be, and am I really now, in the right, as in principle and supreme law; to live for it, to make any sacrifice it will cost me, to believe every thing it will bring me to see, to be a confessor of Christ as soon as it appears to be enjoined upon me, to go on a mission to the world's end, if due conviction sends me, to change my occupation for good conscience' sake, to repair whatever wrong I have done to another, to be humbled, if I should before my worst enemy, to do complete justice to God, and, if I could, to all worlds?—in a word, to be in wholly right intent, and have no mind but this forever?" Ah, how soon do they discover possibly, in this manner, that they are right only so far as they can be, and not be at all right as in principle—right as doing some right things, nothing more. Of course, they are not going to be martyrs in this way, and they have not had a thought of it.

After this there is not much use in looking farther, for if we can not settle ourselves practically in this grand first law which we do know, how can we hope to be settled in what of truth we do not? Are we ready, then, to undertake a matter so heavy? for the struggle it requires will be great, as the change itself must be well nigh total; a revolution so nearly complete, that we shall want every help we can get. And let us not be surprised by the suggestion that God, perchance, may come to our help unseen, when we do not so much as know how to believe in him, only let it occur to us how great a comfort it should be, to have a God so profoundly given to the right; for that subtle gleam of sympathy may be itself a kind of prayer,—prayer that he will answer before the call is heard. And then, as certainly as the new right mind begins, it will be as if the whole heaven were bursting out in day. For this is what Christ calls the single eye, and the whole body is inevitably full of light. How surely and how fast fly away the doubts, even as fogs are burned away by the sun.

Now to make this matter plain, I will suppose a case in which the dissolving of doubt in this manner is illustrated. Suppose that one of us, clear all the vices, having a naturally active-minded, inquiring habit, occupied largely with thoughts of religion,—never meaning to get away from the truth, but, as he thinks, to find it, only resolved to have a free mind, and not allow himself to be carried by force or fear or any thing but real conviction,—suppose that such a one going on thus, year by year, reading, questioning, hearing all the while the gospel in which he has been educated, sometimes impressed by it, but relapsing shortly into greater doubt than before, finds his religious beliefs wearing out, and vanishing, he knows not how, till finally he seems to really believe nothing. He has not meant to be an atheist, but he is astonished to find that he has nearly lost the conviction of God, and can not, if he would, say with any emphasis of conviction that God exists. The world looks blank, and he feels that existence is getting blank also to itself. This heavy charge of his possibly immortal being oppresses him, and he asks again and again, "What shall I do with it?" His hunger is complete, and his soul turns every way for bread. His friends do not satisfy him. His walks drag heavily. His suns do not rise, but only climb. A kind of leaden aspect overhangs the world. Till finally, pacing his chamber some day, there comes up suddenly the question,—"Is there, then, no truth that I do believe?—Yes, there is this one, now that I think of it, there is a distinction of right and wrong, that I never doubted, and I see not how I can; I am even quite sure of it." Then, forthwith, starts up the question, "Have I, then, ever taken the principle of right for my law? I have done right things as men speak, have I ever thrown my life out on the principle to become all it requires of me? No, I have not, consciously I have not. Ah! then here is something for me to do! No matter what becomes of my questions,—nothing ought to become of them, if I can not take a first principle so inevitably true and live in it." The very suggestion seems to be a kind of revelation; it is even a relief to feel the conviction it brings. "Here, then," he says, "will I begin. If there is a God, as I rather hope there is, and very dimly believe, he is a right God. If I have lost him in wrong, perhaps I shall find him in right. Will he not help me, or, perchance, even be discovered to me?" Now the decisive moment is come. He drops on his knees, and there he prays to the dim God dimly felt, confessing the dimness for honesty's sake, and asking for help, that he may begin a right life. He bows himself on it as he prays, choosing it to be henceforth his unalterable, eternal endeavor.

It is an awfully dark prayer, in the look of it, but the truest and best he can make,—the better and more true that he puts no orthodox colors on it; and the prayer and the vow are so profoundly meant that his soul is borne up into God's help, as it were by some unseen chariot, and permitted to see the opening of heaven even sooner than he opens his eyes. He rises and it is as if he had gotten wings. The whole sky is luminous about him,—it is the morning, as it were, of a new eternity. After this, all troublesome doubt of God's reality is gone, for he has found Him! A being so profoundly felt, must inevitably be.

Now this conversion, calling it by that name, as we properly should, may seem, in the apprehension of some, to be a conversion *for* the gospel and not *in* it or *by* it; a conversion by the want of truth, more than by the power of truth. But that will be a judgment more superficial than the facts permit. No, it is exactly this: it is seeking first the kingdom of God, and his righteousness,—exactly that and nothing less. And the dimly groping cry for help—what is that but a feeling after God, if haply it may find him, and actually finding him not far off. And what is the help obtained, but exactly the true Christ-help? And the result—what also is that, but the Kingdom of God within; righteousness, and peace, and joy, in the Holy Ghost?

[There is a story lodged in the little bedroom of one of these dormitories, which, I pray God, his recording angel may note, allowing it never to be lost.]*

Now the result will be that a soul thus won to its integrity of thought and meaning, will rapidly clear all tormenting questions and difficulties. They are not all gone, but they are going. Revelation, it may be, opens some troublesome chapters. Preaching sometimes stumbles the neophyte, when he might better be comforted by it. The great truths of God often put him in a maze. The creation story, the miracles, the incarnation, the trinity, the relations of justice and mercy,—in all these he may only see, for a time, men walking that have the look of trees. But the ship is launched, he is gone to sea, and has the needle on board. He is going now to sell every thing for the truth,—not the truth to keep as a knowledge, but the truth to live by. He is going henceforth to be concentered in the right, nay, the righteousness itself of God; and his prayers he will be hanging, O how tenderly, on

* Y. C. C.

God, for the inward guidance of his Spirit. He will undertake shortly some point that is not cleared at once by the daylight of his new experience, and will, by and by, master it. That will give him courage to undertake shortly another, and he will go to it with new appetite. And so he will go on, not afraid to have questions even to the end of his life, and will be nowise disturbed by them. He will be in the gospel as an honest man, and will have it as a world of wonderfully grand, perpetually fresh discovery. He comes now to the lock with the key that opens it in his hand, fumbling no more in doubt, unresolved, because he has no key.

The menstruum, then, by which all doubts may be dissolved, appears to be sufficiently shown or provided. It only remains to add a few more promiscuous points of advice that relate to the general conduct of the mind in its new conditions.

1. Be never afraid of doubt. Perhaps a perfectly upright angelic mind well enough might, though I am not sure even of that. We, at least, are in the fog eternal of wrong, and there is no way for us to get clear but to prove all things and hold fast. Make free use of all the intelligence God has given you, only taking care to use it in a consciously supreme allegiance to right and to God. Your questions then will only be your helpers, and the faster they come, the better will be your progress in the truth.

2. Be afraid of all sophistries, and tricks, and strifes

of disingenuous argument. Doting about questions, and doubting about them are very different things. Any kind of cunning art or dodge of stratagem in your words and arguments will do you incalculable mischief. They will damage the sense of truth, which is the worst possible kind of damage. False arguments make the soul itself false, and then a false, uncandid soul can see nothing as it is. No man can fitly seek after truth who does not hold truth in the deepest reverence. Truth must be sacred even as God, else it is nothing.

3. Have it as a fixed principle also, that getting into any scornful way is fatal. Scorn is dark, and has no eyes; for the eyes it thinks it has are only sockets in the place of eyes. Doubt is reason, scorn is disease. One simply questions, searching after evidence; the other has got above evidence, and turns to mockery the modest way that seeks it. Even if truth were found, it could not stay in any scorning man's bosom. The tearing voice, the scowling brow, the leer, the sneer, the jeer, would make the place a robber's cave to it, and drive the delicate and tender guest to make his escape at the first opportunity. There was never a scorner that gave good welcome to truth. Knaves can as well harbor honesty, and harlots' chastity, as scorners' truth.

4. Never settle upon any thing as true, because it is safer to hold it than not. I will not say that any one is to have it as a point of duty to be damned, or willing to be, for the truth. I only say that truth brings often great liabilities of cost, and we must choose it,

cost what it will. To accept the Bible even because it is safest, as some persons do, and some ministers very lightly preach, is to do the greatest dishonor both to it and to the soul. Such faith is cowardly, and is even a lie besides. It is basing a religion, not in truth, but in the doctrine of chances, and reducing the salvation of God to a bill of insurance. If the Bible is true, believe it, but do not mock it by assuming for a creed the mere chance that it may be. For the same reason, take religion, not because it will be good for your family, or good for the state, but because it is the homage due inherently from man to God, and the kingdom of God. What more flashy conceit can there be, than a religion accepted as a domestic or political nostrum?

5. Have it as a law never to put force on the mind, or try to make it believe; because it spoils the mind's integrity, and when that is gone, what power of advance in the truth is left? I know very well that the mind's integrity is far enough gone already, and that all our doubts and perpetual self-defeats come upon us for just that reason. All the more necessary is it that we come into what integrity we can, and stay there. Let the soul be immovable as rock, by any threat of danger, any feeling of risk; any mere scruple, any call to believe by sheer, self-compelling will. The soul that is anchored in right will do no such thing. There must, of course, be no obstinacy, no stiff holding out after conviction has come. There must be tenderness, docility, and, with these, a most

firmly kept equilibrium. There must be no gustiness of pride or self-will to fog the mind and keep right conviction away.

6. Never be in a hurry to believe, never try to conquer doubts against time. Time is one of the grand elements in thought as truly as in motion. If you can not open a doubt to-day, keep it till to-morrow; do not be afraid to keep it for whole years. One of the greatest talents in religious discovery, is the finding how to hang up questions and let them hang without being at all anxious about them. Turn a free glance on them now and then as they hang, move freely about them, and see them, first on one side, and then on another, and by and by when you turn some corner of thought, you will be delighted and astonished to see how quietly and easily they open their secret and let you in! What seemed perfectly insoluble will clear itself in a wondrous revelation. It will not hurt you, nor hurt the truth, if you should have some few questions left to be carried on with you when you go hence, for in that more luminous state, most likely, they will soon be cleared,—only a thousand others will be springing up even there, and you will go on dissolving still your new sets of questions, and growing mightier and more deep-seeing for eternal ages.

Now, my friends, it would not be strange if I had in the audience before me all sorts of doubts, and varieties of questions, all grades of incipient unbelief, or, it may be, of unbelief not incipient, but ripe and in full seed. But I have one and the same word for you all, that is, look after the day, and the night itself will join you in it. Or, better still, set your clock by the sun; then it will be right all day, and even all night besides, and be ready when he rises, pointing its finger to the exact minute where he stands, in the circle of his swift motion. Be right, that is, first of all, in what you know, and your soul will be faithfully chiming with all you ought to know. All evidences are with you then, and you with them. Even if they seem to be hid, they will shortly appear, and bring you their light. But this being right implies a great deal, observe, and especially these two things:—First, that you pray for all the help you can get; for without this you can not believe, or feel, that you truly want to be right. Secondly, that you consent, in advance, to be a christian, and begin a religious life, fulfilling all the sacrifices of such a life, provided you may find it necessary to do so, in order to carry out and justify yourself in acting up to the principle you have accepted. Undertaking to be right, only resolving not to be a christian, is but a mockery of right. You must go where it carries you. You must even be a Mahometan, a Jew, a Pagan,—any thing to have a clear conscience. There is no likelihood, it is true, that you will have to be either of these, but there is an almost certainty that you must be a christian. Be that as it may, you must consent to go where right conviction carries you. And there is even some proper doubt whether you can get out of this place of worship without being carried to Christ, if you undertake to go out as a thoroughly right man. For Christ is but the Sun of Righteousness, and you will assuredly find that, in being joined to the RIGHT, you are joined eternally to him, and walking with him in the blessed daylight of his truth.

X.

CHRIST REGENERATES EVEN THE DESIRES.

"And James and John, the sons of Zebedee, came unto him, saying, Master, we would that thou shouldest do for us whatsoever we shall desire."—*Mark* 10: 35.

HAD Christ ever been willing to indulge in satire, I think he would have done it here. These young gentlemen make a request so large, and withal so very absurd, that we at least can scarcely restrain a smile at their expense. "Whatsoever we desire," — what power in the creation could give it? And then it would be strange, above all, if they themselves could endure the gift. Still the Saviour hears them kindly and considerately, only showing them, when they come to state the particular thing they want, that even that thing—the sitting on his right and left—means perhaps a good deal more than they imagine, viz.: that they drink of his bitter cup and be baptized with his fiery baptism. And when he finds them eager enough to answer still that they can do even that, he only turns them off in the gentlest manner, as children that he sees are looking after a toy which it would cost them a tragedy of suffering to accept. I think we can see, too, in his manner, that he regards them with a pity so considerate, simply because the absurdity they are in is nothing but the common absurdity of the whole living world. For what are we all saying, young and old, the young more eagerly, the old more indivertibly, but exactly what amounts to the same thing, under one form of language or another—"Let us have this, that, the other, any thing and every thing we desire." Sometimes, if we could see it, we are really saying it in our prayers; though if we should pause long enough upon the matter to let our apprehension run a little way, I think we should almost any one of us begin to suspect that, having his particular desire, he might sometimes have more than he could bear, and might perfectly know that, if all of us could have it, we should make the world a bedlam of confusion without even a chance of order and harmony left. The first and most forward point accordingly which meets us in the consideration of this subject, is that—

Our human desire, in the common plane of nature and the world, is blind, or unintelligent—out of all keeping with our real wants and possibilities.

I mean, by this, that we are commonly desiring just what would be the greatest damage to us, or the misery worst to be suffered, and do not know it; that our tamest desires are often most untamed as regards the order of reason; and that we are all desiring unwittingly, what is exactly contrary to God's counsel, what is possible never to be, and if it might, would set us in general repugnance with each other, and society itself.

We are apt to imagine that, since we are consciously beings of intelligence, our desires must of course be included, and be themselves intelligent as we are. But we are not intelligent beings it happens in the sense here supposed. We are only a little intelligent, in a very few things, and we do not mean by claiming this title, if we understand ourselves, much more than that we are of another grade in comparison with the animals—able that is to be intelligent if we get the opportunity, as they are not. We get room thus, large enough for the fact of a general state of unreason in our desires. After all they may be about as far from intelligence as they can be—possibly not more intelligent than our passions, appetites, and bodily secretions are. In one view still, they are motive forces of endowment for intelligent action, instigators of energy, purpose and character, and if we knew them only as they move in their law, bound up in the original sweet harmony of an upright state, we should doubtless see them working instinctively on as co-factors with intelligence, if not intelligent themselves. But, in their present wild way, we see them plainly loosed from their law by transgression—heavings all and foamings of the inward tumult—aspiration, soul-hunger, hate, ambition, pride, passion, lust of gain, lust of power; and what do they signify more visibly, than that all right harmony and proportion are gone, as far as they are concerned. Nothing has its natural value before them, because they are reeking themselves in all kinds of disorder bodily and mental. They are phantoms without perception. Even smoke is scarcely less intelligent.

That we may better conceive this general truth, revert, first of all, to the grounds out of which they get their spring. They do not come after reason commonly, asking permission of reason, but they begin their instigations from a fund of raw lustings in the nature clean back of intelligence; rushing out as troops in a certain wildness and confused, blind huddle, that allows us to think of them with no great respect. Understanding well their disorder and confusion, we have it as a common way of speaking that reason must govern them—which supposes, clearly, that reason is not in them. And what do we better know, than that only a very partial government of them is possible; that they swarm so fast and fly so far and wildly, that no queen bee of reason can possibly control the hive.

The next thing to be noted is that they have no respect to possibilities and causes, and terms of moral award. Thus one man desires dry weather, and another rain, one office, and another the same office, one to own a house, another the same house, some to be honorable without character, some to be useful without industry, some to be learned without study. We desire also to own what we mortgage, keep what we sell, and get what nobody can have. We cypher out gains against the terms of arithmetic, and even pray

God squarely against each other. We run riot in this manner all the while, even against possibilities themselves. A child crying after the moon is in the same scale of intelligence.

Causes again we as little respect. Having it as a clear test of insanity to be reaching after what every body knows eternal causes forbid, we are yet all the while doing it. We want our clocks to move a great deal faster in the playtimes appointed for childhood, and a great deal slower in the payment times appointed in the engagements of manhood. We want poor soils to bear great crops, indolence to be thrifty, intemperance to be healthy, and to have all good supplies come in, doing nothing to earn or provide them.

Against all terms and conditions of morality, also, we want to be confided in, having neither truth nor honesty. We desire to be honored, not having worth enough even to be respected. We want the comforts of religion without religion, asking for rewards to come without duties, and that evils fly away which are fastened by our bad deserts. Of course our judgment goes not with the nonsense there may be in such desires, but they none the less make haste, scorning all detentions of judgment.

We get also another kind of proof in this matter, by discovering afterwards how absurd our desires have been—that the marriage we sought would have kept us from a good one, and would have been itself a bitter woe; that the bad weather of yesterday, so much against our patience, kept us from the car that was wrecked, or the steamer that was sunk by an explosion; that the treachery of a friend, so much deplored, saved us from the whirlpool of temptation into which we were plunging; that the failure of an adventure we were prosecuting with high expectation, was the only thing that could have sobered our feeling, and prepared us to a penitent life. Sitting down thus, after many years, and looking back on the desires that have instigated our feeling, we discover what a smoke of delusion was in them, and how nearly absurd they were. How often has their crossing been our benefit, and how many thousand times over have we seen it proved by experiment, that they were blind instigations, thrusting us onward, had they not been mercifully defeated, on results of unspeakable disaster.

There is yet another fact concerning them which has only been adverted to, and requires to be more formally stated, viz.: that they are not only blind or wild, as I have been saying, but are also a great part of them morally bad, or wicked; reeking with selfishness, fouled by lust, bittered and soured by envies, jealousies, resentments, revenges, wounded pride, mortified littleness. Thus it was that even Gœthe, no very staunch confessor of orthodoxy, was constrained to say—"There is something in every man's heart, which if we could know, would make us hate him." And why not also make him hate himself? Hateful is the only fit epithet for this murky-looking crew, that are always breaking into the mind, and hovering in among its best thoughts. Who that is not insane can think it possible to set them in right order, and tame them by his mere will?

What then, is there no possibility but to be driven wild, and hag-ridden always by these phantoms? I think there is, and I shall now undertake, for a second stage in my subject, to show

That Christ new-molds the desires in their spring, and configures them inwardly to God; regenerating the soul at this deepest and most hidden point of character.

We commonly speak of a new creating grace for souls, in the matter of principle, will, the affections, and we magnify our gospel in the fact that it can undertake a work so nearly central. I think it can do more, that it can even go through into what is background, down into substructure, where the impulsions of desire begin to move unasked, and, by their own self-instigation, stir on all the disorders of the will and the heart; that it can go through, I say, and down among them, reducing them to law, and setting them in harmony with God as they rise.

I do not mean by this that we are put on this work of reduction ourselves, under the divine helps given us. Thus it may be conceived that we are only now to undertake, ourselves, more hopefully the government of our desires. But this matter of government begins too late, for it supposes that the desires to be governed, at any given time, are already broken loose in their rampages, so that if, by due campaigning, we should get them under, there will always be new ones, not less wild, coming after. Besides, we do not see far enough to govern them understandingly, or in any but a certain coarse way. Such as are most plainly wild, vaulting as it were above the moon, we can well enough distinguish and repress. We can know something, and can see a little way, but if we could see just one inch farther, how often should we stand back from a desire that seems to be quite wise, even as from a precipice. You would see for example that the horse you are desiring and bargaining for to-day, will kick you into eternity to-morrow. And so a single stage farther of perception would almost every hour, set you back in recoil from some other and still other desired object. We can do something, of course, by self-government in this matter, ought to do what we can, or what God will help us do wisely, but we want most visibly some other more competent and less partial kind of remedy.

Sometimes a different kind of work is undertaken, that is supposed to be more adequate. A certain class of devotees, meaning to be eminently Christian, set themselves to the task of extirpating their desires; counting it the very essence of perfection to have no desires. It is not as if they were merely in a ferment of misrule, but as if they were properties of nature inherently bad. Hence the attempt is, by abnegations, penances, macerations, poverties, mortifications, vows of solitude, and complete withdrawment from the world to kill them off, expecting that when they are dead sin itself will be dead, and all the goings on of the soul will be in purity, whereupon the vision of God will follow. Alas! it is not seen that when these impulsive forces of the soul are extirpated, the corrosive will be left in as much greater activity. And the result is that the imagination goaded by remorse, breaks into riot, and the poor anchorite, how often has it been the fact, begins to see devils, and falls into a kind of saintly *delirium tremens* which is real insanity.

Our gospel, as I now proceed to show, has a better way. It is never jealous of the desires, puts us to no task of repression, or extirpation. It proposes to keep them still on hand, as integral and even necessary parts of our great moral nature. In them it beholds the grand impulsions of activity, the robustness of health, the spiritual momentum of all noblest energies, including even the energies of prayer itself. It even undertakes to intensify the desires, in the highest degree possible, only turning them away from what is selfish and low to what is worthy and good; giving promises for arguments, and saying, "ask what ye will," "open thy mouth wide, and I will fill it."

And it is most refreshing to see how these two young men, James and John, who came to Jesus in their most absurd request, had afterwards got on, and had learned to have not smaller desires, but larger and more free, because now trained to be in God's own order. They write books of Scripture under their names, and one of them says—"Whatsoever we ask, we know that we have the petitions that we desired of him;" "whatsoever we ask we receive of him, because we keep his commandments, and do those things that are pleasing in his sight." He was in God's order, and now his desires went all to their mark. The other in his book is yet closer to the point, saying, "If any of you lack wisdom, let him ask of God that giveth to all men liberally, and upbraideth not. But let him ask in faith, nothing wavering." And again he lectures more at large—"From whence come wars and fightings among you? come they not hence even of your lusts, that war in your members? Ye lust and have not, ye kill and desire to have and can not obtain, ye fight and war, yet ye have not, because ye ask not. Ye ask and receive not, because ye ask amiss, that ye may consume it upon your lusts. Do ye think that the Scripture saith in vain the spirit that dwelleth in us lusteth to envy? But he giveth more grace." Yes, more grace, all the grace that is wanted to set the soul in God's harmony, and give it such desires as he can fitly grant. So these two greedy ones of the former day, we can see, had now made great progress. Living for so long a time in Christ, they had learned to have all their wild lustings put in accord with him, and so to have them liberally filled without upbraiding.

Let us now see how this grace, which is called "more grace," draws the desires, in this manner, into their true cast of relationship with God.

It is done partly, we shall see, by prayer itself; that is by prayer, helped as it is and wrought in by the Spirit of God. For how grand a fact is it, and how full of hope, that the Spirit of God has presence in us so pervasively, being at the very spring point of all most hidden movement in us, even back of all that we can reach by our consciousness. And there by his subtle, most silent, really infinite power, he works, configuring the desires, before they are born into consciousness, to the reigning order and will of God. So that when we know not what we should pray for, he helpeth our infirmities and, so to speak, maketh intercession for us, heaving out our groanings of desire, otherwise impossible to be uttered, into prayers that are molded according to the will of God. And so all prayer is encouraged, by promises that make an institute of it, for the schooling and training of our desires, and drawing them into conformity with God and the everlasting reason of things. In this way of prayer we obtain our request, because we have been drawn closely enough to be in true chime with his will, and so to make an authorized pull on his favor, by our right-deserving; even as the bow-line from a boat, pulling on some object to which it is fastened, draws not so much the shore to it, as it to the shore. In this way it comes to pass, that souls which are much in prayer, and get skill in it, obtain their desires in great part, by learning how to have good ones moderated in the will of God, being drawn so closely to him by their prayers, that bad ones fall away more and more completely, and leave them petitioning out of purity. In passing through which process the Spirit helps them on, preparing them to prayer by the restored quality of their desires.

Again, there is a power in the new love Christ begets in the soul, to remold or recast the desires, in terms of harmony with each other and with God. When the supreme love is changed, being itself an imperial and naturally regnant principle, all the powers of misrule, including the desires, fall into chime with it. The love also is luminous and pure, so that no base underling, that would kennel back of knowledge in the mind, can hide from it. Besides, it does not have to govern or keep down, for it bathes and tinges all through, so to speak, even the desiring substance, with a color from itself. And then it follows that, as the love is, so the desires will be. Loving my enemy, I shall desire only his good. Loving God I shall desire all that belongs to his will, and the advance of his kingdom. And so, indirectly and by association, all the wild ferment of the corrupted nature, all the desires that belong to a sensual, earthly, selfish habit will be gradually changed, and the whole order, and scale, and scheme of desire will be replaced by another. In this love even the drunkard's appetite will be silent; for he will have only to abide in this love, to be free almost without a struggle. For it is a tide so full, that every basest longing is submerged by it. " Breadth, length, depth, heighth, and to know the love of God that passeth knowledge," says an apostle, "that ye might be filled with all the fullness of God." And when the soul is full in this manner, it wants nothing more, because it can hold nothing more, least of all any thing contrary. All the wild wishes and vagrant longings settle now into rest, when the fullness of God is come. Unruly desires will of course begin to have their liberty again when the love abates, but abiding long enough in God as we may, they will even die.

And just here it is that we duly conceive the Christian wise man. He is not any prophet or seer, neither is he any philosopher, but he is a man whose tempers and aspirations have found their equilibrium and right keeping in the love of God. He is called wise because his judgments are not overset by the tempests of wild desire, and because all the gusty instigations of his nature are laid, leaving it open to the sway of right reason and of God's pure counsel.

Our gospel also brings us yet another kind of power by which we have our desire remolded gradually, without superintending the process ourselves. The Christian soul is a soul that by its faith in Jesus Christ is entered into a most dear personal fraternity with him. It walks with him as in a companionship, has its conversation with him, admires him all the while the more, because it gets a deeper knowledge or insight of what is in him, and so, by a kind of social contagion, takes the mold of his feeling, and comes into configurations of temper that accord with his. For what do we better know, than that every man, especially every young person, who is allowed to join himself to any great, much admired character, and pass even years in travel and work, and private counsel with him, takes his type insensibly, and grows into a mold that is largely correspondent. He imbibes, so to speak, the man, and that in matters too subtle even to be noted by himself. Not unlikely even his voice and accent will be affected, when he has no thought of it. How then shall it be with the disciple that walks in the dear great company of his Master? Suppose he has no thought of his desires, will he not be taking the type of his Master insensibly even in these? Is it too much to believe that all his inmost tempers and configurations will be recast, by a companionship so widely different from all mortal companionships, so unselfish and pure and true?

But suppose there still are left some traces of the old misrule and disorder, there is yet a will of Providence put running for him, to reduce all these and finish him, as it were, in God's order. Or it may be, if the sensual and low lustings of his former habit are already somewhat reduced, that there is too much eagerness left in his new Christian habit, and that he is sometimes rushing against God in it, even in his prayers. He loses patience, it may be, and is sorely galled that he can not make the good come to pass as he expected. Beaten back thus and discouraged, he protests that he is almost ready to give over desiring any thing; for what efficacy is there even in his good desires? Or he breaks out in a mourner's grief, perhaps, saying—"Why should God take away my talented and promising son, when I was going to make him such a blessing to the world? Or why my friend who was such a blessing already, and was so much wanted by us all?" By and by, after such sallies, it is discovered, perhaps, that the desires put forward so peremptorily were a good deal more romantic or ambitious, or subtly selfish than they should be, and could only be tamed by discipline. So God has us all the while in schooling under his providence, reducing our foolishness, and wearing out or worrying down our dictations. We roll up tumultuously, as the waves drive up their masses, break into foam and flatten out on the shore, but there is this very important difference, that our desires tire down at last, under God's strong discipline, while the waves never tire, and of course get no such benefit. So there is a grand tiring out principle in this rule of Providence, by which we are all the while being schooled into God's order. And in this manner the old Christian gets, at last, to have a wonderful wisdom in his experience without even knowing it, because it is hid in his more chastened tempers, and never thinks of being a rational knowledge at all.

Pressing on thus close upon his last limit, wrought in by Christ's word and Spirit and Providence, his secret mind, if not perfectly conformed to God, gets to be so very nearly conformed, that when he drops into the river to cross over, and mounts the rampart on the other shore, his last shred of discord dies out in him, and he is everlastingly free. Now that he sees Christ in clear vision as he is, he is thoroughly and completely like him. This now is the redintegration, the restored order of the desires—the most wonderful work, the deepest and sublimest achievement of man's redemption. How it has been done, I have told you in a certain far off way—closer in a more interior way, I could not—for these roots of impulse and springs of movement are clean back of our consciousness. We never saw them, or descended where they are, we only see what wells up from them, and how they jostle us and drive us on, by impulsions first known when they are first felt. Come they whence? out of what murkiness, or steam, or smoke, or night, or morning, or heat, or noonday fire within? Little as we know whence, we do at least know well their awful power, and how they drive on thick and wild, hurling aside, as in storms of the mind, all self-regulative order, will, and principle. They war in our members, they chafe and seethe, and boil, and burn all unsatisfied, all disappointed, and the man wears out, and dies at last of anarchy, not knowing why. They breed aims that are meagre and mean, which is about the worst mischief that can befall any man whether young or old, they blast the affections, they smirch and smoke out the principles, they both drug and stimulate the will, as by contrary instigations, they addle, and muddle, and turn to confusion about every thing in us that belongs to the order of a well-ordered life. Being all in some sense misbegotten infestations of our sin—

foul birds, jackals, hungry wolve packs, let loose in the mind—they cost us about all the worry and torment we suffer, and a great part of all fatal disaster beside. O if this terrible ferment could be stilled, settled in heaven's order, the wildness and bitter nonsense taken out, what a smoothing of this world it would be!

And this exactly is what our gospel undertakes and, as I have shown you, performs, or at least makes possible. I know not how it is that the religious teachers have so little to say of the desires when the gospel grace moves on them, in so great stress of attention. Perhaps it is because they class them with the merely instinctive motions, calling them irresponsible, and letting them be so ruled out of the account. Whereas they are at the very bottom, in one view, of all responsibility cast off, and the soul must be hampered, and galled, and fouled everlastingly by their misdoing, unless they are rectified. They are in fact the hell of the mind, and nothing is salvation which does not restore them. Clearly enough, we can not purge them or set them in order, by any course of training. We educate the intellect so as to harmonize it largely with nature, and law, and truth; we educate the taste, the sentiment, and to a certain extent the affections; also form, color, music; also the hand, the eye, the muscular force—schools on schools, colleges on colleges we organize for these and other such kinds of training. But we have no colleges for the desires, and see not how we could have if we would.* For where shall such kind of training begin, and by what course go on? Where are the diagrams? where is the logic? what objectivities are there to work by? Diogenes, I believe, was the only professor in this line, and he undertook to moderate the desires by his gibes—much as he might still a tempest by whistling it down. And yet it is but fair to say that he did what he could. Should he soberly reprove them, they would only laugh at him. Should he reason with them, what care have they for reason? Inventing a guage for them, where is the guage? who shall keep it? when shall it be applied? No discipline requiring eyes can enter intelligence into these blind factors. Not amenable to reason, or capable of it; able on the other hand to obfuscate all reason; able to be a robber talent as against the strength and fair success and peace of all the others; able, in short, as was just now intimated, to make a hell of the mind, where is the heaven? Here in Christ Jesus, have I not shown you. In him, coming forth to die, have you not, after all, the needed university, the sufficient and complete discipline. Drawing near to him, as he to you, and finding how to walk with him, will not even your desire be learning tenderly to say, "Whom have I in heaven but thee, and there is none upon earth that I desire besides thee." In this most difficult matter come and see what he will do for you; or rather what he will not do. Indeed I know not any other

* Y. C. C.

change in mind that can abate so many frictions, quell so many distractions, invigorate so great concentration of thought in such evenness of repose; nothing in short that will so much advance the possibilities of a good and great life.

And saying this I can not forget or keep out of mind the example of a once dear classmate and friend, who not long ago took his reward on high. He was not a brilliant man as we commonly speak, but there was a massive equipoise and justness in the harmonized action of his powers that was remarkable to us all. The robust life he had in body and mind and moral habit, required him never to be gathering up his equilibrium, for it was never lost. He was not in his own opinion at that time a Christian, but he scarcely could have been a more sound integer, if he had been, to others. A few months after his graduation, he wrote me that he was a good deal tossed by the question to what he should turn himself, as the engagement of his life. We had supposed that he would of course take his place in the law. But "the law," said he, "is for money, and money I do not want. I have enough of that already, (he belonged to an immensely rich family,) therefore I am questioning whether I can do better than to put in my life with the best, even with Christ and his cause. I think I shall there be satisfied, and I do not see any thing else, where I can be." The result was that his whole desire fell into this current, and grew large upon him, getting volume to fill his great nature full; and he went into his clearly divine call as a preacher of Christ, with such energy and such visible devotion, that he was pushed forward shortly into a high, church leadership that widely signalized his life, and made his name, in his death and before it, a name of great public honor. And I think of him now as probably the happiest, best harmonized, noblest keyed man of all my acquaintance here. Would to God, my friends, that in such high example he might quicken you to follow.

And if he should, let me tell you, in this short catalogue of specifications, what the result will be.

You will be wishing less and doing more.

Your momentum will be heavier, and your impulse stronger.

You will have a more piercing intellectual perception.

Your inspirations will range higher, because your desires do.

Your serenity will be more perfect, as the sky of your mind is more pure.

Your enjoyments will be larger and less invaded by distractions.

You will have a more condensed vigor of will.

You will have a great deal less need of success, and a great deal more of it.

You will die less missing life, and more missed by it.

All which may God in his mercy grant.

XI.

A SINGLE TRIAL BETTER THAN MANY.

"And as it is appointed unto men once to die, but after this the judgment."—*Heb.* ix: 27.

It is a form of opinion frequently held, and received with increasing favor in these times, that there is to be some better chance given to bad men after this life is over; a second or renewed trial, that may be expected to result more favorably; a third, possibly a round of trials that will finally wind up all disaster, and bring the most intractable spirits into a genuinely perfected character. This hope I could not encourage, because I see no benefit to come of it—nothing, in fact, but damage and loss.

Observing this word "once," and reading it more exactly, "once for all," we discover an aspect of finality in the declaration that has little agreement with the expectation referred to—implying, in fact, a fixed belief that our present probation, or state of trial, is to be both first and last, a trial once for all. That a great many thoughtful minds recoil from what appears to be the undue severity and rigor of such an appointment is not wonderful. That God should give us but a single chance—one short trial—and hang every thing in our great life-problem on it, indicates, they imagine, some deplorable fault of beneficence. It is as if he had set our trial as a trap to catch us. We begin it, they say, in a state of unknowing infancy, and scarcely get on far enough in knowledge to act our part wisely, when we are hurried away. If God is really willing to do the best thing for us, why does he not, will he not, give us a second trial, or a lengthened, partly renewed probation ; that we may have our advantage in correcting the mistakes and repairing the wrongs of the first ? Do we not learn a great deal from our first trial that could now be turned to account ? And how often are we sighing, all of us, at the recollection of our misdoings, and wishing we could only go over life again. Every thing now would be differently done, we think, because we have learned so much from that experience. We could hardly make any such bad mistakes again as we have made, for we have seen exactly what results follow. The good opportunities we should now value and improve, the temptations that have had their mask taken off we should scornfully reject, the perils that before overcame us we should understandingly face and vigorously master. And so, trying life once more, we should come out safely, one and all, in a character fully consummated and established.

If now this kind of argument were good, if it would be for our real advantage as respects the training of our character, God would certainly allow us to go over life again. He would give us, I verily believe, twenty or a hundred trials, if it were morally best for us, and would secure a greater amount of good or holy virtue as the result. But that it would not, I am firmly convinced, for reasons that I now undertake to set forth. Notice then :

1. The most prominent and forward argument above referred to—viz., the very many valuable regrets prepared by our first trial, which ought not to be lost for want of another, such as will permit us to get our advantage in them. Such regrets in abundance are, no doubt felt; but we must not make more of them than is to be made. A really solid, practical regret is next thing to repentance, and it will not wait, if we have it, for a second trial to give us a chance of amendment; it will seize its opportunity *now,* and be forthwith consummated in repentance and the beginning of a right life. All such true regrets are different from the lazy kind, which want another life to ripen them. Being honest and true, they are prompt also, ready for the present trial, and looking for no other so far off as to let them evaporate. It is, in fact, one of the very precise, undeniable objections to the plan of a second trial, that it is a way—the most certain way possible—of making all our bad regrets barren; for what can spoil their integrity more inevitably than that we are looking for some good time to come, when we shall turn them to account more easily and with less distraction? The precise thing not wanted here is a second trial. The most unpropitious thing possible for a soul, wading deep in the conviction of neglected opportunities, and abused powers, is the proffer of some posthumous,

second-life chance of amendment, that dispenses with the disagreeable necessity of prompt amendment now. Consider next:

2. As a matter partly coincident, the very self-evident fact that, if we had two or more trials offered us, we should be utterly slack and neglectful in the first; and should bring it to its end almost inevitably in a condition utterly unhopeful. For the supposition now, as you observe, is not that a second trial is going to be sprung upon us in the after state by surprise; but that it is to be such a kind of change or transition as we have argued for beforehand. We are to have it here as our deliberate conclusion that, however the present first trial may go, we shall at any rate have another. Be it so; let the argument be sure, and then, if a second trial is certainly to come, what shall hold us to any least concern for the first? The very promise itself is license and chartered recklessness. It even lies in the plan, we may say, that it shall be only a failure; a bad, foul chapter—any kind of chapter we may like in lust and wild caprice to make it. Put into language outspoken, it says, "Plunge thyself uncaringly into evil. Fear nothing, be as irresponsible as you will; and, if it suits your fancy or your appetite, or the wild, bad impulse that takes you, be a devil. And then, when you have burned away your finest capacities and highest possibilities of good in the hells of your lust, know that a second chance is coming in which you will easily make the damage good." Ah? that second chance which is to mend the bad issues of

the first, what is it but a bid for the misimprovement, moral abandonment, irrecoverable damage and sacrifice of the first? It is even doubtful whether Christian men enough could be raised in it to make up, for the present world, a church, or man its gospel offices and functions. Again:

3. It is important or even quite decisive on the question, to observe and make due account of the fact that the second trial must, in any case, begin where the first leaves off. It is *we*, by supposition, that are to go into this second trial; not some other *we*, new-created and set in our place. We carry down with us all the old history lived, and the results matured, as they are garnered in us, and with that dismal outfit we begin again. Righteous men, if such there are, will not, of course, be kept back here in embargo to go through a second trial. Only to the bad will any such going over of the round again have any look of opportunity. And they must be thoroughly bad for that matter, else they will beg to be excused; for such as are only less good than they would be, and have got some tolerable confidence of their future, will recoil from the new trial proposed, with unutterable dread. For one, I should not dare to choose it for my privilege. I should say, and I think a great many would join me in a like confession, that I consciously have made but a poor, sad figure, and seem rather to have slighted than duly profited by what my God has done for me; and yet, having gotten some benefit, such as gives me hope of my future, it is not enough that I might possibly do better

on a second trial; the experience I have had of myself makes me rather afraid that I should do worse, even fatally worse. I can not risk it; indeed, I shudder at the possibility, in such misgivings that nothing short of God's compulsions can ever bring me to it. And yet almost every man who is in the same general state —mortified and troubled by his own short-comings and the self-dissatisfaction he feels—has said, how often, with a sigh, not considering all it means, "O, I should love above all things to live my life over again!" No, I deny it; you would not. Coming to the real point, your courage would utterly fail. If you must begin where you leave off—as you must, if you are the same being—you would see no look of promise or charm of opportunity in the new trial permitted, but would draw back rather in utter revulsion. Possibly certain worn-out hacks of grace and judgment might be so far bereft of perception, as to think it a good thing to have a second turn thus under grace and judgment. But they must begin their second turn where they ended their first, with all their finest capabilities deflowered, and all their sins stuck fast in them—pinned through their moral nature by habit—with a dry, bad mind, and a heart poisoned by its own passion, and a wild, distempered will; and, having only this poor, battered, broken furniture, they must now set themselves to another chapter of trial, and make it a good one. They must, I say; they undertake to do it, but who can believe that they will?

4. Considering the fact that our second trial must

begin where the first leaves off, we shall find it quite impossible to conceive the state supposed, in a way that does not make it utterly unpromising and very nearly absurd. We imagine, it is true, what a beautiful thing it would be to live our life over again, beginning at our childhood and carrying back into it all the experiences we have gained; and we are so much fascinated that we do not see the nonsense of it. We are really conceiving the old spoiled cargo of an old bad life carried onward and put upon or put into a very young child; and are nowise shocked, either by the absurdity of the plan or the woe of the child. What now is the hapless creature going to do, or be, or how to carry himself? Not, certainly, to act his old infancy over again. To handle again, see, touch, taste, question, learn: in that way to stock the mind with symbols, and get in the timber of thought and feeling and fancy and action—which is the beautiful office of childhood—that is no more wanted. The timber is all in beforehand, and the supposition is that the child-soul, thus completely stocked already, will begin to be wise off hand. But look again at this very absurd creature—a little child with a grown man's wisdoms, follies, vices, sins, all packed in, to be the furniture of a certainly wise, good life! Why, the creature is not a child, if you call him so; but a tiny old man, who has worn out one life to no good purpose, and is stocking another out of it to begin again. The unknowingness, the innocence, the sweet simplicity of childhood, the all-questioning observation—none of these are in him; but only what a sinner knew and was, when he left off his former trial and died with the guilt of it on him. We hardly know whether to laugh or be sad when we fall upon one of these premature, old children, seeing him walk and hearing him talk agedly, as if getting ripe in the green. But here we have the oldness without the innocence—a full-grown, rank-grown sinner that was, tottling again upon his tender feet; an old, sixty-year-old man, it may be, who has been actually set up as a child again to make his beginnings of wisdom; all which he is to do by the help of old miscarriages and sins, and it may be vices. Childhood, they say, is the hopeful thing now for him; but hapless, utterly hapless creature, is the child!

Clearly enough there is no such thing possible as a second trial beginning at the point of childhood; that is only a very absurd fiction that we raise when we are playing with our idle regrets. The second trial, if there be one, has, of course, no time of childhood in it. What we call the ductilities, flexibilities, tender possibilities of childhood and family training are gone by. Family itself is gone by, and the family spheres and affections—possible only in the terms of family reproduction—are henceforth left behind. If conscious ties of fatherly and filial relationship remain, they remain as to persons who have already graduated in them, and have them only as in memory. What there is of society now, in this second state, is made up of beings sole and separate; existing in full maturity and coming to their second trial in such characters and habits as they have shaped by their first. Almost of necessity, they will now be more selfish than ever; for, the unselfish industries that, in their first trial, were generously occupied in providing a home—where hospitalities should be dispensed to friends, and wife and children have their free supply—are now displaced by industries that only make dry providence for self. They are now sole monks and nuns, we may say, in their conventual—only monks and nuns that have not found, as yet, their piety—coming hither to see, if possibly the dreariness of their grown-up, blasted condition may not do something for them. To any rational mind the prospect must be dismally discouraging.

Probably the very best arrangement for a second trial that can be conceived will be made by simply giving a new lease of life, that doubles the length of it here; because, in that case, family feelings and connections, and the wonted social relations of time, will to some extent be continued. Add another thirty, fifty, or eighty years, and let the addition be the new trial. And what will be the result? Exactly the same that befel the old primeval race of reprobates before the flood—viz., that having lived out their first five hundred years, they went on to live a second five hundred, and grow worse, instead of better, for their opportunity. If they wanted a second trial, they had it in the very best and most favorable conditions possible—far better and more favorable than if they had passed through death to receive it in the after life; because they are not torn away from their kind, or from the society of the good, but are permitted to enjoy, in some degree, all the tender offices of natural affection, and live in all the bonds of family providence and duty. And what, in fact, was proved by these ante-diluvial men but that, when too much of time or trial is given, no stringent motive for decisive choice in good is left. That last five hundred years was a very generous allowance, given, we might say, for the amendment of their wretchedly bad life in the first five hundred; but, instead of amendment, it only made them more completely reprobate. Too much trial, as they found, is damage—diminishing, and not increasing, the chances of a good result.

Let us not be deceived here by a certain off-hand way of judgment; as if the great shock to be suffered in passing to another world, supposing that we are to have our second trial there, initiated the new experience in a way to make it more promising. Thus, if we had actually gone through death, and begun to live again, having it shown us at God's bar that we have made a dreadful issue of our trial, we should know our immortality, it will be thought, by experiment, and should have our sensibility awakened, as it were, by a shock of tremendous discovery; and so we should be set in a position of immense advantage, as regards the improvement of our new opportunity. Just as every malefactor, I suppose, who is caught in a crime, thinks that he shall certainly make an upright life, if now, this once, he can be respited and allowed another opportunity. No! he will do no such thing; but will pitch himself into any crime that is worse, about as soon as the shock of his arrest passes off, and he begins to act himself again. So, the prison convict goes his dreary round of work and solitude and silence, saying inwardly: "O, what a fool am I to be here! Would that I could live my life over again, and I would not!" But he will be a most remarkable felon if, when his time expires, he does not go out to live his life exactly over again, making good his return within a short six months. So we think a man must assuredly become a saint, if only a second trial after death is given him: when it will turn out as a matter of fact that the saints are not made by occasions, opportunities, or appalling necessities, least of all where the noblest occasions and highest opportunities and most cogent necessities are already trampled and lost. Great shocks felt or crises past have no value as respects the beginnings of a right life, save as they induce consideration, and by such consideration, make a new atmosphere of truth and feeling for the soul's engagement and recovery to good. But where consideration has so often been freshened by new providences and new revelations of God, and all best capacities of truth and feeling have been mocked and hardened by the abuses of a life, what magic is there to be in the strange environments and discoveries of another state of being, that they are going to make men susceptible without susceptibilities left, and turn them back to the right which they have lost the sense of, and from which they have all their life long turned uncaringly away? Their shock of novelty in the transition will pass off in a very short time, and they will settle back into their wild, wrong habit, or willfully neglectful obstinacy, to choose and live and be precisely as before. Again:

5. We have large material for the settlement of this question in our own personal experience and observation. The likeliest times of duty and character we every day perceive are not the last or latest, but the times of youth, and probably quite early youth; for the capital stock or fund most wanted, as regards the finest possibilities of character, is made up of ingenuous feeling, sentiments unmixed with evil-doing, unsophisticated convictions, free and pure aspirations, not of knowledges and wise sagacities, gotten by experience. These prudentials, these wise knowledges, are too commonly bad knowledges, gotten by irrecoverable losses. If we say that a soul must have them, and that, having gotten in a good stock of them on its first trial, it is, therefore, ready, on a second, to act wisely, we very certainly mistake. The sad thing is that a soul may know too much, obtaining knowledges that cost many times more than they are worth—such as come of self-damaging vices and the flagrant excesses of a bad life. All such ways of abuse create a knowledge, doubtless; but what can these desolating knowledges, these burnt-in, branded curses of an old and evil life, do for the immortal prospects of a soul? What, in fact, is the reason why a great many never can, or will, become true men of God here in this life; but that they have been going too deep into knowledge, and have

gotten too much experience at too great cost? Their knowledges are vitriol in their capabilities, eating out and searing over all the noblest affinities and finest aspirations God gave them to be the stock and possibility of their future. And, therefore, it becomes a fixed conclusion with us that a man going into his trial shall make much of his unsophisticated age, and the noble, inborn sensitiveness of his early moral convictions, and be sadly, fearfully jealous of the wisdom he will get by their loss. This dreary and dry wisdom, that is going to be ripened by the practice of unrighteous years, can do little for the subject, however much he values it. His green first third of life has grand possibility of fruit; his wise last third has probably none; and he draws himself very close upon the discovery of this fact as he approaches the end of his trial. The gold-washers of California, having passed their dirt once through the sluice, drop what they call "the tailings" below; and sometimes they discover a very little gold in these, enough to pay for milling them over again. But the tailings of an old, bad life, which has yielded no gold on the first trial—who will go to work on them with any least prospect of success? As certainly as the man understands himself, he will see that his good possibilities will be gone, and will feel the least imaginable desire of a second trial, to mill over the dregs of his unblest experience. We ourselves, at least, know perfectly that nothing will come of it.

But the new state expected, as some will perhaps remind us, is to be a state of punishment, and the pains of it, working purgatorially, must have great and decisive effects. Whereas, the very thing best proved by observation is that pains are nearly unrelational as respects the improvement of character. The fears of pain or penalty, so much derided commonly by these prophets of purgatorial benefit, might do something as appeals to consideration and preparatives in that manner of repentance; but pain, pain itself, nothing. It even disqualifies consideration. Pain is force, necessity, a grinding stress of absolutism, which may do something in breaking down a will, but never in the world was known to lift up a will out of weakness and evil, or ennoble it in the liberty and free ascension of good. Breaking down a will too, be it observed, is not conversion, but catastrophe rather and death—just that which is the undergirding import and reality of second death.

Observation gives us also another fact, which is even more impressive—viz., that with all that is said and assumed and argued for, and stiffly asserted, as regards the fact of a second trial hereafter, the whole world tacitly concedes, nevertheless, that no such new condition is, in fact, expected. For no unbeliever, no practically godless and really apostate believer, no bad man groaning under his vices, no drunkard writhing under his chains, no scoffing Altamont overtaken by remorse, no human creature, whether uninstructed Pagan or best instructed philosopher, and (what is most significant of all) no loosest, largest freethinker, who asserts most confidently the faith of a second trial hereafter, goes out of life—I never heard of such a case—talking of the new chance now to be given him, and the high, free time he is going to have, in the more propitious trial that will suffer him to mend his defects and the consciously bad ways that have corrupted him. All such advocates of a basement gospel, under the world and after the grave, convince themselves, by what they consider most indisputable and profoundly wise arguments, that their ultimation gospel, their posthumous salvation, will have power to mend all damage and smooth away all woes of character begun; but when we look to see those deep natural instincts, which are always the spontaneous interpreters of our humanity, giving out their indications, we find our believers in the underworld opportunity clinging fast to life, as if they had no such faith at all in them, recoiling with instinctive shudder from death, and hailing never in glad welcome the better day now come to help their recovery—in which they may discover, as plainly as need be, themselves, that their arguments are one thing, and the verdict of their immortal, deep-discerning judgments another. They contrive how it is to be, they reason, they promise, they encourage; but their always demonstrative nature nowhere runs up a flag of hope or gives any slightest indication. If the question be whether we are immortal, all the flags of natural hope are out streaming on every hill; but here expectation is dumb and shows no sign!

But my object in this argument, drawing it here to

a close, is not so much to show that no second trial is to be had as to show the undesirableness of it. The matter itself is variously conceived. According to some, the wicked dead will be manipulated by long tractations in the better gospel of the pains, and will so, at last, be purified. According to others, they will be softened by long annealings under undeserved and extra comfortable indulgences. By some it is believed that we were not made immortal by nature, and shall, therefore, cease altogether if we do not take hold of the eternal life in Christ to make us immortal. Others think we were made to be immortal, but fell out of immortality in our sin, and so are to quite die out if we do not forsake it. Some think that the future punishment will itself wear out life in the bad, and finally make a complete end of it. I say nothing of these or any other varieties in the unbeliefs current. I say nothing of eternal punishment itself. One thing at a time, I am saying, one thing at a time; and then, having the one thing settled, as I think it now is, that no second trial hereafter is either to be desired or allowed, we have at least one very great point established, and can well enough allow the other questions to fare as they may. Make what you will of all these other questions, only have it as a fact made clear, which I think I have shown as decisively as it need be, that there is no possible advantage in a second trial promised beforehand, and that we are better off without the supposed advantage than with—have this clear, I say, and all the other last things may be left to find their own settlement. Enough that there is no severity in having but a single trial, and that, if more than one were offered, we should do well to petition against it. Beyond a question, God, in giving us our one opportunity and no more, fixes this close limit because one will do more for us than many. A greater number—two, ten, twenty—we could not have without unspeakable damage and loss.

My argument appears to be thus ended, but I must not shut up the conclusion before it is ready. And is no better account then to be made, some one may ask, of the multitudes brought up under heathenism, or the drill of vice, or the taint of bad society? If there is no second chance for them, what chance have they? I admit the seeming severity of their lot, but a great many things are none the less true because they seem to be severe. They are certainly not as unprivileged as we commonly think. They have all great light. They all condemn and blame themselves. The Spirit of God is with them. Some of them are truly born of the Spirit, and all might be. At any rate, all the arguments I have been urging to show the absurdity of a second trial, apply to them as to others—they have lost the tractabilities of childhood; their staple of good possibility is worn out; they are gotten completely by the opportunity of a new beginning. We must therefore leave them to God, certain that he will somehow mitigate any look of hardship in their lot. Only coming back here on our conclusion, that a second trial can do nothing for them, and that whatever else may befall them this will not.

And since we are looking at questions raised by doubt, I will not shrink from naming another which I can not so explicitly answer; viz., the seeming look of fitness in a second trial, for such as die in their infancy, or in youth, so far unspent as to allow their carrying all best possibilities with them. Why should not such have a state given them, wherein they may unfold the character they are made for? And why, it may be asked in reply, were they not kept here to do it, where the advantages are so many and so evidently great? Perhaps we can as little answer one question as the other. However, we do not certainly know that any one of these infants and youths is not taken away to another and more genial state, there to be unfolded and trained, just because there are seeds of holy possibility already planted in them which might otherwise be extirpated. Their second state is not, in that case, their second trial any more than that of such as die in the full maturity of a sanctified habit. In these young-life souls there may certainly be rich stores of rudimental possibility, waiting for the educating forces of a pure, sweet world, and it may be that so many are carried forward thus early, to make a larger infusion of unsophisticated character than a world of natures fully matured would reveal.

Here, then, we are, my friends, face to face with our conclusion; and a most serious one it is. It raises questions for us that we can not wisely push aside.

All of us are on our way, in our one decisive lifetime trial; and what are we doing with it? How is it turning? Some of us are but a little way advanced in it, and all the fine possibilities of our outfit are still on hand, scarcely if at all abridged. Great, my young friends, is your advantage, greater than if a hundred other stages of probation were promised you. Precious are the gifts, and precious are the moments as they fly. Act, every one, as if this eventful experiment were now on its way and passing rapidly. Allow no expectation of another to beguile you. Bring in all your powers, and center them on this point of crisis, now so close at hand, knowing that God's friendship can not be too soon secured. Others of your number, it may be, are getting farther on. A considerable or even principal part of their trial, it may be, is now gone by. Is it going well? If the tree is to lie as it falls, is it falling rightly? Have you good confidence of the end? Once for all, remember, once for all. And it is appointed unto men once for all to die, but after that the judgment.

XII.

SELF-EXAMINATION EXAMINED.

"Examine me, O Lord, and prove me, try my reins and my heart."—*Ps.* 26: 2.

SELF-EXAMINATION is to many disciples a kind of first point in practical religion. We have also labored treatises from the press, in which set rules are drawn out, whereby the self-examining process may be skillfully and scientifically conducted. In one way or another, this particular type of Christian exercise has come so near being the staple matter of a good life, that any common disciple called to address some brotherhood of strangers, will probably not get on many sentences without falling into the exhortational mood and beginning to say—"Brethren, let us examine ourselves." All which is the more wearisome that it signifies so little, and requires only the dryest kind of sanctimony to carry it on. We might very naturally presume, that there must be a great deal of Scripture for this kind of practice; and yet I do not know more than two passages that can be cited for it at all; one of which certainly has no such meaning, and the other of which has, at most, only a doubtful, or variantly shaded meaning, such as carries no sufficient authority for the practice. The first named passage is the standing proof-text always cited—"Examine yourselves whether ye be in the faith, prove your own selves." (II Cor. 13: 5.) Where it will be seen, at a glance, by the mere English reader, and much more certainly by a scholar versed in the original language, that the apostle is simply referring the Corinthians here to their own new spiritual state, for proof that he has had a power in them for good, and has even transformed them inwardly by his ministrations. "Some of you pretend," he says, "that I am weak, and bring no divine witness in my preaching. Since then ye seek a proof of Christ speaking in me, which to youward is not weak but mighty in you, examine *yourselves* [not whether, but if, or since] you are in the faith. Look into your own bosoms—know you not that Jesus Christ is in you, except you be reprobates." He is not putting these Corinthians on a course of analytic self-study, or self-examination to settle the evidence of their discipleship. He has no thought of it, that is not his subject. His point is the great injustice they are doing him, in running down the significance of his ministry. Therefore to correct them, he says, just look into your own bosom and you will see, that I have not been weak but mighty in you. He assumes their discipleship here, and is not putting them to the proof, but only drawing from it *ex concessis*, an undeniable test of his own apostleship. How this passage ever came to be applied, as it has been, to the testing and self-certifying security of character, I really do not know. There could not be a plainer case of total misapplication. The other passage has a little more show of authority, but is not by any means decisive. It says: (I Cor. 11: 28,) "Let a man examine himself, and so let him eat;" that is, "discerning the Lord's body." But the point here is to merely interpose a caution, an appeal of circumspection, that will prepare the receiver of the supper to partake with reverence—let him put himself to the proof sufficiently to make sure of this—there is no thought of putting him on a retrospective study and testing of his discipleship. At any rate, this would be a very doubtful construction, at the best, and as it puts the text wholly by itself, no other to that effect being found in the whole Scripture, it is certainly more reverent not to force it on a construction so very insufficiently supported.

To make these strictures is not altogether pleasant, for it may even shock the feeling of some, as if it were about the same thing as a virtual tearing out of the most approved foundations of piety. But I hope all such will be sufficiently comforted, on more mature reflection, if I turn them over to God's own way, in what is nearest at hand in the Scripture, and let them have it as a compensation for what has been taken away. The Scripture sends us to God for the examinations wanted, and not, in any case, to ourselves; knowing that when God proves us, we shall be thoroughly and truly proved, and that what assurance he may give us, will be more than a guess, or opinion, or conclusion of our own, a veritable witness of God in our hearts. In this way the Psalmist prays—"Examine me, O Lord, and prove me, try my reins and my heart." And again—"Search me, O God, and know my heart, try me and know my thoughts, and see if there be any wicked way in me, and lead me in the way everlasting." It was also an accepted Proverb even in the same view—"The fining pot is for silver, and the furnace for gold, but the Lord trieth the hearts."

Here then—for I am going to speak to-day, not so much for impression as for instruction—here is the true and proper method of examination; *it must be accomplished under and through the scrutiny, or inspecting power of God; we truly prove ourselves, when he proves us, and may rightly approve ourselves, only when he approves us.* Accordingly—

1. I put forward as a fact, in unfolding the subject stated, that God certainly can examine us, and we can not in any but the most superficial and incomplete sense, examine ourselves. For, in the first place, our memory is too short and scant, to recall or restore the conception of one in a hundred millions of our acts, leaving all the innumerable fugacities that make up our lives, to fly away and print no track of passage on the air passed through. In the next place if we could recall them, every one, we could never go over the survey of a material so vast, and multiplicities so nearly infinite, in a way to make up any judgment of

them, or of ourselves as represented in them. And then, in the next place, since the understanding of our present state is impossible without understanding all the causes in our action, that have been fashioning the character and shaping the figure of it, our faculty is even shorter here than before. Plainly enough omniscience only is equal to that; which is the same as to say that God only is able, or even proximately able. Besides, when we propose to examine ourselves, we do not really mean much by it—only that we propose to question ourselves by certain rules or tests, which in fact would touch and try almost nothing. We suppose indeed that we are going to make very serious and thorough work, when, in fact, we are only proposing to make up a sound verdict on our state, by two or three mere dabs of questioning. How different a matter to be examined by God, who knows all the historic connections by which our present state is linked to our past life, and is able to trace all the nicest shades of our character to the subtleties of action by which they have been sketched and colored in our minds. And yet, again, if we let go all inquiring into the ways in which we have grown to be what we are, the question, what we are, is scarcely less difficult. How shall we fathom the abysses, and distinctly conceive the infinite subtleties of our present state itself—all the more nearly out of understanding, or beyond it, because of the intricacies, disorders, and falsities, bred in us by our fallen condition. "Know thyself" we have all heard was given out by the philosophers, as a first maxim of wisdom. And if they only meant that so we are to get the facts of our philosophy, they were right enough, for these can be gotten, if at all, only by self-observation. But natural faculties and functions are one thing, moral states and spiritual affinities another, and if they imagined that a human creature under sin can know himself, in this latter method, or can so untwist the subtle threads of his motive, and meaning, and character, and want of character, as to really discover the exact import of his condition, they know little themselves of what it is to be men. How much deeper goes the scripture seer, when he protests "who can understand his errors, cleanse thou me from secret faults." And again, "the heart is deceitful above all things, and desperately wicked, who can know it?"

But we are conscious beings, are we not, and what is that but to say that we are self-knowing beings? But in simply noting things as they pass in us, which is all we mean by consciousness, we scarcely do more than to just have a look on the huddle of their transitions. We do not trace their complexions, causes, apologies, deserts, and all the other thousand things concerned in their character. We only look on as we might on the passing of a river, seen from its banks. We examine nothing. Thus if we speak of examining our affections, they are so variable, and changeful, mixed with such multiplicities, and colored by so many crosses, that it is too much like examining the shadows of the clouds sailing, two or three tiers deep, under the sun. Or if we examine our purposes or intentions, we shall know them a great deal better, by just noting what they do, and letting them go; indeed we never know so little about our intentions, and their real desert, as when we are inspecting or handling them, to find how they go—in what temper, by what motive, and the like. Again, it most of all concerns us to know our tendencies, which are the deepest quality and drift of our nature, and they are so very subtle, and twisted together in combinations so intricate, and withal so destitute of harmony, that nothing less penetrating than the all-searching eye of God, can possibly discover, with any real precision, what is in us. Besides, our knowing or examining power itself is in a state of deep spiritual disorder, a creation that groaneth and travaileth in its own discords. And for that reason any effort of a man to adequately know himself, by a direct act of voluntary self-inspection, must be fruitless. He could examine God's great and wide sea in fact from shore to shore and clean down to the bottom ooze, and judge it much more reliably, than he can the abysses of darkness, wrath, and storm, in his own disordered and tumultuating spirit. On the whole it is plain, whichever way we look, or whatever view we take, that God only is able really and discerningly to examine the human soul or spirit. No man thinks it possible, by an act of self-examination, to comprehend the subtle and infinitely multiform processes going on in his body, the contractions, the alternating motions, the secretions, the circulations, the pains, the health whence it comes, the medicine whither it goes. But the soul is a creature infinitely more complex, and subtle, and mysterious, and as much less possible to be read and comprehended by any but the all-piercing intelligence of God.

2. It is a matter deserving of our distinct notice, that in what is frequently understood by self-examination, there is something mistaken or deceitful, which needs to be carefully resisted. In the first place, it is a kind of artificial state, in which the soul is drawn off from its objects, and works, and its calls of love and sacrifice, to engage itself in acts of self-inspection. Instead of doing all the while, and only, what God requires, it suspends, for so long a time, its work, and is occupied with a study of its own figure and character. The will is called off to be questioned, when of course it is out of that engagement where it otherwise would be found—even as a workman might withdraw himself for a day, or a week, from his work, to examine whether he is industrious or not. So one falls to examining his affections, when of course his mind is introverted, and called off from God and Christ, where only right affections have their object and rest. And the result not seldom is accordingly, that persons who become thoroughly bent down upon this matter of examining their affections, are doomed to see them wither and even die out in the process. The wonder then is, that the more faithful they are—and surely they mean to be faithful—the darker they become.

They sigh and groan, they try to be yet more faithful in their tests, and press the search harder, and yet they still lose ground only the more rapidly; till finally they begin to imagine that God has utterly cast them off, to receive them no more. Whereas the fact is simply this, that they have turned away their mind from God, and of course do not see him, can not find him. Then follows a hard chapter. Where is now their love? They do not see that they have any. How can they love God distinctly, when they are wholly taken up with self-inspection? Their mind itself is just as much withdrawn from God as it is occupied with itself, and will of course have just as little outgoing trust and affection, just as little of God's light, as it is required to have, when it is all the while poring over itself, and its own dark shadow.

Many years ago, I knew an excellent, much-esteemed Christian mother, who had become morbidly introverted, and could not find her love to God. Seeing at once that she was stifling it by her own self-inspecting engrossment, which would not allow her to so much as think of God's loveliness, I said to her, "but you love your son, you have no doubt of that." "Of course I love him, why should I not?" To show her then how she was killing her love to God, I said, "but take one week now for the trial, and make thorough examination of your love to your son, and it will be strange if, at the end of the week, you do not tell me that you have serious doubt of it." I returned, at the time, to be dreadfully shocked by my too cruel experiment. "No," she said, "I do not love him, I abhor him." She was fallen off the edge, and her self-examination was become her insanity!

And I must not omit to say, that we may even be so far engrossed, in this matter of self-examination, as to become thoroughly and even morbidly selfish in it; for what can be more selfish than to be always boring into one's self? No matter if it is done under pretext of being faithful to God, still if one wants to be faithful only for his own sake, as he certainly will when neglecting every thing else to do a work upon and for himself, he is as truly selfish as if religion were wholly out of the question. And then if he should perchance bring himself on through this selfish struggle, into the opinion or verdict of approval, which he possibly may—for after all most men are likely to make out somehow that they are right—then he will only have crowned his selfishness, and established the deceit that he will probably carry with him to his grave. No character is more hopeless, as regards the matter of review and rectification, than one that has been smouldering whole years, in a process of self-devoted, self-scrutinizing, introverted life, and has come out in the opinion that he is assuredly right. The conclusion reached is the more certainly irreversible, in the fact that he is wrong; and is reached, not by any act of faith, but by a merely human, and for the most part selfish process of spiritual incubation, separated from God.

3. It is important also, as regards a right impression of this subject, to observe how much is implied in a hearty willingness or desire to have God examine us and prove us. If we undertake to examine ourselves in our own power, it may be to make out a case for ourselves, or, as sometimes happens, in a morbid state of depression, to make out a case against ourselves. False influences in all complexions black and white assail us, and go into the endeavor with us. But if we are ready to have God examine us, and bring us to an exactly right verdict, that is a state so simple, so honest, so impartial, so protected against every false influence, that we scarcely need to look any further; for it is already clear that we are in a right mind, ready to receive the truth, seeking after the truth, waiting on God for the discovery, and prepared to admit his holy will whatever it may be. Indeed I might even go so far as to say, that a soul breaking forth naturally in the prayer—Examine me, O Lord, and prove me, try my reins and my heart, need examine or inquire no farther; it is already found to be in God's friendship, and is sealed with the witness of his acceptance.

The only true and safe conception then of the duty called self-examination is, not that we are to examine ourselves by our own self-inspection merely, but that we are to be rather examined and proved by God. And this brings me—

4. To the point that there is a way of coming at the verdict of God, whatever it may be. None will doubt

the superior ability of God to examine our state, and know what it is, compared with any ability we have to investigate ourselves, but they will see no possibility of making the judgment of God, in our case, available. How can we know, they will ask, what the verdict of God is respecting us, and if it be true, as it must be, how can it be of any benefit to us? Because, I answer, God designs to give us, and has planned to give us always, the benefit of his own knowledge of our state. That we should never be able to make out an accurate or reliable judgment of ourselves, by mere self-inspection, is taken for granted. God has never set us on that footing as regards the conduct of our lives. Many or indeed the general mass of mankind have only the smallest degree of power, in the way of reflective exercise. They are little exercised in this way—almost none but philosophers are thus exercised—their lives flow outward in a way wholly objective, just as the springs flow outward from under the hills and never go back to retrace their courses and inspect their origin. Therefore, God never puts us on the work of testing ourselves. He expects to do this for us, and if we will take his judgment, always to allow us the advantage of it. We are not complete beings or beings perfectly equipped for action apart from God. We are complete only in him. He is, and is ever to be, our light. We are to know ourselves in and through him, just as we are to do our will in his will, and have our majesty in his majesty, reigning with him in his throne.

If then we are in a truly right state towards Him, he will know it, and he has planned to give us witness, infallible and immediate witness of the fact. For as unbelief and wrong separate the soul forthwith from God, so where there is no such separation, or where the separating force is abated, God is immediately revealed in the soul's consciousness. It abideth in the light, it recognizes God as a divine *other*, present within. Even as the Saviour himself declared—"but ye see me," and again—"I will manifest myself unto him." God then is manifested always in the consciousness of them that love him, and are right towards him. They need not go into any curious self-examination, that will only confuse and obscure the witness. They will know God by an immediate knowledge or revelation. They will have his spirit witnessing with theirs. They will have the testimony that they please God. In their simple love they will know God's love to them; for he that loveth knoweth God. For a man then to be obliged to examine himself, and study and cypher over himself to find out whether he is a child of God or not, is no good sign; for if he is, he should have a witness more immediate, and should want no such information at all. God knows him perfectly, and if God has revealed himself in the consciousness, if he has the witness of God and the testimony that he pleases God, what more can he have? and if he has not this at all, what can he have, or what, by self-scrutiny, find to make good the want of it?

But we have a great many defects and errors and bad qualities lurking in us, and here again we shall discover that God has planned to bring us into a perception of these, and set us in the same judgment of them that he has himself. As the fining pot is for silver, and the furnace for gold, so the Lord trieth the hearts. It is wonderful to see with what skill God has adjusted all our experiences, in this mortal life, so as to make us sensible of our errors and defects. As the invisible ink is brought out in a distinct color, by holding what is written to the fire, so God brings out all our faults and our sins by the scorches of experience through which we are ever passing in the fiery trials of life. If we are proud, he has a way to make us see it, and to break down our pride. If we cherish any subtle grudge, or animosity, he will somehow call it out and make us see it. If we are selfish, or covetous, or jealous, or frivolous, or captious, or self-indulgent, or sensual, or self-confident, or fanatical, or self-righteous, or partial, or obstinate, or prejudiced, or uncharitable, or censorious—whatever fault we have in us, whether it be in the mind, or the head, or the body, or I might almost say the bones, no matter how subtle, or how ingeniously covered it may be, he has us in the furnace of trial and correction, where he is turning us round and round, lifting us in prosperity, crushing us in adversity, subduing us with afflictions, tempting out our faults and then chastising them, humbling us, correcting us, softening, tempering, soothing, fortifying, refining, healing, and so managing us, as to detect all our drossy and bad qualities, and separate them from us. He sits as a refiner and purifier of silver, and allows nothing to escape either his discovery or our correction. No self-examination we could make would discover, at all, what he is continually bringing to the light, and exposing to our detection. The very plan of our life is so to handle us that we shall come into the full advantage of his perfect knowledge of our state and character. He is proving us at every turn, making us apprized of ourselves, trying even the reins and the heart, that our most secret things may be revealed.

It can not then be said that there is no way of making God's examination of us available; for he is, all the while, and in every possible manner, giving us advantage of it. If the trial of our faith is precious, he for just that reason leaves it not to us alone to make the trial, but his plan is, knowing what we are and what we want, to conduct every point of the trial himself.

I will only add, and this perhaps I ought to add, that if there be any legitimate place for self-examination, it is in the field last mentioned, where we go into self-inspection just to discover our faults, and the sins that require to be forsaken or put away. This would be a very honest kind of endeavor, and I see no objection to it, save that it is very likely, when pursued too closely, to produce a morbid state, and sink the soul in the disabilities of fatal discouragement. No prudent Christian, therefore, will even dare to set himself down upon the discovery of his sins, and make it his chief engagement. He can not be always looking down this gulf, and not wither in a prospect so ungenial. He must have a little gospel somehow, and if he does not have a great deal, so much sin will starve him to death. It will generally be much better to just let God put him on such ways of discovery here, as will be best for him. But this is not what most disciples go to self-examination, or by their teachers are put on self-examination, for; they are set to it, not to find out their faults, and correct them, but to settle and try out their Christian evidences. Our great and godly Edwards writes his book on the Affections, for exactly this, and taking his book for what he verily thought was to be the use of it, I as verily think it one of the most mistaken books that a good and saintly man was ever allowed to write—it is a kind of morbid anatomy for the mind. And we have hundreds of others in the same strain. Evidences of piety are a great deal more likely to be hidden, or ruled out in that way, than they are to be found, and the most sensitively delicate disciple is the one that will suffer. It is well if he does not push himself into spiritual distraction by it. On the other hand, when evidences are sought in this manner, that class of persons who are commonly finding what they look for, will be almost certain to fish up the evidences they want. This whole method of self-examination, to settle the question of christian evidence, is deceptive, unscriptural, and bitterly injurious.

And it is injurious, I must add, not only in misleading, but also in hindering the disciple. How can he get on with any sort of growth, when totally occupied in the matter of self-inspection? The very engagement becomes a dry and weary fumbling of his own state. Even as the lad I knew, who had undertaken to grow a patch of watermelons, looked to see them ripen long before they were grown; went to them every day and examined and tested them, pressing his thumb down hard upon them, to see if the rind would snap; for that was to be the sign when they were ripe. But the poor things, under so many indentations, fell to rotting, and did not ripen at all. They were examined to death. God's winds, and rains, and suns, and dews, were doing a much better examination upon them—with the advantage that it gave them time to grow, and a chance to naturally live.

The real wisdom of the christian, then, for this is the conclusion to which we are brought, is that he shall be more natural; not facing round as he walks, to examine the tracks he makes, but asking the way to Zion with his face thitherward. This dismal retroversion is the bane of character, giving it a twisted and hard look, a sorely and even selfishly circumspective look. You see at a glance, how often, that the man or woman writes a diary, and puts down all the frames passed through, keeping them in tally, and considering the figure they make. Not that every man who writes a diary does it of course in this self-regarding way. George Fox writes two heavy volumes of diary, and after he has fairly opened his christian story, from its birthday beginning, he scarcely so much as alludes to any frame of feeling, or score of evidence in his life, but simply puts his face right onward, telling where he went, and whom he saw, and what in God's name he did. He never once intimates a misgiving, and when he comes to die, he is so little concerned for it, that in what is called his death, he simply forgot to live! Such a disciple grows less conscious and not more conscious in his habit, and there is such plain, forward-going simplicity in him, that he visibly bears the stamp of God's approving, not of his own self-approving.

God forbid, my hearers, that in ruling out so much that has been held in sacred esteem and reverence, and carefully observed and practiced by the faithful and godly in Christ Jesus, I should seem willing to encourage lightness and looseness of life. Is it a light thing to be said, or only a true, that a man does not want to examine himself to find whether he is cold or hungry, whether he loves his child, whether he is an honest man? No, the sturdy fact is that all such answers sought come and ought to come without seeking, and can only come of themselves in simply being true. And if they do not, if a man has to make a case on the question of his honesty, he is very certainly a good deal less honest than he should be. No, my friends, the thing wanted here, and that which only yields the true evidence, is the genuine down-rightness of our life—that it covers no shams, gets up no mock virtues and no pretexts of proceeding scientifically, but goes right on, putting its face the way it goes, and not backwards. It is consciously right, and God is consciously yielding it his immediate testimony. And let there be no doubt of this, as if it were a way not safe. God will make it safe as he only can. And if you are afraid that some looseness may creep in, or some false hope steal you away, be upon your watch, for watching is one thing, and self-examination a very different thing. Watch and pray that you may not enter into temptation, and let the prayer be this, which God will never disregard—"Search me, O God, and know my heart, try me and know my thoughts, and see if there be any wicked way in me, and lead me in the way everlasting." Then forward, forward in that way.

XIII.

HOW TO BE A CHRISTIAN IN TRADE.

"Then he that had received the five talents went and traded with the same, and made them other five talents."—*Matth.* 25: 16.

IN these words of parable, the Saviour had probably no thought of expressing his formal approbation of trade, as a human occupation; but we only see the more convincingly, in what he says, that he has not even a thought of disapprobation concerning it. His man of five talents he lets go and trade with the same, and regards it as a legitimate or even commendable success, that he returns, after a time, with his little capital doubled by his profits. Taking, then, his words, as a verdict for trade and trade profits, I propose a discourse on this particular calling or engagement, showing—I. *The fair possibility of being; and* II. *How to be, a Christian in trade.*

I undertake the subject, as I ought perhaps to say, because of the immense number of persons who are in this occupation, and are drawing their livelihood from it; and especially because of the great number of young men who are just about going into it, or looking to it with more or less desire, as the probable engagement of their lives. That I can raise any impressions, in minds a long time submitted to its temptations, which will have the power to mend what moral damage and disaster they have suffered, I hardly dare to hope. But the very large class of young persons just entering, or just about to enter, this field—some of them getting under sinister influences even beforehand, from the false impressions they have taken up—these I do hope to set in juster modes of thought, and more christian ways of expectation, that will steady their engagement and make it safe. Some of them are going into it with a purpose wholly ingenuous, and really meaning to be Christian men, if possible, in their now chosen occupation. Others, I very well know, are a little poisoned already by certain false notions they have taken up, and allowed to sharpen their appetite. They do not propose to earn their living in it, but they are going into it to get their living without labor, out of the profits they make by their transactions of buying and selling. And this word *profits* means, they think, no reward of service done to the public, but what they are to get by their sharpness. They expect success just as any specially sharp tool is visibly expecting to cut. Under this profligate and really degraded impression, running, alas! how very low in multitudes of cases, they hurry in to make, as they say, their fortune. Trade, in their view, is illicit, and they go to it in fact as a reputable kind of larceny. They expect sharp practice, or to profit by getting unfair advantages. They would not say it, and probably they do not know it, but they nevertheless really expect to thrive by a strictly filching operation, which operation they call trade.

Now these false impressions of trade, by which so many young persons going into it are so dismally corrupted, are gotten up, I grieve to say, largely by the sophistries and shallow detractions of christian people, who ought to know better. What, they ask, is the very operation of merchandising but a drill exercise in selfishness? And what is the law of price or profit, but the law of possibility; viz., to ask the highest price the market will bear, be the cost what it may, or the value what it may. What too is current price itself, but a market graduation, settled by the contrary bulling and bearing of two selfishnesses, that of the sellers and that of the buyers? And then what is the trader doing but feeling after, all the while, and having it even for his life, to wait on, the adjustments of selfishness, even as barometers wait on the air-waves, and their fluctuating levels?—which waiting always on the unsteady, unsteadies even the sense of principle. Besides the very working of a bargain—what is it but an adroit wrestling match; a talking up of the market and the goods perhaps on one side, and a talking down on the other, or a magnifying by shrewd silences that is even more cunningly and skillfully insincere? There is besides, how often, what a contrary play and parry of opposing magnetisms; the selling airs and plausibilities holding a match with the buying airs and plausibilities, and each watching each, even as an eagle watches the prey, to find how the game is turning, or what will turn it. How often also is it testified, that untruths are a staple matter here, and so far necessary that a clerk or apprentice, who is known to have let a bargain slip for want of a mere lie, will be almost sure to lose his place, as one who has proved his incompetency. By so many poisons, and chemistries of poison, it is imagined that trade is inevitably saturated. Possibly one may be in it, and keep the repute of a Christian. But how many nominally christian merchants will even maintain it as by argument, that a Sunday goodness, a churchly feeling, or prayer-meeting mood, is about the utmost grace of religion permitted them. The man of trade, they will say, is a man sandwiched between such mere times of observance, and the downright selfishness of his engagements. How few young men going into trade, under such impressions, will expect to make their life a properly christian life in it. And of those already in it, not one can be a true living disciple, save under a wholly different set of impressions. Moved by this conviction, I now undertake—

1. To show that there is no necessary moral detriment in trade; that there is quite as good a chance of christian living in it as in any other kind of engagement.

And here I put forward, at the front of all that comes after, the very certain fact that there have been good christians in trade; and if that be so, then it follows by a very short argument, that what has been can be—that is, can be again and often. And what examples of this fact do we meet with in the records of christian living; such as the well-known, much honored father Markoe, the merchant saint of New York; such as our own high-working, nobly christian, trading brother, A. M. Collins. Or such again as the world-famous British man of God and merchant, Samuel Budgett. These I know are superlative examples, and yet we have hundreds in the world's record to match them, and thousands in a grade only one degree below, and millions in a really honorable grade of worth and christian respect that is only a little more common still. There is, in fact, no human employment that has yielded better, and proportionally more numerous examples of christian living than trade. No matter if there be some disadvantages and hindrances to piety in it, the same is true of every other kind of business which can be named. That most tenderly beautiful saint of God, the Quaker Woolman, began with merchandise, and being apprehensive lest he might find it "attended with much cumber," drew off to another occupation that was like to be more simply industrious in the sense of labor, viz., that of a tailor; but he left that even more speedily, because the call of God that was on him put him in silent affinity with another, which I have no doubt was to him more wholesome than either of his two former callings, because more congenial to the sacred bent of his nature. Otherwise he could have been as good a christian in either as in that.

Sometimes it is urged as a proof of the anti-christian affinities of trade, that the man who gets deeply engaged in it becomes eager and sharp, dropping out the soft amenities and charities, and carrying his points of mercantile justice, with a peremptory squareness and mechanical hardness not pleasant to encounter. That exactly was the accusation most commonly set against two of the distinguished characters just named, Mr. Collins and Mr. Budgett. And the reason was wholly to their credit. They were never known to veer by a hair from integrity in any transaction of business, but they would have veered a hundred times a day, falling into a muddle where all distinctions of principle are lost, if they had not done their trade as trade, under the law of trade, and reserved their charities—all their sympathies, allowances, mitigations, merciful accommodations—for a separate chapter of life. But here it would come out how surely, that no tenderest, most simple hearted child was more easily moved in his compassions, or more unstinted whether in gifts or favors. And for just this reason it is, that so many of the best and most valuable christian disciples we have, are such as come up out of the walks of trade. They do not dawdle in their life-work, but they mean business. They know how to engineer operations, how to move with alertness, and turn their hand nimbly as things require, keeping every thing still in the training of order and practical system; playing in, under these, and as it were to fill them out, all most practical mercies and tenderest graces. So that if we want the best engineering of counsel, and the most energetic flexibilities of movement, we are more likely to get our supply from the class of disciples in trade, than from any other. Operations are their study, and they get limbered in it for all most cautiously safe and practically efficient operations, in religion.

The next point to which I ask your attention, is that all apprehensions of a specially harmful exposure in trade are mistaken. What it calls profits are just as truly earnings, as any of the fruits of hand labor. For it is a calling grounded in nature, even as mining, or agriculture, is conceived to be. Thus one clime produces ice, another oranges and figs, another sugar and coffee, another cotton, another furs. In like manner iron, gold, silver, salt, and coal, are distributed locally in spots, on different or distant shores. Medicines are sprinkled here and there, some in one region and some in another. And then all these supplies and comforts of the different regions must be gathered by the merchants, transported to the parts where they may be wanted, distributed into small parcels, and sold out to customers for use. All which requires a great risk of capital, great contriving, long correspondences, expensive transportations, adding as much and real comfort to the uses of life, as if the articles were drawn out of the soil by the hand labor of the persons engaged. They do, in fact, a work very much like that of the rain, or the rain clouds, which instead of leaving the world to be watered by waterspouts falling here or there once in a thousand years, take up the water that is wanted in parts remote from the sea, carrying it off thither by their wind sails, and there, making small the drops for a gentle and general distribution, let it fall on the ground, sprinkling it all over. These rain-clouds are the merchants of the sky, and trade is distribution in a like beneficent way. *Trade* in things is the kinsman of *tradition* in facts, as any one may see on the faces of the words, and there is a commerce of delivery and distribution in both, that fulfills a like beneficence. And if any one doubts whether the goods distributed can be rightly sold for a profit, or at more than their cost, let him go without these conveniences of trade and its distributions for a few months, let every product stay at home, every box and bale unbroken, every piece uncut, and he will begin to understand what work trade is doing, how real it is, how deserving of profit.

But granting there may be some service rendered by trade, what price shall be fitly paid for it, and to what is this matter of price left, but to the rapacity of the merchant? Just contrary to that, in the common articles of traffic, almost nothing is left to him; for he can not much advance upon the current price, which is always determined, so to speak, by the common vote of the market. A conspiracy may be gotten up by some merchant, to buy the market bare of some necessary article, or he may do it as a single operator by himself, but then he ceases from any thing which can be properly called trade, and becomes a robber. His very operation casts off the laws of trade, and prefers the chances of plunder. Or, again, it may sometimes happen that a blight, a frost, a fire, disturbs the ratio of supply, and gives opportunity for exactions that are cruelly extortious. Doubtless it is sometimes possible, in such a case, to carry prices up to the pitch of starvation, but the man who does it is sure to discover, at last, that he has offended against the laws of trade at bitter cost to himself. Who will come to him for trade, after he has shown himself a pirate? Much wiser, and in how much better keeping with the laws and possibilities of trade, was the course of that rough lumberman of a large mountain village of California, who could say to his townsmen driven out by a fire which, in a single hour, had swept every thing bare—"here is your material, give me just what price I have been receiving, no more, and it is yours." This man, be it noted, was the man, after all, who best fulfilled the laws of trade.

Ordinarily the transactions of merchandise encounter no such temptation. The undertaking is to sell under and by the laws of current price, and the productions of agriculture, and the wages of hand labor, go by exactly the same law. Nor is it any objection that current price is being all the while adjusted, by the contrary pull of two selfishnesses, for it is even doubtful whether two benevolences could do it any more justly. The seller does not settle the price, and the buyer does not settle it. It is finally settled in despite of both, and by those higher laws that make the contrary pull of the parties about as good a measure of want and supply as can be contrived, even though—perhaps because—it settles the price at just that point which is disliked by both. And if men were angels, there would really be no likelier and juster method than to let supply and demand work at the case each on its side, and make the prices vibrate by their oscillations, in just this manner. There is now and then a case, it is true, where some merchant very nearly fixes current price, for the time, under the autocratic principle, putting it down thus and thus for himself; which is understood to be the manner to a principal degree of a certain immense trading house, too vast to have a rival, in the city of New York. But even this almost dictator of prices has a very close eye to what is possible, and what is not, sometimes marking up his prices, and sometimes marking them down; consenting virtually to the fact, that price is not by him, but by what after all is above him.

But what shall we say of trading under variable prices, and practicing on the customer accordingly as he will bear it. The guage of price is not, in that case, in the goods, but only in the unquestioning facility of the customer—a way of trade that even proposes to fleece all the customers best entitled to favor and protection by their generosity, and make up the general score of the profits at their cost. At the same time it is a very hard, forbidding way of trade to maintain prices absolutely invariable. It is even doubtful whether variation, within a certain small range, may not best serve the flexibilities of courtesy, and best serve the interest of both seller and buyer. Possibly some very great millionaire of trade may set his own prices, and mark off his goods to be sold only by the mark. But it must be said in justice to the small trader, that he very often can not well ascertain what the current price really is, and is even obliged to do it by feeling of his customer, and giving a certain faith to representations brought him thus, of what is going on in the street. Perhaps the current price itself has veered a little since yesterday. But this is a very different thing from having no price at all, and going for such amount of prey as the customer will suffer. That is not trade, and there is no bad effect of trade to be thought of in it. It is the way of a knave, or a jockey, and these are not included under any proper definition of trade.

As little room is there, under any thing properly called trade, for what many seem to regard as the necessary skill, in raising color by glosses of false recommendation, or by small lies sprinkled in for the due stimulation of the customer. That is not an accomplishment belonging to the genuine operation of trade, but only to the low-lived, inbred habit of the man. Such arts I know are practiced, but never to advantage. They are sometimes even a fatal hindrance to success; for as certainly as what is contemptible carries contempt, the man who is willing to sell his integrity with his goods, will appear to be just the character he is. Undeviating adherence to truth and justice may possibly lose to-day's customer, but in the long run it will bring as many more as it is more implicitly trusted. There is, I know, a certain, low-minded folk who have a general liking to high talk, and can hardly imagine they have made a good bargain, till they have gotten the price down a great way below the talk. And yet most men are wiser, loving to buy of one who puts them at their ease, by his quiet ways of integrity. They make a study instinctively of the salesman, and if they find him pressing his point by much talk, and that which is manifestly reckless, they are taken both by a disgust and a caution, and leave him to the knavish airs of his practice.

Of course it will be understood that no one, caring to be a christian in trade, wants to be certified of any such possibility in sales and distributions that are themselves illicit, or immoral. Moreover trade itself is a grand republic of commerce, under laws of use and beneficence. These illicit engagements are outside of morality, doing no service, satisfying no beneficent use—outrages often of liberty, insults to purity, instigations of appetite—and of course are just as far outside of trade. They are even mockeries of it in its prime idea; selling what they call goods, which they know to be evils.

There are then, as we have now discovered, no reasons why a young man going into trade, may not expect to be a christian in it. The contrary impression so often held is without any sufficient foundation.

But the possibility does not make sure of the fact, and we now pass on—

II. To show how the trading man may be surely christian, and more decidedly and strongly christian for his engagement.

At this point we ascend of course to a higher point, above the plane of morality, and begin to look after what belongs to the life of religion. No man of course expects to be a christian in trade, without being a religious man in it. And just here, alas! is the difficulty most commonly encountered—the difficulty, viz., of continuing to be a christian without beginning to be; the difficulty of being kept safe in religion, or religious character, by a business carried on without such character, and wholly outside of religion. I even suppose it will be objected mentally, at least, by some, that after all I only undertake to show how a man may be a christian in trade by being one. Undoubtedly I do; for it would be a very singular thing if I could show how one may be a christian in trade, without having it on hand to be, or without any responsibility accepted for being a christian at all. No, the point I undertake to show is how a man, who is in the beginning of a christian life, or seriously bent on such a beginning, can maintain the love of God, and grow up into God, by faith and prayer, and go on to make all most solid attainments of character, in the life-occupation of trade. And then when the question how is raised, the very first, always indispensable, thing is that he shall be faithfully set to it, and expect to succeed only by making cost for it—by enduring hardness, by fighting out the great human battle with self-seeking and the love of money, and by standing fast in God's name in all holiest integrity. He must not go into trade as any sharp work, to be sharply, shrewdly done, he must not pitch himself recklessly into making his fortune, he must not look upon his business future with a mind wholly slack towards God and religion, willing to be floated whither the tide will carry him. No true character is ever made in that way, in any employment. A going in upon chance, with a slack mind submitted to the drift of the occupation, is enough to make sure as possible of not being a christian any where. And it is precisely in that way that trade has come to be regarded as a kind of life so preëminently hostile to the interests of character.

It is also another very important consideration that you are permitted, if at all, to go into this occupation by a really divine call. Not many, I suspect, ever think of any such possibility for a merely secular employment, or for any but that perhaps of the christian ministry. And very few, I fear, thoroughly believe in even that; simply because it is held to be a thing so entirely special, a call of God that stands by itself, with no other to match it, or keep it company. Whereas the real and really grand truth is that God has a place for every man, in what is to be his particular employment, as he has a place for every rock, and tree, and river, and star. And exactly this we assume, perhaps without knowing it, when we speak of this or that man's employment as being this or that man's *calling*. We use the word as in a smothered meaning, to signify only his engagement or life-occupation; but there lingers in it, we may see, a certain divine recollection, as if he were in it, or it were his privilege to be, as by God's personal and particular call. He may not so believe, himself, but just as surely as he is in his own right place, he is in that to which he is called, whether he has ever thought of it in that way or not. Some are not in their place, and it is their sad infelicity that they never can be. But the great majority of men I do think are led, drawn, beckoned, whispered into their calling, some pushed in by stern necessities, some by urgent wants or incapacities, some crowded in by Providential circumventions. Meantime a blessed few find their places by going to God for them. And this most sublime and really glorious privilege is for all, and for all kinds of places and employments. There is such a thing as spiritual guidance for men. You can form some judgment of your calling by finding what others think of you; by considering also your tastes, and tempers, and capabilities; what kind of loads you can carry; what kind of annoyances you can bear; also by considering what opportunities of good are afforded; and where you can make yourself of greatest consequence to mankind, and the salvation given to mankind; but then, when all such inquiries are ended, you can be absolutely sure of your calling, by seeking unto God's oracle for it. Tided inwardly by his divine Spirit, as you may be, you will flow in sweetly, as by silent drift, into the very thing which is to be your calling; whether it be trade, manufacture, or any other calling. And then having found your occupation, and come into it by the calling of God, what satisfaction will you have in it! how reverently, lovingly, safely, will you invest your life in it!

Now, again, after being thus installed in trade, as by the call of God, how surely may you have God's help in the prosecution of it. How surely, that is, if you ask it, and train your ways of practice so that you can fitly receive it. Here, too, I shall encounter, as I well understand, a certain kind of unbelief that makes it extravagant, or even a merely pietistic illusion, to be looking for God's help in such a matter as the carrying on of a trade! As if the Spirit of God, by his private concourse, or the Providence of God, by his government of the world, could descend to the care of the very small, very secular matter of helping a man succeed in a concern of traffic! Of course he can not and will not, if traffic is the really selfish and low concern we are all the while assuming it to be. But if it be a proper and most real industry, if it undertakes to gain a profit by doing a service, and a profit proportioned to the service, if it is and is to be a beneficent matter, such as any call of God must be; then I see not why even God should scorn it, or refuse to be a helper in it. He did not scorn to give a special inspiration to Bezaleel the artificer in brass, and Aholiab the carpenter, filling them "with the Spirit of God, in wisdom and in understanding," to "devise cunning works," "in all manner of workmanship." God indorsed the patriotic prayers of Nehemiah and sent him back with money and much timber to rebuild the city. Paul commanded in the shipwreck, by the Spirit, even down to the matter of dining before the break. If we think that all things secular are too common for God's care, we dishonor both ourselves and him. God helps nothing wrong, and omits to help nothing right. All right employments are callings into which he puts his servants for their good, and what will he more surely do than help them to find their good! The trader is not a man by himself, and yet in some sense he is; for his purchases are often a very blind problem, his rivals are many and sometimes bitterly unjust, his risks depend on things exceedingly occult, his liabilities of panic when great storms of revulsion overturn the confidences of credit, are such as not even military commanders often encounter in disastrous campaigns. Customers too are how often unreasonable, creditors unjust and rapacious, the laws a trap, and the courts more careful to be ingenious than to be just. In all which, as by these mere glances we discover, the merchant, going into trade, most truly goes to sea. His calling is verily on the deep—unstable, stormy, set about by combinations and complexities that require high courage, a firm, steady-judging mind, a perception that is next thing to a prophecy of event. Therefore he wants, if any man does, true God-help always at hand, and much of it. He needs, for his mere business' sake and the solid composure of his counsel, a steadfast grounding in God, and a conscious strengthening with might by God's Spirit in the inner man. Scarcely does even an apostle need it more.

It is another consideration also that reaches far, that the merchant in his calling of trade is put in a relation to God so inherently religious, if he will undertake it in that manner, that he is justified in passing his vow not to be in trade, or even for a day to stay in it, if he can not have the enjoyment of God in it. This is true of all legitimate occupations, and all right works of industry, and not less true of trade than of any other, that the man who is in it can have and is bound to have God with him in it; to begin his day with God's smile, to end it in God's approbation, and to pass it all through in the testimony that he pleases God. Going thus into and onward in trade, he will have no difficulty in being a christian in it. He is fast anchored in all right practice and right living, by holding himself to courses that permit the enjoyment of God, and then the enjoyment of God will in turn hold him to his courses. Doubtless a man may be a very poor christian, who settles by mere hap-hazard into such kind of courses as will fill up his money-making days; a great many poor christians are made in that way, and a great many more that are no christians at all. And so it is in every lawful business the world knows. No carpenter, blacksmith, weaver, clothier, no simplest and purest of all tradesmen, gets on well as a christian, who does not set himself to such a kind of living that he can have the enjoyment of God in it. But having that, how smoothly does he sail out on his course, and how sweetly do the gales of the Spirit waft him on. Such a man can be a christian any where, and will as certainly be in trade as any where else.

Again there are even special advantages in trade as regards the development of a christian life, which do not occur as largely in any other employment. The transactions are many, crowding thick upon the shelves and counters all the day. The temptations of course are just as much more numerous as the transactions; and it must not be forgotten that the more tempted a man is, the more opportunities are given him to grow. Scarcely could he grow at all if none at all were put in his way. Besides, the thicker temptations are huddled, the less chance they have to prevail; there is no time in fact to do much more than to reject them. Whereas if temptations only come single, one a day for example, hanging round the mind in still approaches of seduction, and holding as it were all day their magnifiers up before it, the poor disciple's chances of resistance are how greatly diminished.

There is also a considerable christian advantage in the relation that subsists between the merchant and his customer. To be a customer signifies more or less of favor and confidence. The customer, in being such, commits himself in a large degree to the honor of the merchant, and then the merchant in turn accepts him naturally as a man who comes in expression of trust, and is fairly entitled to generosity. And if the customer is an old customer, coming to his old haunt of trade, where the old fair-dealing trader has for so many years been proving his integrity, you will see that they meet as friends, and not as sharpers coming to the prey. And if they are christian men, you will see that also, even though they do not say a word about religion. There is no barrier visibly between them, but a perfectly open confidence, and their meeting does them good, as truly as if there were some grace of communion in it—as, in fact, there is.

Sometimes again the proposed transaction of trade includes a question of credit. And here the merchant is put to a trial that always yields him benefit. He is getting insight thus into men, and learning whom he may safely trust. His whole exercise goes to sharpen his perceptions of character. He learns in it also to respect modesty and neatness of person, with plainness of dress. And above all he learns to observe who a man's friends are, as the most significant token of all. He gets a way of moral sharpness in this way that has an immense value in his understanding even of himself. Specie payments and pay-down trade would make a very stupid and morally stupefying element in comparison.

Trade also furnishes occasions of beneficence to the

poor, which are all the better for both parties, that they make no parade of charity, but may pass for a buying and selling between them. The merchant, I have said, should do his trade by the strict law principles of trade, and never let his operations be mixed up with charities. But how many beautiful charities may he dispense under the nature of trade, which not even the receiver will know, and which he himself will enjoy the more, that he has them for his unknown secret before God. Thus he parcels off what he may consider to be more or less nearly the waste of trade, all which he would otherwise put in auction, and sell at great loss to himself and great profit to the buyer, and marking it down to the very lowest rate he could hope to receive—remnants, faded, and smirched, and smoked, and shelf-worn-goods, and styles of goods gone by—gives his silent order to sell in that mark, to chosen candidates hard-pressed by want, and ready because of their want, to find a relief most welcome in the opportunity. It is trade on one side, and trade on the other; only that on one side it is so near to the confines of beneficence that it consciously passes over. A more gentle, genial, and genuine influence on the man could hardly be devised.

It is yet another and very great moral advantage of trade, that it is just the calling in which a christian man will best learn the uses of money. If he began as a christian at the true principle of christian living, he put himself in bonds, so to speak, to consecrate all his successes to God. And then, from that point onward, he has not been after money for money's sake, but as capital for other kinds of works; sometimes secular and sometimes religious. He handles what he gains by trade in turns of nimble investment, and never hoards it. The agriculturist and the small artisan handle money slowly in restricted quantities. It stays long in their hands before expenditure; they look at it often, and begin to think fondly of it. In this way they very often become misers. But the merchant almost never is a miser; for the money that he gains signifies nothing to him, save in the footing of his balances. It freely comes and freely goes, and he turns it as readily into goods as goods into money. Money in fact is to him but one of the kinds of goods; more valuable if at all than any other, because it is more easily convertible. And for just this reason it is that our freest and largest benefactors in the matters of public charity and religion, are commonly men who have gotten their success by trade—because their notions are not stunted by the small amount of money needed in carrying on their transactions, and because what they get is expected to go and not to stay.

Hence, I conceive, it is going to be discovered, that the great problem we have now on hand, viz., the christianizing of the money power of the world, depends for its principal hope, on the trading class in society. Talent has been christianized already on a large scale. The political power of states and kingdoms has been long assumed to be, and now at least really is, as far as it becomes their accepted office to maintain personal security and liberty. Architecture, arts, constitutions, schools, and learning, have been largely christianized. But the money power, which is one of the most operative and grandest of all, is only beginning to be; though with promising tokens of a finally complete reduction to Christ and the uses of his kingdom. In our late civil war, the money power, for the first time, so far as I know, since the world began, laid itself fairly on the altar, and gave itself, in heartily-pledged devotion, to the public welfare. It even took up, we may say, the nation's heavy and huge bulk, and bore it grandly through on its Atlantean shoulders. Every thing we have for public love, was the maxim even of money, and there was never before a fiscal campaign to match the sublimity and true majesty of the spectacle. It was the money power standing sponsor for the nation, in its terrible baptism of blood. Now what we wait for, and are looking hopefully to see, is a like consecration of the vast money power of the world, to the work, and cause, and kingdom of Jesus Christ. For that day, when it comes, is the morning, so to speak, of the new creation. That tide-wave in the money power can as little be resisted, when God brings it on, as the tides of the sea; and like these also it will flow across the world in a day. And such a result, I conceive, we are to look for largely, to the merchant class of disciples. Trade expanding into commerce, and commerce rising into communion, are to be the outline of the story. When the merchant seeking goodly pearls—all the merchant race, find the precious one they seek, and sell their all to buy it, they will make it theirs.

The question I began with—"How to be a christian in trade?" is, I think, now sufficiently answered. At the end of this review, I think it will be agreed, that there is no calling in which a christian may grow faster, and rise higher in all holy attainments. After he has once learned how to enjoy God in his calling, how to carry Christ directly into his works, and do all in the higher consciousness of Christ revealed, his satisfactions will be great, his increase rapid, his strength immovable, and his very sleep elysian. And what is a nobler sight to look upon, than a christian merchant, standing at the head of his operations; thriving in the small, or rolling up his immense income in the large; doing every thing squarely, as in terms of business, and not in a fast and loose manner, yet with a christian heart as flexible and free, and as little hampered by the mechanism of trade, as love itself must ever be; then passing out among his kind, to look about for objects wanting his aid; standing as a bank of charity for all good necessities to draw upon; resorted to with confidence by all who are forward in good works; spreading his generosity well up toward the limit of his surplus means; firm in credit; honored for his word of promise; sought unto in trust by the righteous, and remembered in the prayers of the poor—is there on this earth a character more to be envied, or more genuinely Christ-like than he?

XIV.

IN AND BY THINGS TEMPORAL ARE GIVEN THINGS ETERNAL.

"While we look, not at the things which are seen, but at the things which are not seen; for the things which are seen are temporal, and the things which are not seen are eternal."—2 *Cor.* 4: 18.

THERE is a great deal said about looking away from the things of time, to the things of eternity; and Paul, I suppose, is credited with this idea on the score of the language here cited. Whether he would accept the credit is more doubtful. It certainly is no conception of his, that we are to ignore the temporal, and go clear of it, in order to being fixed in the eternal. Indeed this kind of prescription, so constantly reiterated, and soaked in, as it were, by a long dull-minded usage, is really about the sleepiest and most noxious drug that Christian living has ever had put in its way. I acknowledge that these temporals are often too much like the temporalities of the Pope, and keep the eternals a great way off. But if we lay it down, that we are to really look away from time, when we look at, or in order to look at, eternity, we make a very hard case for practice; for what figure is any one likely to make in the realizing of things eternal, when he has even to push the world out of sight, in order to see them. Have we not also a suppressed or subtly instinctive sense of something unpractical in the attempt; as if it were a forced view of life, more ascetical than practical. How can we think, in real earnest, that such a world as this was made just to be looked away from? And if we try to do it, tearing our mind away from the visible and the temporal, and requiring it to see only what is invisible and eternal, how certainly do we find the air too thin to support our flighty endeavor, and drop away shortly on the ground, held down to it, after all, by temporal weights and visibilities we can not escape.

And just here I apprehend is the reason in great part of that inability to realize, or give a sound existence to spiritual things of which so many complain—they misconceive the problem. It is not to literally look away from temporal things in order to see the eternal, but it is to see the temporal in the eternal, or through it and by means of it. These temporals I conceive are the scabbards of the eternal, or the capsules in which it grows, or the matches whose fires are kept hid in their bodies. Paul I am sure had no other conception. By not looking at the temporal things, he means simply not fastening our mind to them, or upon them, as the end of our pursuit; for he calls them "things that are *seen*," which implies that, in another and more simply natural sense, they are looked at; for how can they be things seen if they are not?

There is then, I am going now to show, a *fixed relation between the temporal and the eternal, such that we shall best realize the eternal by rightly using the temporal.* We shall best conceive the true point here, by observing the manner of the apostle himself; for it was one of the remarkable things about him as a Christian, that he was so completely under the power, so sublimely invigorated by the magnitudes of the world to come; longing for it, testing himself in it, and carrying the sense of it with him, into the hearts of all who heard his preaching. Things temporal he saw a great deal more penetratingly than any mere worldly mind could; saw far enough into them, to discover their unsolidity, and their transitory and ephemeral consequence, and to apprehend just so much the more distinctly, the solid and eternal verities represented by them. Things and worlds are passing—shadows all that pass away. The durable and strong, the real continent, the solid landing-place, is beyond. But the present things are good for the passage, good for signs, good as shadows. So he tramps on through them, cheering his confidence by them, having them as reminders, and renewing, day by day, his outward man by what of the more solid and glorious future is so impressively represented and captivatingly set forth in them. He does not refuse to see with his eyes what God puts before his eyes. He has noted the successions, and phases, and forms of things. He distinguishes God's stamps and signatures upon them, takes the whole order and architecture of the creation as a type of God's great mind, and rejoices that the invisible things of God, even his eternal power and Godhead—all the truths eternal—are, from his creation, clearly seen. He loves society also; rejoices in its new prospects, now that the eternal kingdom of the Lord Jesus is set up in it. And what is more than all,—more than the creation, more than society, more than all things temporal and visible, Christ, the Son of God himself, has come out in his eternity, to be incarnate in these scenes, and live in them and look upon them with his human eyes. And so these all are hallowed by the enshrining, for a time, of his glorious divinity in them, becoming temporalities redolent of his eternity. And so, as every thing was raised in quality, even from the grave he perfumed by lying in it, up to the stars he looked upon, all, all, this wondrous furniture is changed and blessed, and hallowed by the life he lived here in the flesh. In a world thus glorified, it would not have been wonderful if Paul had even been ready, looking round upon these ranges of things we call idols and hinderances to religion, to say, "let us make tabernacles and stay." And yet he did it not. If Christ had been here, Christ also had gone; to go therefore and be with him was far better. Christ had come too, not for society's sake, not to beautify and heal and gild society, or to get up any paradise in these temporalities, but only to bring us on, or rather off, and establish us in the grand eternals of his kingdom on high. Our apostle looked thus on the things that are temporal as not looking on them, but as looking straight through, on the things eternal, which they represent and prepare. He looked on them just as one looks on a window-pane, when he studies the landscape without. In one view he looks on the glass. In another he does not. Probably enough he does not so much as think of the medium interposed at all. Or, a better comparison still is the telescope; for the lenses of glass here interposed, actually enable the spectator to see, and yet he does not so much as consider that he is looking on the lenses, or using them at all—he only looks on the stars. So also the apostle looks not on the things that are temporal, even while admiring the display in them of God's invisible and eternal realities. He looks on them only as seeing through; uses them only as a medium of training, exercise, access unto God. Their value to him is not in what they are, but in what they signify.

Thus it is a true use, I conceive, of things temporal, that they are to put us under the constant all-dominating impression of things eternal. And we are to live in them, as in a transparency, looking through, every moment, and in all life's works and ways, acting through, into the grand reality-world of the life to come.

Having gotten our conception thus of the apostle's meaning, as well as a good argument from his religious habit and character to prove it, let us next consider the fact, that all temporal things and works are actually designed or planned for this very object; viz., to conduct us on, or through, into the discovery of things eternal. Every existing thing or object in the created empire of God, all forms, colors, heights, weights, magnitudes, forces, come out of God's mind, covered all over with tokens, saturated all through with flavors of his intelligence. They represent God's thought, the invisible things of God; and an angel coming out into the world, instead of seeing nothing in them but only walls, would see God expressed by them, just as we are expressed by our faces and bodies. The invisible things of God, all his eternal realities, would be clearly seen. No, we do not become worldly by looking at things temporal, but by not looking at them closely enough, and with due religious attention. We first make idols of them for their economic uses and their market value, and then, having begun our worship, we go on with it, having our eyes shut. Why should we look in, to see divine things in them, when we are already so far captivated by what they are worth in possession? How different, for example, would they be, if we could but stay upon them long enough, and devoutly enough, to see the prodigious workings hid in them. We should find them swinging and careering in geometric figures, weighed and spaced in geometric proportions; and what are these but thoughts of mind and laws of thought—eternal in their very nature? It comes out thus to us, in these stellar magnitudes and motions, that they must be somehow rolling and wheeling inside of some mind, as if they were its proper thinking—which indeed they are. Again what do we find as regards material substances, save when we are just hoarding them for gain, or devouring them for pleasure—uses that adjourn intelligence—but that they are composed of atoms joined by count in the exact notations and formulas of arithmetic? So that, in our chemistries we think out the world—all the orb-matter of the sky, all the earths and rocks and crystallizations. The significance, in this manner, of the substances is not so much their substance, as the eternal laws we behold in them. Mind, we see, penetrates them all; they are all bedded in mind. Necessary truth, the eternal absolute truth of mind, that which being must be forever, fills and orders them all, visibles and temporals though we call them.

The same is true of all the multifarious, seemingly inexact orders of animated nature. Bone, flesh, circulation, innerving force, what do they make but a composition that appears to almost think aloud. And so evident is it, that these classifications of life, animal and vegetable, are related to mind, that Mr. Agassiz puts them down as premeditations of God, eternal orders of the thoughts of God—which, ruling creatively in them, make them, in that manner, not visibles only, but intelligibles, possible objects of science.

There is yet another and more popular way, in which these temporal and visible things carry forces and weights of eternity with them—they are related as signs or images, to all the most effective and most glorious truths of religion. They are all so many physical word-forms given to make up images and vocables for religion; for which reason the Scripture is full of them, naming and describing every thing by them—by the waters and springs that quench our thirst, by the bread that feeds our bodies, by the growing corn in its stages, by the tares that grow with it, by the lilies in their clothing, by the hidden gold and silver and iron of the mountains, by the sea, the storms, the morning mist, the clouds, the sun, the starry host, the deep central fires of the ground, and the sulphurous smoke they expel—every thing we look upon is an image of something otherwise not seen, a face that looks out, as it were, from God's eternity, and carries God's meanings on it. Our complaint therefore that temporal things hide the eternal and keep them out of sight, is much as if one should complain of telescopes hiding the stars, or window-panes shutting out the sun, or even of eyes themselves obstructing the sense of things visible. There is a way, I know, of handling these temporals coarsely and blindly, seeing in them only just what a horse or a dog might see. A brutish mind sees only things in things, and no meanings. If it were possible for us to ignore every thing but what is temporal, we could be as perfectly unspiritual as the animals themselves. And a great many minds wholly given to things are doing what they can to make this attainment. But it can not be said, without the greatest wrong to God, that he has given us these temporalities to live in for any such use. It would even be impossible to make up a world of so many temporal things and so many temporal occasions, and keep God's light shining on their faces more visibly, or keep his everlasting verities more effectively present to every soul. Spirituality of habit and thought could not be made more possible, or the lack of it more nearly impossible.

Hence also the fact so often remarked, that forms, colors, objects, scenes, have all a power so captivating over childish, and indeed over all young minds. Thus we note the irresistible impulse of infants to handle every thing, which means, in fact, if you study the matter a little, that every thing is handling them, looking into their hearts, filling them with images and shapes, and all the various timber of thought. At first they will cry after the moon, or the fire; next they will run after the rainbow; and then, as in high youth, will see all things dressed in such colors of delight, as to be almost bewildered in their eagerness to be everywhere, and seize all things at once. Now we are not to think that it is the mere quantities or substances of the things, but their senses or significances, that take such hold of the soul's appetite. They captivate, because they are related all to thought, truth, feeling, and offer a drapery to the inborn, scarcely waked affinities of the mind; because, in fact, they are the faces and forms of God's thought; existences analogous to whatever is highest and closest to divinity, in our human mold; poems for the eyes, in which the subject is God.

The child or youth thinks not of it, and yet the

power of the fact is on him. The real and true account of the fact is, that the eternals are in the things looked on so eagerly by these young eyes, shining out, filling them with images, starting their thoughts, kindling fires of truth and eternity in their spirit. As age advances, the eagerness of observation slackens, but the old man who has lived on many years, wondering all the while where God is, and where the eternal things are hid, has all the images in him, so that when the Spirit has opened his understanding to their significance, it is as if the visible things of God had been pouring all their contents into his bosom, and he did not know it! O what a glory, what a power of eternity is in them now—strange that I should have chased these things so eagerly in my childhood, not knowing why; stranger still that I should have sought and followed and worshiped them so long in my manhood, and valued them only as things!

Again, it is the continual object and art of all God's management, temporal and spiritual, secular and christian, to bring us into positions where we may see, or may rather be compelled to see, the eternal things of his government. So little reason have we to complain, as we do continually, that our relations, occupations, and works, take us away from the discovery of such things, and leave us no time or capacity for it. Thus, at our very first breath, we are put in what is called the family state. In the providence of it we live. By the discipline of it we learn what love is, in all the severe, and faithful, and tender offices of it. And so, as it were from the egg, we are configured to the eternal family state for which we are made.

So, also, if we speak, or revelation speaks, of an unseen government or kingdom; where we get the very form of the thought from our outward kingdoms below. So if we speak of law, punishment, pardon, or judgment-seat justification—these all are notions prepared in us by the civil state, and by that means inserted in our thought, for the higher uses of the eternal government in our souls.

Meantime the ordinance of want and labor, and all the industrious works and cares of life—fearful hinderances, we say, to any discovery of God—what are they still but works and struggles leading directly in to his very seat? What do you do in them, in fact, but just go to the earth and the great powers of nature, to invoke them by your industry, and by your labor sue out, as it were, from them, the supply you want? And when you come so very close to God, even to the powers and laws which are his reigning, everlasting thoughts, what temptation have you to lift your suit just one degree, and make your application even to God Himself! It is the beautiful characteristic of industry that, instead of taking us away from God, and things eternal, it takes us directly towards Him, and puts us waiting on the seasons, the soil, the mechanical powers, which are but the faithful bosom of God Himself; and there we hang, year by year, watching for our supplies and the nutriment that feeds our bodies. Our very industry is a kind of physical prayer, and the business itself of our busy life is, to watch the gates of blessing he opens upon us. His smile feeds us, and his goodness ever before us leads us to repentance.

His scheme of Providence also is adjusted so as to open windows on us continually, in this earthly house of our tabernacle, through which the building of God, not made with hands, may be the better discovered. God is turning our experience always, in a way to give us the more inward senses of things, acting always on the principle, that the progress of knowledge, most generically and comprehensively regarded, is but a progress out of the matter-view into the mind-view of things; for all the laws, properties, classifications of objects, as we just now saw, are thoughts of God made visible in them; so that all the growth of knowledge is a kind of spiritualizing of the world; that is, a finding of the eternal in the temporal. For God will not let us get lodged in the temporal, but is always shoving us on to what is beyond. Whoever undertakes to build him a paradise in things and stay in them, is either defeated and driven out of his project, or is compelled in deep sorrow to find, that what he took for pure delight is destitute of all satisfaction; a dry cup, or even a condition of bitter suffering. The fires that fell on Sodom are scarcely a more visible sign that Lot's family are to be dislodged and flee, than these scorching fires of Providence, falling on our temporal state, are that we are not to stay here, and shall not? And so God is commanding us off, every hour of our lives, toward things eternal, there to find our good, and build our rest. Sometimes he does it by taking us out of the world, and sometimes by taking the world out of us. Or again he sometimes does it by breaking in a way for his divine light, through the incrustations we have formed about us. Thus, living in the temporals and for them, we call them nature, and nature we conceive to be a wall impervious to God and Spirit, and all supernal visitations. And therefore he sends down his Son from above, to re-reveal and re-empower the eternals we have ceased to see. And it is as if he came tearing open the wall, riddling it as it were with interstices all through, letting in the love of God, the mercy and salvation provided, and calling us to come up through into the eternal life.

Besides, once more, we have eternals garnered up in us all, in our very intelligence; immortal affinities, which, if we forget or suppress, are still in us; great underlaid convictions also, ready to burst up in us and utter even ringing pronouncements; and besides there is an inevitable and sure summons always close at hand as we know, and ready for its hour; whose office it is to bring the great eternals near and keep them in power. True this instituted fact of death does not logically prove any thing as regards the existence of realities unseen, or of a second life. It may be that we drop into nihility. But we are very little likely to think so, if only we can fully admit, what we so perfectly know, that these temporal things are only a snow-bank, dissolving under us to let us through. No man is likely to miss the eternal when once he has let go the temporal. Consent that you are dying, and that time is falling away, and your soul will arrive at the conviction of God's eternity, and of things beyond this life, very soon. Nay, she will hear voices of eternity crying out in her own deep nature, and commanding her on to a future more solid and reliable than any mere temporalities can afford.

Here then we are, all going on, or in rather, to be unsphered here, and reinsphered, if we are ready for it, in a promised life more stable and sufficient. The eternal has been with us all the way, even when we could not find it. Now it is fully discovered, and become our mansion state. The fugacities are left behind us. The poets, too, we leave chanting their sad refrain,

"Naught may endure but mutability;"

the disappointed and world-weary, sighing over the mere shadows which they say were all that was given them to possess or pursue; the groping ones praying as it were to the darkness, "O that I knew where I might find him," and complaining if there be a God, and things eternal, that they should be so strangely hidden by the curtains of sense, so dimly seen, so completely shut away by the coarse temporalities of things—all these we leave behind, with only the greater pity, that they are so miserably defrauded and deplore so bitterly the not seeing, of what they simply have no eyes to see. We did see something, and we now see more. The eternal things are now most distinctly seen, and the temporal scarcely seen at all. So that as we now look back on the old physical order, it was arranged, we see, to be a kind of transparency, and we were set in among and behind its objects and affairs, before open windows as it were, there to look out on the everlasting and set our life for it. These temporal things, we now perceive, were sometimes dark to us, just because we insisted on using them as they were not made to be used, even as a telescope is dark to them who will only look into the side of it. How could they be otherwise than dark, when we never sought God in them, but only the things themselves. Or if we sought him only a little, with a clouded and partly idolatrous love, how could they be much less dark? God, as we now see, meant to have the eternities stand up round us, even as they do here; so visible and tall that mere temporalities should dwindle and become shadows in comparison. To the truly great and godly soul they always were so, as they now are to us.

Two things now, having reached this point, let me ask you to note, or have established. First, that you are never to allow yourself in the common way of speaking, that proposes to look away from the things of time, or calls on others to do it. Never speak as if that were the way of an unworldly christian, for it is not. The unworldly christian, if he has the true mettle of a great life in him, never looks away from the things of time, but looks only the more piercingly into them and through. He does not expect to find God beyond them, but in them, and by means of them. Besides, this call to look away from the things of time, good enough as a figure sometimes, has yet a weak and sickening sound. It is not a living piety that speaks in this manner, but a frothy and debilitated sentiment. God help you rather to be manly enough to use the world as it is, and get your vision leveled for eternal things in it, and by it. You will come up unto God by uses of mastery, and not by retreat and feeble deprecation. These are they that endure and faint not. This world has no power to baffle them, or turn them away. They live in it always, having a sound respect to it, because they see God in it, and love to watch his footsteps. O these grand, unworldly souls, how majestic their aspirations, how solid their objects, how firm their sense of God. They live in the present as a kind of eternity, never sick of it, and never wanting more, but only what, this signifies.

Another correspondent caution, secondly, needs to be noted, and especially by those who are not in the christian way of life. They inevitably hear a great deal said of spiritual mindedness, and they see not any meaning to give it, which does not repel them. What are called spiritual things appear to them to be only a kind of illusion, a fog of mystic meditation, or mystic expectation, which the fonder, less perceptive believers press out thin, because they have not strength enough to body their life in things more solid and rational. Living therefore in this spiritually minded way appears to be living in phantasm, or breathing only hydrogen, or some kind of fetid air, which can not sustain a properly vigorous life. There could not be an impression farther from the truth. For the spiritually minded person spiritualizes temporal things and the temporal life, by nothing but by just seeing them in their most philosophic sense. He takes hold of the laws, finds his way into the inmost thoughts, follows after the spirit-force everywhere entempled, and puts the creation moving, at every turn, in the supreme order of Mind. If this be illusion, God give us more of it. The spiritual habit is, in this view, reason, health, and everlasting robustness.

XV.

GOD ORGANIZING IN THE CHURCH HIS ETERNAL SOCIETY.

"But ye are come to Mount Zion, and unto the city of the living God, the heavenly Jerusalem, and to an innumerable company of angels, to the general assembly and church of the first born which are written in heaven, and to God the Judge of all, and to the spirits of just men made perfect."—*Heb.* 12: 22, 3.

WHEN we read this passage of Scripture, we seem to scarcely know what world it is in or about, and not much better what world we are in ourselves. "But ye are come," says the apostle,—*are* come, in the present tense—that is, come already. And yet a great part of the terms that follow,—city of the living God,—heavenly Jerusalem,—innumerable company of angels,—general assembly and church of the first-born whose names are written in heaven,—appear to be upper-world terms, proper only to the kingdom of God above. Which blending, again, of celestial sceneries, in terms of the present tense, with sceneries partly terrestrial, is permitted the apostle, it may be, on the ground of a large analogy and comprehensive unity, including both spheres of life together. All the more competent and commensurate is the grasp of idea in the specification given; all the more fit, too, we shall see, is the double compass of the language, to the purpose I have now in hand; viz., to magnify the church of God, and freshen up, if possible, some due conception of its universality and of our responsibility for it.

It is one of the remarkable, and, it seems to me, gloomy signs of our time, that we are so evidently losing interest in the church and respect for it. It is not a thing so very new, that a great many persons outside of the church take up a prejudice against it, and begin to prophecy, with airs of exultation, its shortly going by, to be among the things that were; but it is a matter of far more appalling significance that so many of its own members appear to be somehow losing out even their confidence in it. They do not really care much for it, and for this reason probably, appeals of duty made for it get as little fixed hold of impression, or practical conviction, as in such a case they must. Even if they pray for it, and occasionally speak in a way to magnify the duties we owe it, there is yet a certain slackness in their manner, which indicates rather a wish to have some concern for it, than a real concern. I sometimes hear the question raised by such, what, after all, is the use of the church? Would it not be just as well if it were given up, or disbanded? Is it not in fact gone by already?

No, it is not, I am sure,—and never can be. Do we not know that Christ gave himself for it, that he purchased it with his own blood, and set it on a rock, and declared that not even the gates of hell should prevail against it? Is it then going down just now? Is it coming to be an outgrown fact? Not unless Jesus Christ is outgrown and his kingdom antiquated, which I do not think will very soon appear. Until then, be the look just now as it may,—until then, the church will stay, and we may as well be sure of it. Besides, I think we shall finally discover, after we have fairly worn out our extempore and shallow strictures, that there is interest and meaning enough in it, to make it the grand, everlasting fact of the creation of God—all which I now proceed to show.

The church is bottomed, for its final end or cause, in society. Man, as we are all the while saying in the tritest manner possible, is a social being; only we conceive but very partially and dimly what we are to mean by it. We ought to mean, as regarding both him and all other like moral natures in other like worlds, that they are items only or atoms—incomplete beings, and scarcely more than candidates for being—till they become organically set and morally joined in society. Existing simply as units, in their natural individualities, they are not of much consequence either to themselves or to each other. In that kind of merely sole existence they have nothing to raise the pitch of their consciousness, no moral dues of brotherhood or sentiments of justice and charity, no religious affinities that put them reaching after God and things above the world, and no high sense of being approved by God and other kindred beings. They make, in short, no part of a divine whole or society, sweetened by the possession they take of it, and in being taken possession of by it. As being merely creatures made, they are scarcely better than nobodies waiting to get some consequence, when society arrives at them, and they at society. Calling them men, they are not so much whole natures related to society outside, but they own, as we may say, scarcely a one-tenth part of their personality, and society the other nine-tenths. Or if we conceive that they own their complete whole constitutionally, that whole, existing chiefly for society, is chiefly owned by society. They are made for society as a moral affair, and have their property in it as being owned by it, and morally configured to it. In their natural instincts and family affections and such like fellow-fondnesses, they begin a faint preluding of society on the footing of mere nature; but this is only the sign, so to speak, or type, of that vaster, nobler society, which is to be fulfilled, under and through the great love-principle that claims their moral and socially religious nature. In this love principle they are kindled as by a kind of infinite aspiration, wanting in fact the whole universe—all there is in it, or can be, of righteous mind—each to possess it, and in the possession be himself complete. And it would even pain them to know that there is or can be any living nature which they can not touch, or be touched by, any society that must be unrelated to them, in any outmost world, or kingdom of God, known or unknown. The principles that are to organize the society are of course identical in all worlds, and the love by which it is organized is an all-worlds' love. Hence, the society organized must be an all-worlds' society.

Inasmuch now as the great society is to be, and to have any real significance can only be, a moral affair, it will be seen at once that it could not be organized by mere natural constitution. The animals could have a certain rudimental show of society prepared in their natural instincts. But when we speak of moral society as appointed for men, the most that could be done for its organization was to make them capable of it—capable that is of acting themselves into it, in all the qualities, and tempers, and divine principles, that compose it. They must be capable, that is, of law, truth, love, and sacrifice; and then the whole body of the society will be fitly joined together and compacted by that which every joint supplieth. Creation first, then society—this much we say preparatory to any right and living conception of the church, such as we are now after.

And here we strike into the text we began with, proposing henceforward to keep the vein of it. It is, we have noted already, a kind of both-worlds' Scripture, bearing, as it were, a church celestial and a church terrestrial on the face of its terms. And the distinction of the two is, that heaven, the upper-world church, is Society Organized; and the church below, Society Organizing—both in fact one, as regards their final end or object, and the properties and principles in which they are consummated. Of course the incomplete society below comprehends aberrations, misconjunctions, half conjunctions, and a great many mere scaffoldings which the other does not. Let us look now at the two in their order.

I. The Society Organized. It is called a city, the city of the living God; because it is the most condensed, completest form of society. It also includes or takes in "angels an innumerable company," some of them, we are to believe, from worlds more ancient than ours and from empires afar off, quite unknown to us. It gathers in also "the first born" of the church, and puts their names in register on the roll of the grand all-worlds' society. And "the spirits of just men made perfect," are either there or on the way up, to be joined in the general city life and order, for which they are now made ready. All the indications are that a complete organization is so far made, and all its distributions and relations adjusted; as when men of all grades and races are gathered into and unified in, the state of city organization.

In this organized society it is one of the first points to be noted that there is no distribution by sect or sectarian names. Not even the peoples of different worlds, and of old-time, gone-by creations come in as sub-societies, under names to be maintained against other names, though it will not be strange if matters so grandly historical are somehow kept in memory, as by calling these Uranians, these Saturnians, these Orionites, these the Earth-born people; for in being so represented, they are not antagonized, but are only made to show the variety of their populations. Meantime the myriads that arrive, new comers from the church below, drop off the names of their sects, having left them in their graves not raised—for there is no resurrection promised of these names. They are not Romish any more, not Anglican, not Calvinistic, not Arminian, or Wesleyan, their general assembly is not the Presbyterian, their crowns are not brimmed as being Friends, and since baptism is no more wanted, there are no Baptists. But they are all earth's people and Christian to a man, all other names being sunk and forgot in their now complete society.

Again, the organization is not bodied under official magistracies. There are no pontiffs, patriarchs, or prelates; no bishops, priests, deacons. Probably it was so bodied, in what was called the church order below, and the magistracies too were in a large variety. But the organization was never in any respect from them, but from God and the headship of his Son; in being joined to whom—every man by his faith—the whole body was fitly joined together and became the fullness of him that filleth all in all. Still the magistracies had their day and their uses, not equally well appointed, perhaps, but sufficiently authorized in all cases when doing a good work. They were not mere straws on the flood, and yet the flood has moved directly on, leaving them we know not where. In the completed society they are all gone by and forgot, and not even ministers, in the cleric sense, any longer remain—only all are made priests unto God in their ransomed state of exaltation, and all do service work, as ministers for the common good of all. I do not by this intend to say that there are no precedences in stature, and personal weight, and consequent dignity and power. They move in great quaternions doubtless, and holy satrapies—thrones, dominions, principalities, powers—but we are only to see, in this, that they are all regnant alike in their order, which is what these figures signify. Some of them are as much above all priestly and pontifical orders, and carry a sway as much more advanced, as they are more transcendently advanced in thought, and weight, and character. And yet they fall into their places, unenvied, undecried, there to be admired and loved, and had in reverence gladly, because they are wanted for the perfect society by the humbler natures themselves. In one view these more advanced ones are lifted into virtual leadership, because they have such weight of being and true counsel as makes them leaders gladly accepted.

It is another point to be observed, that there is no theologic base in the society thus organized. Because the new faith now is alive all through in the society finished; which is itself a confession unwritten, only more full and perfect than there could be in any most rugged articulations of doctrine. They require of course to be fastened by no bonds of catechism or creed, in order to keep their liberty safe; for being the truth themselves they can bear to be free. Some of us here below are much concerned for these matters, much concerned for theology; and perhaps with reason, considering how much of trammel is wanted to keep organization safe among creatures that are unsafe. But there is no such concern above. Theology is there even quite gone by, and nothing but truth remains. And there is more truth alive in a single one of the now free saints, than there ever was in all the fathers, and councils, and schools of the world. These are grown up now into Christ the head, from whom the whole body is fitly joined together.

But these are negatives mainly. Passing over then to what is more positive, we begin to look after the crystallizing power in which the grand celestial society is organized. And—

First of all and at the base of all we find the righteousness and love of God. The righteousness of God is God in everlasting, absolute right, and all created beings who are with him in it, standing fast in sinless integrity, will be organized by it, as their common inspiration. For not even they will be self-righteous in their integrity, but will have the righteousness of God by faith upon them—an everlasting inbreathing, or influx, an eternal radiation from the central sun—and be organized by it, as the common bliss of their conduct and character. But as far as the great all-worlds' society is made up of spirits that were fallen, these could not be organized till the righteousness gone by is somehow restored, and become a new inspiration. And here comes in the love of God as the quickening grace of the cross, for it is at once the wonder of God's love, and the organizing power of it, that he loves against all unloveliness, loves what offends him, what disgusts his feeling, the wrong, the cruel, the abhorrent, descending to any bitterest sacrifice that he may gather even such into his family and friendship. Could he only love the lovable it would not signify much; and not any more, as respects organization, if we should do the same. The society organized would only be a society of mutual admiration—a picture gallery in perfect good taste and nothing more. No, there is a grandly tragic side of God's glory which is not here. That can only be seen when his love takes hold of the bad, the wrong, the shameful, and defiled, able to suffer cost and be redeeming love. Only blood can show these tragic depths in God. Of course we can not congratulate ourselves that we have sinned, but if there be vast orders of being, as many think, who have not, one can not but regret the very little knowledge they must have of what is in the love of God. All that is deepest, grandest in God's character must be to them, so far, a hidden book. And if they have not learned themselves to love, and suffer cost for the bad, even their noble integrity will leave them something to regret, though perhaps they will make up in chastity what they lack in experience, and obtain also by their questions what they have not learned by defilement and sorrow.

Again the great all-worlds' society is still farther advanced in organization by worship. It coalesces in worship; and worship, as it is the grandest felicity, so it is the most effective spell of organization. Of course we do not take the impression that singing hymns about the throne of God and the Lamb, is the total occupation of the everlasting society. We only take such representations of concord in song as figures that completely express the glorious harmonies of feeling, and the common felicities and homages by which it is swayed. Worship is the highest joy of mind, because it is the looking up to behold and feel what is highest and most adorably great. Thus we take long journeys, to just behold and feel what of physical grandeur there may be in a cataract; which feeling of physical grandeur is a kind of natural worship, a feebly effective symbol of what takes place in the worship of the adoring, all-worlds' society. And in that common joy of worship—oftener silent probably than expressed—they are forever coalescent in closer and more powerful bonds, because they feel themselves together everlastingly in it.

Again they have also common works, no doubt, in which they are yet more practically organized, even as a team is brought into line by the stress of a common draught. What their works are we do not know, save as we catch brief glimpses here and there; sometimes sent forth as for guard and watch, also as couriers, also as convoys home of spirits departed, also to be escort trains for the Almighty—chariots of God counting twenty thousand, even thousands of angels. One of them, great Michael, is sent forth to head a war against the dragon power of persecution, though exactly what that means we may not know. Perhaps they go forth on excursions among distant worlds and peoples, reporting, for new study, what of God may be discovered among them. Doubtless they have all enough to do forever, and that which is good enough and high enough for their powers.

They are united and consolidated also in the society life by their victories; for whether they have vanquished all sin, or all temptation, or great forces of hate and cruelty banded against them, they come in all as victors bearing palms, to be organized by the common all-hail, and the *te deum* that celebrates their story. Indeed they come in like an army in register, "the church of the first born whose names are written in heaven;" and no organization is so completely made up as one that shows a complete register. As God's register also is true, there are no hangers on, no pretenders, or doubtful members. Their enrollment is by inside knowledge, and allows them to know even as they are known.

And now it only remains to note, in this connection, the very remarkable fact, coincident with what I said at the beginning, that when the Revelator John shows the grand society emerging full organized, in his last two chapters, you hardly know what world it is in, whether in the upper descending upon this, or this borne upward to the other. No matter; enough that now the eternal city-life is come, a state of exact society, represented by the figure of an exactly cubal city, as many hundreds of miles high as it is broad and long. An image that is hard and violent, and yet on the second view, wondrously significant; as if society, that loosely-shapen factor of the creation, were become the perfect cube of order, in exactest and most solid measurement.

Thus we sketch, as in stammering words, our conception of the church above, the society organized; and from this we descend to a relative conception—

II. Of the church below, the Society Organizing. It is, in fact, the same as the other, and is pouring on its trains continually to be merged in that other, and become a part of it. It is even called a family—"of whom the whole family in heaven and earth is named." Just as we sing in our sublimest of all hymns—

> One family we dwell in him,
>   One church above, beneath,
> Though now divided by the stream,
>   The narrow stream of death.
>
> One army of the living God,
>   To his command we bow,
> Part of the host have crossed the flood,
>   And part are crossing now.

The supposition here is, that in what we call the church on earth, the peoples composing it are being organized in, or into, the state of everlasting society just now described.

And here the first thing we have to settle is, that the church is not properly what we recognize under this and that formula, meeting in this and that place, presided over, taught, confessed, or kept in discipline, by one or another kind of church magistracy. The church, as we are now speaking, is what is called "the communion of saints," and the saints themselves, in their union to Christ, are the staple matter of it—all in training here for the complete society. I am not questioning, observe, the right of their covenants and cures, and forms, and ministries, or even of their parishes and bishoprics and councils. I only say that these are at best only scaffoldings all, and that the real import of what they are, and what they are for, is in the souls who are training under their husbandry. And they undoubtedly have great uses often in this way. As to there being intendencies divinely authorized and the only ones to be allowed, composing, as it were, the whole church institute in their own official right and sanction—of all this I know nothing. I suppose that it would be competent for any brotherhood, meeting in the Spirit, if not already organized, to organize in what form, under what offices and rules they please, and that in this manner any known form of organization is allowable, even that of the Quakers; if only they can find how to grow in it, and make an ever-spreading society in the communion of saints. These regimental machineries are none of them the church, they are only the scaffolding of the church, and are all alike to be done away, when that which is perfect is come.

Furthermore it is difficult to admit that what are called sects have no positive use, in the organizing way. If they are divisions and not distributions, they are so far evil. But if they are only distributions, they furnish by their mutual reactions the conditions of close thought and compact feeling. Frictions too, it may be, are necessary to much life in souls partly benumbed by sin. And besides it is a fact not often observed, that these distributions, under different names, do really help out the enlargement of our charity. If we stood related only as individuals to individuals, our charities could run out but a little way—just as far as our acquaintance runs, and no farther—but when we push out our charities, as in this day we are learning to do, on so many sects, we make a sweep for them as large as the sects are,—counting them all in to be the body of Christ, the fullness of him that filleth all in all.

But the power that works towards organization—let us inquire after this. The lowest form of it will be seen in the expense, and labor, and wear of contriving we submit to, in the way of providing preachers and church edifices. For our whole strain of endeavors in this lowest key,—in which we make ourselves responsible with others for the provisioning and perpetuating of the gospel institution,—has a steadily condensing efficacy of organization in it.

Then again, to go farther inward, our relations of church brotherhood are a continual drill in and for society. In this we are schooled in fact, into the very love of God; for the whole body of our fraternity is tinged with badness, troubled by disorder, damaged by sore faults, hurt by offenses. Envy looks up with bitterness, pride looks down with contempt, jealousy looks every way snuffing the scent of wrongs that are only to be. Some are covetous, some are mean, some are passionate, some are sensual, some are strong only in hate, some are weak only in principle. A great many things are coming out thus, every hour, that are very unlovely, and quite likely some of us lose our patience at times, and begin to protest that the church after all is made up of such kind of material as looks really worse than the world. But we come back shortly to the living love of God, and take a new lesson; where it is opened to us that we ourselves are in this divine society just because it is God's hospital, where he is watching and nursing his poor morally broken children, loving them never at all for what they are, but only for what he can make them. And so we learn to love with patience, and to bear even as God does, loving what we do not like, and can not approve, and can only hope to benefit. The whole problem of our church-life is a problem of divine society working towards completion.

Then again we have the bad, outside, to work for; and here we are drawn to the closest sympathy inside, that we may find how to gain, by our love, those whom Christ's love died to save. And this brings us ever into the closest sympathy with Christ, so that our hearts are melted often, even as his was, by our compassions for his rejectors. Coming into this labor, as we ought always to be in it, we are in the closest, tenderest way of society. We are even configured to each other as we look in each other's faces, and behold the glow there kindled. Our assemblies are all contempered by the heat of God's living sacrifice for the transgressors. Are we not so getting ready fast for the perfect society?

I say nothing here of our common repentances, and common sorrows, when we find that we have fallen away from our calling. We confess how much of the bad together, and our sorrowing clears up, in new discoveries of what God has undertaken to endure by his love. So the ebb of our tide brings on a flood once more.

And then again, perhaps, we have our times of inspiration. And they are all the more significant that we have them in society, and have our hearts burning in the same divine fire. We sit in heavenly places now, and have the heavenly good by anticipation. Our testimonies are bright, our songs make melody in our hearts. Brothers, is it not good to be here!

The common hope we have in our brotherhood, is also a great consociating and consolidating power. Thus in hope, as our apostle says, we are come beforehand to the city of God, the heavenly Jerusalem. What we so much hope, he imagines to be already taken possession of, even as it has taken possession of us. And then what possesses us together, fills our eye, kindles our expectation, draws us towards or into a closer band of society. Even as we sometime see, when our birds of passage, hastening on to the lands where they summer, hook themselves to each other, as they fly, in lines of order, pulsing on the air in a common time-beat of their wings. They fly as if drawn by the hope of a city, or populous new nesting-ground unvisited by enemies. Trail on thus, ye citizens to be, of a city that hath foundations, knowing that your blessed conjunctions in hope will there be issued in society, everlasting and complete.

But we do not finish our conception of this all-worlds' society, without naming two points that were not, and could not be, named before; because we did not know the "society organized" sharply enough to see the necessity for them. But we discover it now in the society organizing; for these two things, we see, are even made a part of our training, and go in, as restrictions, on organization, to save us from being totally gulfed by it. First we must have times of solitude and spaces of withdrawment; and secondly we must have the liberty of our own thoughts; to keep them back, or give them out, or give them by selection. There must even be room left for opinion. To be always out in publicity, to be on parade, so to speak, everlastingly, to have joys ventilated always by expression—the same expression, or the same roundelay of praise—would drug our sensibility, and become wearisome beyond endurance. We are trained for no such thing. Such perpetual out-door life, such living in transparency, would even be intolerable. The grand organization therefore will be perfect, only and because it is shortened back by fit limitations; allowing all the innumerable personalities to have their own field to themselves, enjoying themselves the more that they have ways of withdrawment, and enjoying each other the more, that they have such confidence in all as to know, that never, in their most secret moments, will they even think any thing, having full power to do it, which is not sweet, and friendly, and right. Which confidence they can have, because their own thoughts have no war, run to no bitterness, flowing as it were in the rhythm of a perpetual hymn.

Having outlined, in this manner, the society organized, and the society organizing—the church above and the church below—it remains to distinctly state some of the points of benefit I have been having in view; which I shall do in the most nearly staccato manner possible.

1. Let no one disrespect the church because there is evil and sometimes real baseness in it. That is exactly what there should be, and in that works the brave purpose God has in it. What is it but a mill that runs for the grinding out of evil? What enters here, enters for love to work in, and to work upon—such love as can have patience and forbear, and new-conform in good. Doubtless God is proposing, in this, a glorious church, not having spot, or wrinkle, or any such thing; but when it comes to that, it will not be here and is not meant to be. It will be graduated and brought home. And what is there in all this, but the grandest possible title to respect?

2. It is neither wise, nor right, to be fastidious here.

You do not like churches, you say; they are not the sort of people here that suit you best, and you do not like to be brothered by all kinds of good folk that happen to be disagreeable—as a great many of them are. And what if God, and Christ, should have happened to be fastidious, unable to love, and seek, and bear the unworthy—how would it be even now with you? Besides, what kind of world or society are you going to hereafter? Is it anywhere provided, in the good society of God's kingdom, that there shall be no little ones, no humble minded, no sweet, low children of sorrow? Do you not see, in the very idea of the church, that your fastidious feeling is the very lowest and most cruelly bad of all feeling? What, on the other hand, can be more honorable to God, than that he is fashioning a great all-worlds' society, that shall set the weak in due honor, and repay the dejections of an adverse lot by deserved and really great exaltations.

3. It is every good man's duty to acknowledge the church, and be a hearty, faithful member in it. No, you say, it may be; for what we call churches have magistracies, articles, laws of discipline and a sectarian life. Yes, and since the society organizing is for the partly bad, and not for the just made perfect, how could it be otherwise? Not that these church forms and magistracies are themselves organization, as we often hear. The President of the United States and all his subordinates, down to the tide-waiters, do not organize the nation. Not even the laws organize it. It is done, or can be completely, only when the people

are right, and true, and just, and good, and that without any laws. Meantime the magistracies and laws are only hampers, added to substitute organization, where there is none. Have you then no duties to the state or nation? So it is your duty to be openly joined to the church of God under some frame of order and rule. These frames are only shells in which the egg is kept. Say not that you belong to the church universal, counting that to be enough. Enough, that is, to be an egg without a shell! You are going to get ready, you imagine, for the perfect society out of all society, making common cause with nobody! That is, you are going forward into the everlasting society, there to meet no solitary creature with whom you stood shoulder to shoulder in love and sacrifice. Forgive me if I greatly mistrust whether you will meet any one there that knows you at all—save as a contemner of the society from its beginning onward.

4. It ought, by this time, to be clear, my brethren, that there is no other cause, compact, institution, now on foot in the world, which is at all comparable for benefit, and dignity, with the church of God. It has outlived the great empires, three or four tiers of them in succession. It has created new empires, such as this of ours. It has leavened all human society with elements of advancement—by which educations, laws, liberties, sciences, inventions, constitutions, have been coming all the while into flower. It would take whole hours just to give the shining roll of names that, in worth and genius, and true sainthood, have been

marching out into their great history in it, for these almost nineteen hundred years. The history, I grant, is in some sense an awful history, having, as it were, Jacob and Esau struggling in it for the birth. The woes are sharp, the fires are hot, the prisons are burst-ed with wail; women-martyrs, child-martyrs, the general bleeding host of persecuted merit move on, as it were, in procession to die. From age to age it has been rock, as the Saviour promised, to the wrath surging heavily against it; rock, also, which is yet more strange, to the horrible rage of cruelty and crime within. Unable to be shaken by either this or that, it still stands firm as no political state or kingdom could have stood, even for a generation; till now we see it emerging, as we think, in the grace alone of the cross; in that to be full-organized—society complete—everlasting, universal, inviolable brotherhood.

Do we then some of us ask what cause, engagement, work is for us? to what we shall best give our talents, our inspirable youth, our courage, our powers of devotement and fires of sacrifice?* To what surely sooner than to the church of God? If we have talents to spend, where else can we spend them in a braver, more unselfish devotion? And if our talents are only moderate in their measures, how shall we more certainly enlarge them than to put them at work in God measures,—in his subjects, his charities, his contemplations and causes—putting our whole nature at school by his. Besides, the church is everlasting, the only fabric,

* Y. C. C.

structure, institute, society or state that is. And O, how grand a thing it is that, going in hither, we can build ourselves into the eternal. Against all else a statute runs of limitation. Getting wealth we get no charter for breathing. Getting fame we shall not be on hand to hear the ring of it. Going into the healing of bodies we can only patch them up for an hour. Going into the law we give ourselves to what was made last year, and will be unmade the next. Public honors vanish, and statesmanship and states are only for a time, and commonly a very short time. Not so the church of God, the great, everlasting all-worlds' society; that remains, and if we put much cost and sacrifice into it, all the better. Many I know are chaffy enough just now in their conceit to prophecy the date of it. Do they not tell us it is close at hand? Yes, and they shall see the end of it just when the blue fades out of the sky, when the mountains drink up the sea, when the heat of the sun freezes in, or better still when God's predestinating will breaks down—then, and not till then. No, it exists for God's whole future and as long as that will last. God help us all to have our future in it—every man established, by the law of social right, in that universal ownership conferred on each, by the everlasting society of all.

XVI.

ROUTINE OBSERVANCE INDISPENSABLE.

"Give us this day our daily bread."—*Matth.* 6: 11.

We have two opposite varieties in religion that are about equally mistaken; one that puts every thing in rounds of observance, as in fasting on Fridays, and repeating *paternosters* so many times a day; and the other in having no times at all, only doing acts of duty and devotion as and when we are inclined to it. This latter misconception belongs more especially to us of the Protestant family; though to us not equally, but in different degrees. We all appear to be indulging ways of relaxation which we call our advance in liberty. And the more impatient of routine we become, the higher conceptions we think we are holding of the Christian life. Falling away from all fixed times and rounds of observance, and learning to hold them in a certain disrespect, we go more clear, perhaps, than we mean to be, of the sturdy old habit of Puritan law, and drop into a looser way that is more agreeable. And have we not reasons to offer, that indicate advances made in religious dignity? Are we not casting off our unnecessary bondages? And what kind of meaning, or sincerity can there be in observances or acts that we do not feel inclined to? What moreover is prayer but a merely cringing way in us and a real mockery to God, when we are moved to it by no disposition to pray, but are rather strongly disinclined to it, and set ourselves to the observance only because the prescribed time has come? Family prayer, as a daily observance, fares in the same way. No matter what the ground of disinclination may be —circumstance, convenience, pressing engagements— why make an unalterably fixed ordinance of it, even for the children's sake, when, at any rate, God will bring up his sun, and load the morning table with food, and set his flowers blooming at the door—all punctual and true to their times? So in matters of charity, so in church-going, so in the stated times of conference and prayer; and then why not so in the going to school of the children, and their punctual times of returning, in their street hours for the evening, and their late hours running into even the far off times of the night.

What I now undertake therefore is to show the necessity, in religion, of a more or less rigidly appointed routine practice; beginning at the petition cited from the prayer which our Lord gave his disciples—"give us this day our daily bread." We do not really understand him, unless we distinguish a mental reference in his words, to the customary observance of morning prayer. For it is a prayer for each morning that he gives; a daily prayer for daily bread, even for this day's bread. To offer this prayer, therefore, as many do, after the day or every repast of the day is finished, is to make it a thing for the form, when it is nothing in the fact; which is about the worst dishonor that could any way be done it. The supposition is that the soul is to have every morning, as a sunrise of religion—punctual and bright as the morning. Conceiving a prayer to be used for the noon or the evening—even as the Psalmist says, "evening and morning and noon will I pray," he would certainly have done what the Psalmist did, adapted his prayer to its time. At any rate nothing was farther plainly from his thought, than to say, "pray when you have a mind to it, and let it pass when you have not." Whether he means his prayer to be used every morning or not, he does, at least, give honor and sanction to the daily observance of morning prayer. And it is under his sanction, thus given, that I draw out now, for your consideration, this great law of practical christian living—

That we need to keep fixed times, or appointed rounds of observance, as truly as to be in holy impulse; to have prescribed periods in duty as truly as to have a spirit of duty; to be in the drill of observance, as well as in the liberty of faith.

In other words, I am to show the place of what we sometimes call *routine* in religion, and as we are constituted, the profound necessity for it. And by way of preparing you to a just impression of the subject, I ask you—

1. To notice the very obvious fact that the argu-

ment commonly stated, as against the obligation of fixed times and ways of observance in religion, contains a fatal oversight. It is very true that mere rounds of observance, however faithfully kept, have in themselves no value, nothing of the substance of piety; but they have an immense value, when kept and meant to be, as the means of piety. It is equally true that nothing is acceptable to God, which is not an offering of the heart. But it does not follow, by any means, that we are therefore to wait, doing nothing till the inclinations or impulses of the heart are ready. Thus, when the disciple says, "Why should I attempt to pray? what is my prayer but mockery, when I go to it by fixed times without or against inclination?"—he overlooks entirely what belongs to the very economy of prayer, and constitutes its highest practical value; viz., that not being an exercise to merely play out impulse and inclination, it is also an exercise to kindle impulse and beget inclination. This, in fact, is the very particular blessing of it, that when we are averted from it and slacked in all our inclinations towards it, we may still get our fire kindled by it. When we go to it, therefore, by fixed times of observance, we do just what is necessary to beget fixed inclinations, and train the soul into a habit of abiding impulse. Otherwise, or desisting because we have no inclination, we consent to have no inclination, but that which wavers fitfully, and probably, at last, no inclination at all. The whole argument turns here just as it does in other matters. There is no genuine prayer, for example, that is not offered in the Spirit, and yet God promises the Holy Spirit to them that ask Him. Shall we then decline to ask because we have not the Spirit already, and because such kind of asking will be only mockery! No! for the very design of God is to meet us *in* the asking, and to enter his Spirit into the asking itself. He puts us to the asking for the purpose of getting us open to the Spirit, and accessible to his holy inspirations. We go to obtain inspirations, inclinations, gales of impulse, and not simply to play out such as we have already. Nothing in this view is weaker, more unpractical, closer to a shallow dissipation, more certain to end in a dreadful collapse in character, than this most treacherous doctrine, which makes it even a law, that we surrender every thing to our inclinations. Let me ask your attention now—

2. To the grand analogies of time and routine movement in the world you live in. Nature is, on one hand, a world of routine or of prescribed times and recurrences, and on the other a realm of versatile changes and endlessly varied occasions or appearances. The days and years, the moon and tides, the mornings and evenings, the eclipses and even wandering comets, have their times exactly set, and their rounds exactly measured. We can even make up their almanac for the most distant ages and cycles. What we call the almanac is, in fact, an exhibition to the eye, of the grand principle of routine in nature. So far the vast empire of being is grounded in a sublime principle of routine

everywhere manifest; it is ordained for signs, and for seasons, and for days and years. And without this, or apart from this, it would be only a medley of confusion, a chaos of interminable disorder. What could we do in a world where there are no appointed times, no calculable recurrences, no grand punctualities, where the seasons are moved in different orders of successions, days and nights coming at random, and staying for such time as they please, the heavenly bodies a chapter of celestial accidents in their motions, the moon quartering once a month, or ten times a month, the tides rising with or without the moon, the dews falling on the snows, and the snows on the verdure of June—such a world would really be valueless; we could do nothing with it, and simply because it has no fixed times. And for just this reason God has consented to inaugurate the sublime routine necessary to its uses, determining the times before appointed, and the bounds of our habitation.

And so very close does God come to us in this matter of times or of natural routine, that our heart beats punctually in it, our breath heaves in it like the panting tides of the ocean, and the body itself, and with it also the mind, yes even the mind, is a day's man only in its power, a creature of waking and sleeping, of alternating consciousness and unconsciousness, like the solar day and night of the world.

And yet some can not think it a matter sufficiently dignified to have any prescribed times in religion. Though God himself is a being of routine, though the everlasting worlds are bedded in routine, though their very bodies and minds are timed in it, like a watch, or the earth's revolution, still they are jealous of any such thing in religion, and refuse it, as an infringement on their liberty! Is this, I ask, the lesson which they draw from the great teacher in whose bosom they live? And if the world itself, apart from its fixed rounds, or prescribed times, were only an uninhabitable chaos, what greater value is there like to be, in their own acts and doings, when there is no fixed time for doing any thing.

3. I refer you again to the analogy of your own courses in other things, and also to the general analogies of business. As we are by nature diurnal creatures in the matter of waking and sleep, so we are voluntarily creatures of routine and of fixed hours in the matter of food. In this respect the wild Indians of the forest differ, we are told, from us—eating immensely when it is convenient, or the necessary game is taken, and then fasting even to the door of starvation, till the fortune of the hunt brings another supply. We, on the other hand, have our appointed times—just so many times of repast each day, at an exact hour by the clock—and we take it as a hardship, or a constraint on our liberty, if we are obliged, by any circumstance or pressure, to fail of our time. Which then do we suppose to be in the best conditions of comfort, dignity, and good keeping, the savage tribes that have no times, or we that feed in the exact routine of the civilized table? How is it also in the

matter of business, or the transactions of trade and industry? What figure of success will any man make in business, who has no fixed hours; who goes to his work, or sends out his men, at any and all hours of the day—five o'clock, or ten, or two, as best suits his convenience, and despises the oppressive and slavish law of prescribed times—as if a man who respects himself could submit to be wheeled on through his works by the tick of the watch, or to keep time with the shadows of the sun! Or suppose he is equally averse to the bondage of times in his engagements, gathering his dues when they chance to come, expecting his interest money at just such times as he pleases, and paying his notes when it is convenient—will such a man succeed, or will he find that in refusing any law in times he refuses all success, all credit, name and character. If then there is nothing men do with effect in the world of business, despising the law of times, how does it happen that they can expect, with any better reason, to succeed in the matter of their religion—their graces, charities, and prayers? Wherein does it appear to be absurd, to assume that the soul wants times of feeding as regular, and frequent, and punctual, as the body? Again,

4. Consider the reason of the Sabbath, where it is assumed that men are creatures, religiously speaking, of routine, wanting it as much as they do principles, fixed times as much as liberty. Indeed a very considerable part of the value of the Sabbath consists in the drill of its times; that it comes when we do not

ask for it, commands us to stop when we desire to go on, calls us off to worship by a summons astronomically timed, and measured by the revolutions of the world. In this view it is, I conceive, that the fourth commandment is set in the decalogue. The design is to place order in the same rank with principle, and give it honor in all coming ages, as a necessary element of religion, or the religious life and character. And what we discover in the reason of the Sabbath holds equally well of other observances and duties. As we are creatures of impulse, inspiration, liberty, so also we are creatures of drill, and there was no way to perfect or establish us in any thing, unless we could be required to do what we are not inclined to do; to appoint our times of prayer, keep ourselves in rounds of observance, and hold fast in the punctual discipline of times.

Indeed we could not have any fixed appointment of public worship, or common prayer at all, under the mischievous doctrine I am contending against. There is no true worship, I agree, in public more than any where else, unless the heart is in it. Why then should we give attendance, you may ask, in public worship, when we have no heart in it? Why keep one day in seven, if we have no inclination for it? And so common worship goes down, the prayer meeting falls out of possibility, and all the powerful means of piety thus ordered, is even lost to the world.

5. The Scriptures recognize the value of prescribed times and a fixed routine of duty, in other ways more

numerous than can be well recounted. Thus in the old religion, the sacrifices, the great feasts or festivals, all the observances and forms had a fixed rotation, and the power of a military drill on the mind of the people. The entire calendar, in fact, was set off in sevens of days, and years, and the sacred number seven was carried so far that even the march about Jericho was to be in it, in order to the mystic sevenfolding under God that winds up the spell of its fall. The holy men had all their times; one was accustomed to observe the sacred number in his worship, having it seven times a day, as the fixed order of his life. Another went to prayer three times a day. In the New Testament the observance of fixed times appears less distinctly; and partly because many of the zealots and precisionists made a righteousness of their observances, apart from any meaning or honest purpose in them. Wherefore Paul was obliged even to rebuke this kind of superstition—"the observing days, and months, and times, and years," the respecting "holy days, new moons, and Sabbaths." To break up this subjection to ordinances, the new religion even went so far as to abolish the seventh day. Not however because the routine was itself evil; for the first day was, at the same time, substituted as a time of stated worship. The object was to strip away the bondage that had come to be an oppression, because it was a superstition—in that view a beggarly element. And that only this was the object is made clear, in the fact that Christ himself, in the interval between his resurrection and ascension, keeps day with his disciples, meeting them by a weekly manifestation of his presence, as if purposely to give them stated times—even as he had taught them in his first sermon to have each day their time of prayer, saying, "Give us this day our daily bread." All the teachers after him made it a point, in the same manner, to institute a piety whose rule is order, and whose liberty itself is regularity. Thus John is in the Spirit, and meets the vision even of his prophecy on the Lord's day. Paul observes that day, and gives it as a good rule to lay by what may go for charity on that day, that so there may be order in charity; remembering, also, in the very chapter that forbids the observance of holy days, new moons, and Sabbaths, to commend the brethren, "as joying and beholding their order, and the steadfastness [or regular working] of their faith." Had they no fixed times and rounds of duty, doing every thing by impulse or fancy, or caprice, he would have found any thing but order to rejoice in. Which—

Again brings me to say that if we have no times in religion but such as we take by mere impulse, or inclination, we shall fall away, at last, from all times and all duties. Let any one take the ground, for example, that he will never pray except when he is drawn to it, and he will less and less frequently be drawn. If any one tells me that he can not pray, when he is disinclined, or not moved to it, and would feel it even to be an act of insincerity, I understand that he prays very seldom, and perhaps never. Such a rule of prayer would gradually let down the best Christian, and finally take him quite away from the exercise. In his ordinary state he may have been commonly inclined to the exercise. But there will be times when he is not, and then, if instead of girding himself to what interest he may find, he yields to his mere self-indulgence, that self-indulgence will rot away his confidence, exterminate his peace, turn itself into habitual disinclination, and so, by a fixed law, put an end to his praying altogether. Doubtless he will have a great many plausible reasons to comfort him, as he goes down the descent, but the descent he will make. Though he is now sure he practices no insincerity, and does not force himself in that which ought to be free, he will also be as clear, that he has not the nearness to God he once had, and is losing the relish of God's friendship, by which he once was drawn so fondly to the exercise.

After all, however plausibly we may reason about forced exercises, or a want of sincerity in them, we have really never any great sincerity where we do not sometimes cross our inclinations, by the salutary compulsion of prescribed times and duties. A scholar is not in the true idea of scholarship, till he becomes able to bury himself in study for the pure love of knowledge. But no scholar ever comes to that, who does not put on the harness of work, and set himself to the drill of regularity, and the fixed routine of the class or the school. A merchant is never deep enough in his engagement to have any title to success, or chance of it, who does not set his times and proceed by system, and when he feels a little disinclination, does not use compulsion enough to hold himself to his engagements. And if he has not manliness enough or energy enough in him to do this, we take it for granted that there is no earnestness in his engagement, and never can be any real success. In fact, no man ever does any thing which he has no times for doing. And if a man is too delicate to suffer any fixed times in religion, it will fare with him as it does with other men, who are always about to do some great thing, but never find the time for executing their romantic intentions.

Once more the true way to come into liberty and keep ourselves in it, is to have our prescribed rules, and in some respects, at least, a fixed routine of duties. I do not say or suppose that a mere round of repetitions can accomplish any thing, or that any mere observance of times and years can, of itself, produce in a soul the grace of a true discipleship. Nothing done as a matter of mere observance is better than the fasting Pharisaically twice in a week, which Christ condemned. But if any Pharisee had taken it upon him to fast twice in a week, not for the merit of the fasting, but to have it as a means and exercise of repentance, looking unto God, in the engagement, for grace to make it effectual in the renovation of his life, no matter how distant he may have been at the beginning, from the state of faith and liberty, he would assuredly have found a living grace of piety in it.

Many a child brought up to begin and close each day with prayer, is guided by that simple routine exercise, connected with the other influences of life, into the true spirit of a disciple, and grows up in the kingdom as one imperceptibly initiated. Let any most dull and worldly minded christian gather himself up to the established rule of prayer for three times, twice, or even once a day, determined not to have it as a mere observance, but as an exercise of grace and practical waiting on God, and it will not be long before he is truly restored and walks in liberty. So that if we grant the inherent defect of any and all prayers in which there is nothing better than a forced exercise, no impulse, no liberty, the true way to be in liberty and be kept habitually there, is to live in that holy routine which is the bond of all true application, and the certain method of all earnestness and fidelity. And accordingly it will be found, as a matter of fact, that they who are readiest to endure hardness, and have least delicacy about forcing themselves in constrained exercises, have really most liberty, live closest to God, enjoy most of his smile, and as they keep up the rounds of duty most faithfully, will have really least feeling of constraint, or even think of it as no constraint at all.

I need not undertake to show you how exactly what I am here saying is borne out by the experiences of holy men. I will simply note one or two examples. Thus when you find young Taylor recording it as his rule, "the last thing before retiring every night, to commit to memory a portion of scripture, and rejoicing in the computation of what this may amount to in eight years," the time of his preparation, now begun, for the ministry, you will discover that spirit of application that augurs infallible success. And this is not the man to wear out his life in a drill of legalities, but he will be one of the freest, most joyful and jubilant of the saints. So also when you find a Jonathan Edwards, at the age of twenty, recording it as one of his fixed resolutions—"Resolved to ask myself at the end of every day, week, month and year, wherein I could possibly, in any respect, have done better," you may see a great mind engineering in the solemn routine of appointed times and fixed methods, to keep himself in the way of fidelity; so to be a living and free soul in the faith, and fill up his life with holy impulse, and cover it with the radiance of God's free manifestation. Few men have enjoyed more of God on earth, or been less drudged by the punctuality and system in which he so cautiously lived. There is, I know, such a thing as a legal, barren, painful observance, which like the sorrow of the world worketh death, just as there are martinets in place of commanders, and regiments in drill that will be cowards in the fight, but of this we may be sure, there never was or will be a successful man in any thing, least of all in religion, who can not gird himself to application by some fixed rules and times of action.

I regard this subject, my brethren, as one that has a

most intimate and vital connection with all sound advance or possibility of advance in your Christian life. Most true it is that God has no pleasure in any mere formalities or observances you can offer him. He demands the heart, he looks with respect and favor on no tribute which is not the tribute of the heart's freedom—unless it be that he lovingly draws nigh to them that are pining and sighing for the want of such a gift. It is no tread-mill service of routine that wins you his friendship. Inspiration, impulse, liberty, a service of freedom and gladness, this only is his delight. But in order to this, there must also be subjection to his rule, a systematic care, a prescribed obedience of duty, a holy drill of times patiently accepted. The way to find liberty is to come into the schooling of order and law, and let our will be harnessed in a punctual keeping of holy times.

Have you never observed that where there is no order, there is no piety; or if any, none but such as represents the confusion, the irresponsibility, the looseness and chaotic chance-work of the life?

You have noticed with wonder and sorrow, it may be, the fact that so many Christians have no reliable exactness in their dealings with their fellow men. It is partly because they have no exactness with God. They are loose in their representations, grazing close upon the gates of falsehood, and sometimes hard against them. They are not reliable. They are as loose in their times and engagements as in their statements. Their honor is not maintained. And the reason is that they are loose with God. They do not keep their vows. They have no times of prayer. They let their life float on as it may, or as self-indulgence or convenience will determine. There is, in fact, a very close sympathy between punctuality in routine, and exactness in principle, such that no man will ever be a man of principle who has no times. And then again there is a sympathy equally close, between high principle and God, for it is only a very exact conscience that is capable of a sharp confidence, and then it is only a delicately sharp confidence towards God that can have a clear and glorious access to his presence and his smile.

If a Christian shuns routine, therefore, having no times of prayer, observing with his brethren no appointments of prayer, praying in his family only now and then, or perhaps never, because he may not always be inclined to it, you can easily see why he will get on poorly in his piety, and why his light will be darkness. Because his conscience will be loose, and his confidence low, and his will in no keeping, and as no pains are taken for Christ, no sacrifices made, no fidelity observed, he will of course be as ignorant of liberty as he is ambiguous in duty.

Brethren, how is it with you in this matter? Do you live in the girdle of law or without? Do you give your charities when some fit of the impulse takes you, or when some hard importunity presses you, or do you try to settle carefully before God your measures, and times, and objects? Do you have your times of prayer, and keep them, cost what it may, or do you pray by the rule of inclination or convenience? Do you keep time with your brethren, in their weekly hour of prayer, or do you fall in late, or fall utterly away—excusing yourself from attendance because the place is dull, making it more dull by a lack of attendance? Do you lag and grow slack everywhere, and contrive to think you are waiting for God to give you appetite?—such waiting will be long before it wins. If the sun waited below the horizon for fair weather, fair weather would certainly wait for the sun. Ah, it is a greater thing than you imagine to stand fast in your order, and the system of a faithful life. Half the benefit you get in holy times, and punctualities, lies in the fact that for Christ's sake you keep them. You can not be too rigid in this matter. A loose way makes a loose man. Prove your fidelity by your painstaking, and it will be strange if you do not stand fast even though you stand alone—blessed and great honor this, to stand alone! Such a man has no dull time any where, his inspiration is full, his confidence sure, his peace the calm deep flow of a river.

I knew a man of fortune, whose business was a care equal to a small kingdom, and who had it as the rule of his life, to be always up in the morning before the day, or by the early dawn, and to spend one or two hours in the exclusive exercises of religion—reading, meditation, and prayer. The result was that what was begun as a law, became, in a short time, his privilege. He had such enjoyment, such delight in the unmolested good of the time, that it became the chief blessing of his day; and all its works were done under the sacred impulse, and the smoothed flow and buoyant spring of the sense of God there received. It was in fact his luxury; just that luxury which every humblest, poorest saint could have as well as he; and in which all the gifts and orders of life are how nearly equalized.

Now there may be some of you that have never had so much as a question about these routine observances in duty. What is there for you in them, when, as respects the matter of religion, you have never come into that kind of duty at all? What can you do in religion, having no heart to it, but wait till the heart is given? What are your sacrifices, till then, but an abomination? Of course your prayers or sacrifices are an abomination, when they are offered in a wicked and abominable spirit. But not so if they are offered in a real desire to get help in clearing the bad spirit, and beginning a right life. Considering then calmly the fact, that religion is the first errand of existence, and the chief import of your life-charge itself, give yourself to it in set times of thought and spiritual endeavor. No matter what your present feeling may be, or how great your want of feeling; no matter how indifferent you may be, or how dark as regards all christian subjects. Set your times of prayer not for a mere experiment, but as a fixed appointment never to be discontinued. Go to it in the cold to get heat. Go to it in the dark to wait and watch for the light. Go to it without inclination, pleading the promise of God's Spirit to give you inclination. All this in the rational conviction that, as religion is your greatest practical concern, God will be waiting, on his part, to open the gate for you; to greet, accept and bid you everlasting welcome. Now, doing this, I can not tell you precisely in what manner God will deal with you. I can only promise that, as certainly as your times are kept, and kept in a desire to find him, he will be found—discovered suddenly, it may be, in a revelation unexpected; or you may be drawn along in a way more nearly imperceptible, till finally, you scarce know when, the conclusion is upon you that you are somehow changed. What you began with constraint, you somehow love. Your affinities, feelings, principles, motives, aspirations, you know not in what way, are certainly recast, and become wondrously new. Thus in one way or another it will be with you. According to the fidelity of your times, and the steadiness of your meaning in them, God will give you, and with that you must be content. There is no person living, as I verily believe, who will not thus, after some due time, be established in the faith, and filled with the revelation of God. Your dawn may come straightway like the sun flaming over the horizon as an outbursting power of day; or it may take even three or four whole days to bring it; but it will come. After two days he will revive us, in the third day he will raise us up, and we shall live in his sight. We shall as certainly know as we follow on to know the Lord, for his going forth is prepared as the morning.

XVII.

OUR ADVANTAGE IN BEING FINITE.

"Thou madest him a little lower than the angels; thou crownedst him with glory and honor, and didst set him over the works of thy hands."—*Heb.* 2: 7.

Because we are created and finite, the conclusion is sprung at once, by many, that we are insignificant. And sometimes they will even make a merit of it, counting it a way of doing honor to God, that we draw as dejected and sorry a figure as possible of ourselves. Even as we see in Job's friend Eliphaz, one of those old-time sophists of the East, whose trick it is always to be laying, first, their slant of contempt on whatever is finite, and then spreading themselves out in high airs on the infinite, as if it were altogether in their province! "Behold he put no trust in his servants, and his angels he charged with folly. As to them that dwell in houses of clay, whose foundation is in the dust—they are crushed before the moth." I read from Umbreit's version. But the sophist keeps on with his prating as he began. He not only puts down the poor mortal under such frailty that even the moth will trample him, but goes on to add that he perishes without any regarding it,—lives in but the empty show of excellency, and dies without wisdom. I do not call the citing of this libel on God's work in man, quoting Scripture. I only do it, that I may controvert and refute the libel. Putting with it also what our new-time Eliphazes add, in what they conceive to be their more sovereign philosophy; showing that our finite consciousness is only a pleasant conceit of being something we are not; that what we think our liberty is only fate; our sin a thing of circumstance in which we foolishly make ourselves guilty; our immortality a merely fond illusion. So we get a last shove towards nothingness, and in that we go down, sometimes quite out of sight of ourselves; saying, how often,—"No matter, let God, or fate take care of us; for we are really too nearly nothing, to be of any great consequence, whether to ourselves or to each other." Atrophy, complete moral atrophy, is the certain result of this most unnecessary and unjust self-depreciation; and there can be no other.

In the passage from which I speak, I begin at quite another point, where God's well authorized teacher shows Him magnifying his creature—putting even glory and honor upon him, enduing him with prerogative, setting him in dominion. He is not proposing to magnify God by crushing down his creature, but by raising him up, rather, into power and majesty. When I read this passage of Scripture, indeed, I am not quite sure that the Uncreated being is more privileged than the created; and it is this grand positivity of privilege that I now undertake to show. Distinguishing between the two great conditions or kinds of being, the Uncreated and the created, the Infinite and the finite, the Supreme and the subject, I propose, using these terms interchangeably,—for they mean, as far as we are now concerned, the same thing,—to give a merely calm, just statement of the created, the finite, the subject, which will show them in place, as the geologist might say, and will practically magnify their significance as no most flaming and declamatory exhibition possibly can.

It is a very conclusive and short argument that I put at the head in this discussion; viz., that all the wisdom and character there may be in the Uncreated, will of course be entered somehow into the advancement of the created. So that whoever depreciates his work, depreciates him. Of course he has not put his infinite quantities into every or any finite creature, but all the wisdom he has, all the goodness, all the privilege of nature that he has in himself, is just so far entered into his creature as it can be. It is not so with other kinds of creatures, such as animals and stones, for they are not reciprocal natures. But the moral nature of man is reciprocal, and is, by supposition, open as by right, to all there is of good in God that can be communicated, or received. In this simple fact, of answering property and perpetual participation, what a conception have we of the privilege of every created moral being, as related to the Uncreated! What is it thus for any created mind to be, but glory, and honor, and dominion over God's works?

But we have a specification to make, in which we may begin to see, more distinctly, what advantage we have in being finite, or created. I begin with the fact that we have a whole class of virtues permitted us which are interesting and beautiful in themselves, and yet no wise pertinent to God. *Temperance*, for example, is one; a self-containing, manly habit, as respects the uses both of mind and body, that has been abundantly admired and praised by the ripest teachers of philosophy. *Contentment*, in like manner, is a virtue that has no place with God, because he has no uneasy, malcontent properties in his nature that require any such kind of self-regimen to compose and sweeten them. *Candor* is a lovely and just character, that is able to hold the reins of judgment impartially, against the sway of prejudice and passion. Having no such liabilities, God wants no such virtue. *Courage*—we make heroes of courage; but as God has nothing to fear, no perils to subdue, he is eternally out of range, as regards this noble virtue. *Gratitude*, most honorable to show, and a real beatitude to feel, is no privilege of the supreme, or of any but a subject nature. So of *prudence, fortitude, economy*, and a great many other like qualities; all humble flowers, yet even such as God will look upon with delight, though not in dignity for Him—crocuses, blooming in the low chill air of human life, anemones, violets, arbutuses, of virtue, pricking out close down in the margin, as it were, of the snows; fair as they know how to be, fragrant as they can be, tokens, in that manner, of our finite privilege.

Next as being creatures and finite we are allowed to grow, as the Supreme Infinite, can not. He encounters no new ideas, acquires nothing which he had not before, beholds what he beheld, and is ever the same that he was. We, as being finite, have our best enjoyment in the sense of progress. We advance in thought, we accumulate force, we run with larger volume and momentum, as rivers fed by new and larger tributaries on their way to the sea. It is very difficult for us to conceive the Infinite being as existing in a way of eternally stationary completeness, without associating some concern lest he be staled in the exactly full orbed perfectness of his knowledge and power. Thus the scholar, the clerk, the apprentice, who should have it forced upon him, that he is going never to take a new idea, never to acquire a more ready dexterity in his employment, never to advance upon himself, would be utterly crushed by the discovery. Of course it is in point to remember that the Eternal Wisdom wants no new ideas, because he has all that can ever be true already gathered in; fresher too in their oldness, than any that are newly arrived and not yet half apprehended can be. He wants no growth, because he is full grown already, and like truth itself, he never can be staled in ripeness because he is in beauty everlastingly fresh born. But since any such mental stock is impossible for us, what is it but our noble privilege, to advance upon ourselves, in a more phenomenal and transitional way?

Again, it is a very great advantage of our subject and created state, that it has a perfectly unknown future. I know it is not so regarded. It even chokes our patience, that we can not tear away this veil, or fly over this mountain. We worry ourselves in throes of curiosity and auguries of would-be divination, and break into bitter complaints, that we can not know what shall be on the morrow. But we must be infinite, by definition, to have all the future commanded by our knowledge, and that by supposition we can not be. Most happy for us too, it is. For if we could know things future by direct inspection, as God does, it would rob us of a great part of the satisfactions of our life, and reduce us to a condition of dullness and dryness quite insufferable. Now, as we have it, every moment is rolling up into knowledge out of the unknown, and to live is to discover. We are greater discoverers in fact than Columbus, discovering, each man, his own new world every day. The very zest of life as things are now is enterprise; that going upon a venture, which dares the unknown, to wrest victories from it. Hope is now the consummate flower of life; whereas if we had the future mapped distinctly out to our knowledge, we could hope for nothing. Now among all the felicities of God, there is to him no place for hope. It is the uncertainty also of life, as a future unknown, that constitutes the ever-pressing argument for faith, shoving us out upon the help that is invisible, and the good that is unseen—which faith-power is the grand sixth sense of life, outreaching all the other senses, and grasping worlds of reality that lie beyond their compass altogether. The Infinite being doubtless dwells in other felicities that are proper to his all-knowing state; but any such kind of knowledge of the future would plainly enough be a suffocating knowledge to us.

Again, we have relations to equals, and vast opportunities of happiness proper to such relations, which of course the Infinite being has not, because it is impossible for him to have equals. How much this means we can easily discover, if we note what kind of unsociety we suffer when we have about us only persons very unequal—too far above us, or too far below. These great inequalities it is that furnish picturesque opportunities of favor bestowed or benefit received, and so impart a high-toned relish to life; and yet our staple enjoyments come, for the most part, from such as are more nearly our equals, and there is a peculiar and most welcome flavor in such. The acts we perform and the sentiments we cherish towards such, are what they perform and cherish towards us. No immensely superior being among ourselves could give us any such common-level tributes of respect or approbation; and we could not easily aspire to render such to him. We are commonly jealous, too, of what we imagine to be patronizing airs. Or perhaps these high ones flatter us, to win our returning suffrages of applause. It is not as when old comrades in school, in suffering and labor, in shipwreck and battle, come to us in their unaffected, unexaggerated offices of friendship. On this plane of mortal equality, therefore, we have a whole set of principles, virtues, and felicities, that belong to our finite privilege, in a way that is exclusive; duties and deeds of courtesy, society, voluntary differences, hospitable customs, modes, manners, entertainments, generosities and ways of freedom, that have no fear of cringing, or desire of being cringed to, no thought of trespassing, or being trespassed on—all which belong to equals only, and become a virtue in them that is strictly their own. Thus it is the privilege of men, and a very great privilege, to know what equals think of them. God has no such privilege. It is even impossible for him to value what any but creatures vastly inferior, and comparatively low, can think of him, for there are no other. We have a certain value of some men's opinion, but God never valued the opinion of any body, unless it were to somehow mend it and make it more adequate. He may enjoy us certainly, and he does, but only as enjoying weakness to make it strong, or such as grope that he may give them light—much as we value the tottling of a child when we help it to walk.

Meantime it is another privilege related to this of having equals, that our finite range permits us to have superiors, and especially to have and enjoy one great superior, the Universal and Supreme Himself. Whereas He, whatever joy beside is allowed him, can never know what it is to look up to, rest in, or enjoy, any being greater than himself. As being infinite, he is shut up to the solitude of his own incomparable and immeasurably transcendent greatness. Therefore, some have been so much concerned for his felicity, as to be set on contriving how he gets society in the everlasting Three; supposing that to be even the necessary condition of his comfortable bestowment. But a trinity not viciously conceived makes God numerally one, not any such plurality, or congress in society. And even if it made him three co-equal Gods, it would not give him a superior. In that respect we still have our advantage. We are set thus everlastingly, in a most dear relation to one, who can be, and is, our Infinite Friend. His all-seeing eye keeps watch. His all-hearing ear listens. His all-governing power is regnant in us and about us. In him we have a grandly fortified state. We dwell among magnitudes and in masses that are centered in his will, as secure from injury by them, as if we had infinite power and wisdom in ourselves to manage them. We live, as it were, in dialogue with infinite greatness. Small in ourselves, we have contemplations, and contacts of it, that are putting us always in the sense of majesty and strength everlasting, and giving us an experience above our own measures. We are complemented, infinited, so to speak, in our Great Superior. The having such a superior is, in fact, our principal significance. Better not to have eyes and never to see the sun, than not to know this blessed relationality with Him. O what beauty, what ever-during freshness, what satisfying fullness, what depth and height of measure, does it give to our otherwise little affairs! Our sceneries have thus an overtowering summit, but the lowly valleys and green dales we live in are not the less gladdened by warmth, that they are sheltered by heights that look solitary and cold. It would of course be freezing cold to any one of us, to be shot up, in our littleness, into such solitudes of preëminence. But we must not allow the impression, that infinite being is of course unprivileged by reason of its own magnitudes; for God is not any so cold mountain peak of greatness in the world as we may think, but a sun of goodness rather, above all worlds, having heat in himself for his own everlasting comfort and ours besides. Only he can never have the peculiar kind of joy in us or any other, that we have in Him; because there is and can be no other high enough to command his admiration, or support his homage and trust.

At this point, again, we naturally pass to a notice of the great and even immeasurable advantage we have in being such as may fitly have our opportunity in worship. Here we go beyond the mere sense, or certified consciousness, of relationality just spoken of. We pass into act, and set ourselves adoringly before the object of worship. We regard, too, not so much his preëminent order and the natural greatness of his person, but we are occupied more with his holiness, and the beauty and majesty of his moral greatness. To worship is to find a joy in prostration before a being infinitely pure and perfect. It is to say and to sing "hallowed be thy name," and be hallowed by it ourselves. Brought up, as we are, under the blue heaven, symbolizing always the purity of God, and letting fall its image to waken correspondence in our feeling, we are trained, so to speak, for worship. I believe it is not commonly thought of, as being in itself a privilege to worship, but it is considered to be only a good much commended, because it comes along as a prescribed part of our duty in religion. On the contrary, as we are constituted, there is nothing to be thought of, or desired, or done, out of the most licentious liberty of choice, at all comparable to the exercise permitted and provided for, of worship itself. In it we rise highest, think the noblest things, burn with the divinest fires our nature can support. Even as we receive the highest, dearest, sentiments that visit our eyes, in the ranges of nature, making long journeys, and putting ourselves to undertakings most exhausting and perilous, just to get the privilege of wonder, and have the sense of beauty and sublime admiration stirred in our feeling. The joy we obtain thus is a kind of natural worship, paid to sceneries and sounds, to waterfalls and heaven-piercing mountains, and storms of the land, and storms of the sea, to wrath, and thunder, and power, and color, and beauty. In all which we discover, in a lower key and a comparatively feeble example, what joy we are made for, in having our finite mind exalted by the contemplations, and kindled by the glow of worship. And it is a joy of the finite and created only. The Infinite being has of course no right or possibility of worship; for there is nothing above him to move his homages, or set him in the beatitude of praise. The glorious Amen, the awful joy of worship, is permitted creature minds alone.

Not to multiply points of advantage in the finite, without limit, there is yet one other which is not strictly incidental, it may be, or necessary to, the relation of infinite and finite being, like the points already named, but is even instituted or appointed by God's will and counsel. It is referred to by the apostle himself, wonderingly and with praise, when he names the very impressive fact that our Creator has set us over the works of his hands. For it is most remarkable that finite creatures have it given them, on so vast a scale, to come in after Him and put their finishes on his works. Thus he becomes Creator and we sub-creators; Saviour, we sub-saviours. In almost every thing, finite being is set of course in a subaltern office, where nevertheless it is called to fulfill or complete what the infinite has begun. Thus God creates in the rough—land, sea, rivers, mountains, and wild forests. So far only does he make scenery, but he never creates a proper landscape. The rich fields, and gardens, and green meadows and lawns, the open vistas of ornament, the road-ways, bridges, cottages and cleanly dressed shores of water—all that constitutes the special beauty of the world, is something added, as finish, after the world is made; even as our first father was set to dress and keep the garden, and make a finer and more properly artistic scene of it. We look abroad over almost any landscape, and every thing we see, except the mere skeleton form, is from the finite creators who have taken up the rough work that was given them, to put their final touch upon it. So of all fruits, grains, animals of use; taken as being made, they were only wild, half-begotten, misbegotten creatures—apples that were crabs, wheat of a bitter wild-rice-looking kernel, horses of the mustang type, and size. Not even the flówers, lurking in the woods, could show much beauty till they were transplanted and taught what shape they might take in their kind, and into what colors they might blush. So again of government, the infinite of it is represented far back, in moral natures, simply configured to right, and then it is their finite action that is to build up codes of manners, duties, and rights; framing also states, and laws, and constitutions, and setting all the ranges of family care at work, as so many mills of discipline, to mold and model the manhood, that shall be, in the childhood that is. In like manner, mind, in its rough original, is but a ray of possibility from the infinite, which can never be intelligence, in fact, till it struggles forth itself, or is brought forth by some educating help from its kind. Here too laws are from the infinite, science from the finite—coming out after a long time, but always expected to come. So of all high culture, in thought and art, and language. What a magnificent temple is built in every great language.

Passing, last of all, to religion, or the christian form of it, what do we see, but that when it is done as to the making, it is yet to be finished by the propagation. It does not even propose the conversion of the world, save by men themselves. It must have its ministries in them; it must be reincarnated in the finite generations, age upon age, and theirs it must be, to live its divine beauty into the world, to preach, and sow, and cultivate, and suffer, if need be, till they have leavened all sin, by the love that is in them. And so it comes to pass universally, with how great honor, I might almost say deference, shown to creatures in the finite, that God, who is the infinite beauty Himself, wants to see it bloom in his children. Perhaps it could not be distinctly apprehended till they had given it their touch themselves.

But if there be so many advantages in our subject nature, and finite order of being, an objection will most likely be interposed, asking what of sin, or moral evil, and the liability under which it appears? Is it not the natural and all but necessary incident of our limited and progressive endowments. I have no time or space here to discuss so large a subject. It is in this fact referred to, as we can not but see, that our existence becomes a tragic affair, and are we not aware that all greatest movements, and highest exaltations, whether of action, or sentiment, are closest bound up with tragedy; yielding, in this manner, the tenderest and most thrilling delights. Even its woes are delights. Shall we not also come up out of our shame and sorrow, knowing good by the fiery scorch of evil, and have it better good because of evil? Have we no grand privilege, in this bitter and deep story? Of course we are not put into it as privilege, for, in some principal sense we put ourselves into it; but the very unmaking of it—what can it do but make us gods, climbing up out of it into God's plane, as not even the lying serpent imagined. One thing, at least, is clear, that our eternal Word can never know, as he has given us to know, what it is in so great mortal shame and hopelessness, to be visited by a superior nature's love, sorrowing tenderly about him, and dying into him, as it were, to rally him and win him back to life. That is a felicity most grand which never can be his!

It will probably occur to some of you, in the tracing of these illustrations and discovering in them what dear privilege there may be, in our subject form of being, that possibly we are to apprehend some secret reason herein of the incarnation, which is not often adverted to or conceived. Thus over and above what benefits of grace and salvation were proposed, it is not absurd to imagine some attractiveness felt in our subject conditions themselves. Just as some great hero, or apostle, now and then, will love in mere tenderness to become a little child among children, and have his part and place with them as an equal. Nothing is more evident from Christ's own word and way, than that he had great satisfaction in it. Did he not come for the joy set before him—set before him, not as in prospect, but as a table is set for a guest? Was it not confessedly his meat and drink, to be subject thus under the Father? Was he not tasting finite privilege in it? Was he not acting himself into the created, and harvesting in it the fruits of a sweet human obedience? In what deep welcome also did he receive the witness—"This is my beloved son in whom I am well pleased;" remembering just there, we may suppose, how a good, right *man* of the old time felt, when he had "the testimony that he pleased God." Not that any such humanized privilege was needful to him, but that he might magnify our finite lot, by letting the joy of it beam out through his sorrow, and so might give us a sufficiently dear, and really divine, opinion of it. And so praying that we might have his joy fulfilled in us, what did he mean, but that what he found himself, in our finite molds of good, we also might find? What honor therefore did he put on our human form of being, that he came into it in such ready humility, and went through it so gloriously himself. And what has he done for us more impressively, than by setting his own divine honors on all our duties and trials and even tears—tempted as we are, faithful as we should be, joyful as we may be. Is it then a low, dull life, that is given us? Do we long for higher ranges of experience? Do we disesteem the scale of our engagements? Far be it from us, since our own great Lord is with us, and every thing we look upon here is honored by his part with us in it. If we think it trivial and low to be finite, it was not so to him!

At the same time, while we dare to magnify our finite privilege in this manner, let it not be with offense. If we count it a great thing to be finite, and sometimes even a condition of privilege beyond what belongs to the infinite, we only take the honor and the good that are given us. There is no frothiness or conceit, in this boasting. No, we magnify humanity overmuch only when we praise it for a goodness it has not, or cover with vain words the sin it has; when we make it our gospel to have faith in the dignity of human nature, apart from any dignifying power of grace and salvation; when we puff ourselves up into magnitude, by recounting possibilities of greatness already trampled and lost, or dress ourselves in shows and draperies of virtue too thin to be soundly respected. None of these will at all advance the proper estimate of our quality. We rise highest, when we discover what grand privilege belongs to our finite range itself, and level ourselves up towards it in the recovery of what we have lost; when we settle into modesty, and set ourselves hopefully down to the honest sorrows of repentance; when we have it as our just ambition to be completely, perfectly finite, filling out the privilege of our creature being, in exactly the measures God has set for it. Then too we have gifts how many, and virtues how beautiful, and joys how blessed, that do not some of them belong even to Him—having no longer any good to hope, or desire, in the conceit of merits and virtues that do not anywise belong to us. This in fact is the real faith in man, though not exactly that of which we hear so much. It is that man can reach high enough in his repentances to be so full and great, and be drawn relationally so close to the All-Father, as to be complemented everlastingly in his nobler measures.

It ought also to be added in this connection, that our very subject should itself sufficiently humble us, to keep off any thought of pride for our humanity; for behold what revelation it makes of the sin of sin, showing us exactly what it is, and wherein its criminality lies; viz., in the refusal to be lovingly and justly finite. It refuses control, and will not have God to reign over it. It does not formally undertake to be infinite, for it would see the absurdity of that, but it does undertake, in the negative way, to be exactly that, in refusing to accept the conditions of a merely creature life. It shakes off allegiance, it is annoyed by commandments and claims of authority. To be controlled in duty, to be limited in opportunity, to be restricted in liberty, provokes irritation. It bolts, in fact, the finite state itself; calls it a chain, tears its law aside and breaks away. What could be more grand, or a higher appointment, than to fulfill just the true creation-measure of God, and be his created, such as he has meant and means us to be. Ah, we do not understand, my friends, what sin there is in this our sin—how perverse against reason it is, how unjust to God, who is only contriving in all he appoints for us, and all he requires of us, to bring us in, just where we shall be most truly and completely ourselves. Without being infinite, and plainly enough there can be only one that is, we can not even conceive a state more advantaged, than this in which we are set. In a great many points it has seeming advantage over even Supreme Being itself. And yet this horrible riot of our sin spurns all such advantage, refuses to be so exalted, and lets us down, below limitation itself, into woes of self-extirpation, such as we must suffer from the waste of our disorder, and the bitterly consuming pangs of our remorse. God forgive such madness. Still the really sad bent of our time, I grieve to say, is towards the denial of sin; we resolve it into circumstance, we call it a necessity, we even think it a good misnamed. In one way or another, we contrive to let down the guilt of it. I confess that when I draw out this conception of advantage in our finite order, I feel a more unspeakable horror of this wrong than I know how to express. It throws me back on those oft-derided words of Scripture, "the exceeding sinfulness of sin." After all, there is no so faithfully just and soundly significant testimony as that.

There is yet a particular point, on which this subject has been pressing from the first, and I can not fitly close without demanding for it your special attention; I speak now of the immense and really religious significance it gives to human education. It is in this fact of our being finite progressives, that we are educable; capable that is of being drawn out towards the infinite. Thus, in our human scale, we think one thought at a time; the infinite Father all thoughts at a time and forever. Our thought runs in successions, making only rills or rivulets of motion; his broader, vaster measure holds all thoughts in static equilibrium together, as an all-comprehending sea, towards which our rivulets run. We begin at some given date thinking our first thought, and going on thus, in our human curriculum, we try things, we discover, we deduce, we memorize; all which is finite operation; the infinite has none of it. But there is attainable and is to be, and that is what all education reaches after, a condition of correspondence, where every subject thought answers exactly to what is in the Supreme thought; even as David's, when he sang, "how precious are thy thoughts unto me, O God," or as Kepler's, when he sprang up in the fresh discovery of his problem and cried, "O God I think thy thoughts after thee!" So it is that all the truth we find is truth to God, and if we find any thing which is not truth to God, it is a lie. The same is to be said of moral opinions and principles; we find no law of righteousness which is not a law for all beings and worlds; for the finite, and as certainly too for the infinite. Science makes no true discovery save as it opens into some law, which is God's thought threading the creation.* Learning or literary culture approaches its true end only as it attains to ideas, inspirations, and modes of skilled composure that belong to the everlasting proprieties. All true education travels up thus towards the infinite reason, and the culmination of it is religion; other

* Written for Y. C. C., but not delivered.

culmination it has none, and without this it is altogether headless and chaotic.

How grand a thing then, in this view, is education, and withal if we could see it, a thing how nearly sacred. It is even a kind of church life in the temple of knowledge, whose inmost shrine contains the ark of God; and if it does not bring us finally to Him, the *cultus* operated by our study is but a kind of nonsense. To make a study of astronomy, without looking up, is not a whit more absurd. All knowledge that refuses to know the highest, and be ended off in the highest, is but a sham, a living in the bran that rejects the flour. We encounter also just here in this low feed of knowledge, and also in the non-improvement or misuse of educational advantages generally, the further, more appalling mischief of a stunting of our souls; in which we suffocate the very highest functions of our intelligent nature. Uncreated being, as we have seen, has no attribute or possibility of growth. Insensate things, such as rocks, and seas of water, do not grow. Animals and trees grow a little, for a little time, and come to their limit. But the grandest attribute of our created minds, one that belongs to no other finite creature whatever, is that they have the gift of a growth everlasting. A fact which makes it only the more dreadfully appalling, that they can so easily and also fatally shorten back this capacity, and give it a forever stunted force; for no really stunted creature, whether animal or plant, or mind, after a certain early period, which may be called its growing day, is over, is ever set back to its full growing rate again. Even the faithful scholar gets through growing size and staple force in a very few years, and, after that, only gathers in further contents without much enlargement of volume. And what an argument have we here for the faithful improvement of all opportunities; always and every where too for a sound self-discipline; for a nobly pure life; for a godly habit, and a vision purified and cleared by the grace of religion. For these helps of education rightly improved, propose as we have seen, a larger man, and to give him everlastingly enlarged consequence to himself; while the poor idler, the light-headed trifler, who rejects application, gadding always after pleasures and dissipations, goes forward into his future to be as insignificant there as here, as incapable of thought, as insipid and trivial as any growing creature that has lost its day, and stopped short in making volume, inevitably must be. To break out there, after his education day is over, and recover his lost volume, is as little to be expected as that any dwarf will grow up into a hero. O my friends there is no question for a finite creature, in his schooling day, like this—what shall my nature be worth, and what amount of being shall I carry with me, when I enter the great world before me? The old trivialities are now gone by, the nonsense hours are over, and now it only remains to be set down in such quantity of being and character, as are left—and what shall it be? His privilege was to make volume for himself; to be so far a voluntary re-creator of himself; for his education-right was to be summed up, not in his acquirements, but in his enlargements. Is he then to be a stunted child when his education day is over?—that is the question—or is he to be a MAN? Ah, my friends, that is what you will very soon have decided.

XVIII.

THE OUTSIDE SAINTS.

"Of a truth I perceive that God is no respecter of persons. But in every nation, he that feareth God and worketh righteousness is accepted with him."—*Acts* 10: 34–5.

THIS most grandly catholic platform of salvation, Peter the apostle derives partly from his vision of the sheet, and partly from the outside brotherhood which his vision of the sheet has prepared him to know and acknowledge; the brotherhood, I mean, of Cornelius. This man is a born Pagan, a military captain brought up doubtless in the superstitions of the Pantheon, who yet gives our apostle to see plainly that he is, in heart, a Christian—a Christian, that is, outside of Christianity. He has been largely known for a long time as a man of prayer, and a thoroughly devout character. He is also discovered and approved by God, before he is by Peter; for God even sends an angel to tell him —"thy prayers and thine alms are come up for a memorial before God." And as there is always something better coming, when a man gets heaven's indorsement in this manner, word is given him to send to Joppa after Peter, and receive from him a more competent knowledge of these things.

Peter then goes down to Cæsarea at his call, and becomes a guest with him in his house; where he hears the whole story of his faith, and learns apparently about as much from him, as he from Peter—brings out, or matures by his Pagan brother's help, the great banner-principle, from which I am now proposing to speak.

In it he corrects the superstition by which his own apostleship had been disfigured; viz., the Jewish notion of an exclusive right in Israel to the salvation of God; taking the broader doctrine of a salvation everywhere, and for every body who truly seeks God's light, or whom God's light effectually finds.

Have we no similar misconceptions that require to be corrected? When we assume, as we do, the inexcusable guiltiness, and the certain exclusion from God, of all idolaters, and all the born subjects of the false religions, as in fact we very often do, is not Peter's vision of the sheet as truly for us as for him? Neither does it signify any thing, in this matter, that we can cite so many denunciations of the Old Testament, to just this effect, against the idolaters; for these denunciations were not made to the idolaters—they never heard of them—but to the people of God, dwelling in God's own light, to deter them from lapsing into idolatry. So when we cite the declaration of the New Testament, that "there is no other name given under heaven among men, whereby we can be saved, but the name of Christ," do we not fall into just the same mistake, of not observing, that it is we who have heard of

Christ and known his gospel, that are put under this ban of exclusion, and not any Pagan people, who have never heard of him, or seen any light but what they have in a way more immediate? Nothing is more certain than that Peter's grand charter-principle forbids any and all such denouncements. If, in every nation, he that feareth God and worketh righteousness is accepted, how many may there be that never heard of Christ, and scarcely know God more sufficiently than as the unknown God, who yet are so far right with God, and so truly found of God, as to be fitly joined with us in the common hope of life. We hope from within the Bible and the church, and they from without, or on the outside of the same. They compose the church beyond the church, the unhistoric discipleship, sprinkled over the world in distant ages and realms of idolatry, who, without a gospel, have found a virtual gospel by their faith, and learned to walk in God's private light. That private light is truth unstated probably even by themselves, beginning at the feeling, more or less distinct, that there is some Father of all whose offspring they are, which unknown Father loves them, and has set them down here, in the grand trial of life, to feel after him and, if they may, to find him. They are such as have come into the way of holiness by invisible God-help, which God-help way of living is in fact a living by faith. Such examples may not be numerous, and yet they may be more numerous than we think. If they were only such as seek after God of their own motion, they might be very few, but since God is seeking after them—after all men everywhere—it should not be incredible that some are found by him, and folded in his fold, which they do not so much as know. A glance also at certain great first principles, particularly the three that follow, would induce the hope that many more than we commonly suspect, are thus harvested for the kingdom—

First. That God loves all men impartially, and is no respecter of persons; having the same desire to be loved by all, and be known as their Friend.

Second. That he is never afar off from any, but is close at hand, putting them always on seeking after him, in a desire to have them find him.

Third. That the Spirit of God is present, going through all minds, all over the world, moving them inwardly, in a way to kindle their yearnings, and draw their inclinings towards the inborn grace, that will be in turn his finding of them.

Do not imagine that, in stating these three particular premises, I am preparing to discuss the possibility of a salvation for the outsiders of the gospel. My object is different; viz., *to show how God finds access to such, or by what methods and means works their piety and engages them in a felt devotion to his friendship.*

The method I propose to adopt in this inquiry will perhaps not be expected. I shall not spread myself on nature and Providence, showing what truths of natural theology and practical discipline are set open there to all, and how the outside men have, to this extent, precisely the same revelation that is given to those of the inside. Neither do I propose, in looking after such examples, to range the general field of profane history, and draw out the characters, here and there, that appear to have a tinge of goodness and religious devotion. Making the most we can of such examples, there will yet be reason left for a good deal of doubt in regard to them all. I am going therefore into the Bible itself, to find our outside brethren; just where we so often assume that we are not of course to look for them. I do it because I shall have them here on a right orthodox footing of trust, and shall have nothing in fact to do but to consider them, in their supernatural relations, receiving their calls and private lessons, and finding how to know God in the unwritten bible of their own personal experience.

I begin with the case of Enoch. There was no written Scripture in his day, and probably no church. He appears to have lived a kind of solitary life, which is therefore called his walking with God. He was probably much derided by the men of his time, which made it the almost necessary comfort of his days to live "in the testimony that he pleased God." And this testimony was not any audible witness, but the witness of the Spirit, who came in at the open door of nature set open wider by his faith, till finally he became so permeated and leavened by the divine affinities, that he went up, and could not any more be found.

Noah appears to have been a character not less separated from his time. He was a preacher called to preach without a Bible—a preacher of righteousness, even as God taught him to be. But there were no ears to hear. Society itself was a godless and wild crew, given up to all kinds of wrong and violence, and lost, as it would seem, to even the distinctions of virtue. It does not appear that there was any single person, out of his own family, that knew any thing about God, or had any care for religion. And the oracle that found him, and that he himself had no skill of his own to find, improbable as it was, so verified itself as to put him on building his ark, amid the jeers of his people; for God by a process strangely mysterious, which he could only trust, and could not understand, was preparing him to be the new-stock father of a new and better age.

These two examples belong to an outside life, when there is no church. We come down next to Abraham, who stands at the fountain head, or on the frontier line. In him the church begins, and so far he is inside of it. And yet he is prepared, in all important respects, by a previous outside training. He had no written revelation, and had seen no organized form of religion. But he came out of the east, a profoundly religious and nobly just character, so far opened to God's Spirit, by his acquaintance with God, that he could receive a life-call at first hand, and take the necessary guidance in that call. It finds him at Haran, far back in the plains of Syria, and going forth in it, he begins the church history. Under what kind of training, uniting what kind of advantages, he had been brought up, in the far east, we do not know; but it afterwards appears, when he sends his servant back to the east country, to obtain a wife for his son, that all his relations there are, in some sense, religious people. Thus when Abraham's servant arrives, he is welcomed in the name of Jehovah, and in some, at least, of the proprieties of religion. Still there was a mixture of idolatrous corruption that largely infected their Jehovah worship. Thus when Rachel came away, a generation later, pursued by Laban to recover the lost gods of his religion, it appears that she had hidden among her effects certain little idols, or amulets, called teraphim, that were much in vogue, at least, among the women. And the coarseness of Laban, as also the petty thieving of the gods by his daughter, indicate the general style and merit of their religion. But how grandly marches out Abraham into his call, clearing forever all such trumperies of idolatry, and growing into such high intimacy with God, that a pure divine religion crystallizes, and begins to be organic in his life. He knows nothing of piety by definition, or intellectual dissection. He has never read Edwards on the Affections, and knows not how to square his life by distinctions of motive; has no tests of regeneration, practices self-abnegation artlessly, without analysis, or even asking what it is. But God has him in training, and knows exactly by what lessons to bring him on, as we see in the story of his sacrifice. The problem here is to teach what is yet unformed in thought, by what is done as in act. The two great elements of obedience and trust are set in, as by a tragic practice. He is held in deep maze all the while as he goes on, emerging at last and brightening out in the discovery, that what God is most exactingly demanding, he is always providing himself a lamb to supply. It makes no great difference whether we conceive this lesson by action, to be given outside of the church or in it; for it could have been there and is wanted here. It is alphabetic, any way, and the book is to come after the alphabet is made.

Having given us five books of scripture, Moses will naturally be put down as a scripture character. He was born moreover of the Jewish stock. And yet, as he was a foundling, picked up in the flags of the Nile, and carried directly into the Egyptian court, to be brought up as the son of Pharaoh's daughter—nursed meantime for only a little while by his own Jewish mother—and largely separated afterward from his race, scarcely knowing more, it would seem, than the fact of his mere blood connection; as he was entered directly into the Egyptian schools, and applied himself with such enthusiasm as to master all the learning of the Egyptians, who at that time were the foremost of all peoples, especially in science; and as we find him afterwards building a close commonwealth, that is not in any sense Abrahamic, or pastoral, but territorial, and legal, and penal, set off in orders and tiers, both priestly and civil, and having incorporate in its laws all the Egyptian therapeutics, and partly their notions of clean and unclean food—having all these facts to be digested, our minds preponderate in the conviction that he is to be conceived, up to early manhood, as a properly Egyptian character. But the fact of his Jewish origin had reached him, and by force of that he broke out in the naturally explosive heat of his youth, to be the avenger of a much abused kinsman of his people. From that moment he was launched in his mission, as yet even to himself unknown, and being obliged to flee for his life, he is taken far away to the region back of Horeb, where God has him forty years in training, to get him qualified in the matter of a religion. There also it is that afterward, Jethro, his father-in-law, a priest of Midian, intervenes to be his teacher and counselor, and Jethro is a wholly outside man, grandly religious and nobly just, able also to help him in his religious development. He also comes back to him after the exode, with his nobly paternal and statesmanlike advice, sketching for him—Midian for Israel—a complete and masterly outline of his whole civil service plan. So that, on the whole, we are led to look on Moses as a virtual outsider himself, down to the time of his call in the burning bush. His religion, as we can see, is mainly by God's immediate light, getting apparently no help below, save from a man whose religious traditions, if he has any, are as far out of all historic connection as his own.

A strangely curious episode challenges our attention next, in the case of Balaam, the eastern soothsayer.

This man is a great problem, any way, and specially in his religious inspirations. The sharpness, and beauty, and truly evangelic richness of his oracles, are really inimitable. There is nothing finer in the Scripture, or at all more vigorously self-evidencing. Nor is it any objection that divination was forbidden, about this time, by Moses, and declared to be an abomination to the Lord; for it had not been forbidden to Balaam and the Mesopotamians. And therefore it was only natural, perhaps, that he should mix, or be supposed to mix enchantments with his oracles—just as our astrologists and alchemists sought religious light with mixtures of incantation. He was certainly faithful to his convictions, against all the blandishments employed to win his consent. On the whole, I think this man would be acknowledged universally, in his truly weird story and character, as a man profoundly enlightened by God's secret revelations, if it were not for the very harsh strictures put upon him afterwards, by the perhaps unjust prejudice of the Jews.

In the book and character of Job we have another and more grand episode, so to speak, in the historic train of the Bible. Job is not a Jew; the book is clearly not a Jewish book; for there are, in fact, no Jewish references or allusions in it. The world of thought which it opens is a new, unjewish, outside world. The piety is real and profound, but unhistorical, out of all connection with the Bible history. The argument is a matter by itself, supposing a debate with opinions not Jewish. And thus you have one of the most remarkable books of the Scripture—a book that reveals the clearest evidences of inspiration, and presents the highest summits of sublimity in thought and diction, which is, in fact, the book of an outsider; some prince of the Land of Uz, some Arabian or Mesopotamian poet, some Persian or Babylonish teacher, wrestling with the great themes of God and human life, in the uncovenanted mercies of an alien, framing thus a theodice or vindication of God, for all the after ages of the world and the church.

At a later period we have the example of Cyrus, one of the most remarkable and best characters of the ancient history, a great commander and conqueror, a great statesman, according to Xenophon a great benefactor to his people, humane and just, and withal a protector and firm friend of the people of God. He it was that gave the decree to Ezra, providing him with funds and forces to go back and build the temple of his religion, saying—"the God of Israel he is God." And the reason of his conduct is given by the prophet, who declares that God unseen has holden his right hand, raised him up in righteousness, and directed all his ways. He was a monotheist in his religion, as all the Persians were, and was therefore conscious of no change in the favor he showed to the people of God; but the prophet declares that God has all the while been visiting him unseen, and tempering him to his own high counsel—"I have called thee by thy name, I have surnamed thee though thou hast not known me." And it is a great felicity in this example that the unseen access and visitation of God are so grandly affirmed in it. What better footing of original, first-hand discovery could be desired.

At the very opening of the New Testament we encounter the Magi, religiously related, in a sense, to Cyrus. They were priests of the Medo-Persian religion; astrologers living among the stars, and watching there, to spell God's oracle, in the changing motions. And many of them too became so raised and spiritualized in habit, as to be not unfitly honored by the guidance of a star, and led in to offer the world's first tribute of worship to the new-born Messiah.

The Syrophenician woman, whose faith the Saviour so heartily commended, was a Pagan-born woman probably, and by some heavenly guidance, not unlikely, went to Christ for help.

The case of Cornelius we have traced already. That of the centurion was like it. And in deliberate comparison of his character with that of his own countrymen, Christ says—"Verily I say unto you, I have not found so great faith, no, not in Israel." And he can not stop there—"I say unto you that many shall come from the east and from the west, and from the north and from the south—all these from the outside—and shall sit down with Abraham, and Isaac, and Jacob, in the kingdom of heaven. But the children of the kingdom shall be cast out into outer darkness."

I might also turn off here and gather in a roll of names from classic story; such as Numa, Marcus Antoninus, Plotinus, Plato, and his master Socrates; the list fully given would be a long one, and I have no room left me to sketch the persons, or verify them as men whom God has called to be partakers in his private light. I can only say that the Greek and Roman literature, still preserved to us as that of most Pagan peoples is not, allows us to look directly into the working of the religious nature, in multitudes of serious, thoughtful men outside of revelation, and to see just where they are—their notions of God and the better notions they are struggling after, their half-discoveries, their expressed longings after a revelation, their sighs, suspirations and prayers, their belief in dreams and lying down for dreams, their gropings or almost findings, their premonitions, their sturdy argumentations, their trances of contemplation. Instead of finding them quite dead to such themes, it is as if their religious nature were packed full of questions, and the Spirit of God were just about to burst open their prison and let them out into the day. They even go long journeys, hoping to find perchance some one who can tell them what they want to know. Their own yearnings sometimes put them in a state in which they lay hold of Christ, at the very first discovery, even as a starving man of bread. Thus it is that multitudes of souls without a Bible, are turning Godward here and there, as being inwardly sought after by God. Even as Paul says to the Athenians—"though he be not far from every one of us; for in Him we live, and move, and have our being—for we are also his offspring."

If accordingly we go apart still further from the region of mental life and culture, among the savage tribes, for example, of our own North American continent, we shall find many traditions that seem almost to have the sanctity of a revelation; and now and then a character appears springing up as a strange solitary flower in the wilderness, and assuming all the most remarkable distinctions of a genuine piety—as for example in the wild Indian disciple of Brainard; a man who lived apart, as it were, from his time and people, coming out among them now and then as a kind of saint, to restrain their murderous passions, or call them away from the ruinous vice of drink; and when he could not prevail, running off into the woods in tears of grief which he could not restrain. "Ah, there must be some one," he would say, "who thinks like me; where shall I find him?" So also there came to light not long ago in the wilds of Africa, a woman who had been praying many years to some Power Unknown, and who, as soon as the story of Jesus was given her, exclaimed—"O that is he, the same that I have found, and now have always with me." And what should be more credible than just such visitations, occurring here and there among peoples most unfavored? If God is a being whom we need to know and naturally yearn after, and if he wants to bestow himself on us, why should we wonder that he sometimes finds a way through even incapacity itself, bringing his unchurchly help and sympathy to the miserably forlorn one in his outcast lot?

I will not pursue this exposition farther. I have undertaken to show you what God is doing and can do, for the outsiders of his Bible and church. And to make the exposition more convincing, I have taken my examples almost wholly from the part such outside men have had in the Bible story itself. God has had his witnesses, you now see, in every age of the world, apart from all connection with his covenant, and the organic institutions of his grace in the earth; men that have been visited and called by him in the solitudes of nature, and there have burned as the silent, separated lights of their times.

It now remains to say that, in tracing this subject, I have had deliberate respect altogether to uses needed by ourselves, in our inside field of gospel truth and privilege. My object has not been, to answer the perhaps merely curious question, what possibilities are given to idolaters and heathens, but to gain a position of discovery in regard to the Bible itself—how it came, how to use it, what to get under it, and do for it; what need of it, in a word, the inside people have, and how they are to get their best advantage from it.

First of all, then, we are not to judge that the mere possibility of a revelation outside of the Bible supersedes the want of it. That was not the opinion of God when he sent his angel, even by miracle, to Cornelius, to put him in the way of an apostle, who should teach him Christ and baptize him in the faith of a disciple. The souls most enlightened too by culture have been most apt to sigh for authorized teachers and appointed rites, and a veritable revelation. Having gleams of insight, and almost visions of God, they wanted it the more. They sighed, and waited, and even groaned for it, knocking piteously at the gate they knew not how to open. And such as neither sighed, nor groaned, nor cared, only wanted it the more. Christ not wanted! the Bible not wanted! just as well to be without a revelation! What could show more affectingly the insupportable destitution of such a state, than the gropings and only casual findings of its hungry millions? Doubtless there is a possible salvation for all men without a revelation—I verily believe there is—but a naked possibility is alas! how slender a footing, where the interest and peril are so great.

Then again, secondly, having reached this conclusion as regards the immense want of a revelation, and of Christ as a Saviour, let no one turn the blame upon God, that what is so much wanted everywhere, is not everywhere given. Doubtless God might rain showers of Bibles, just as he does the showers of rain all over the lands and even seas of the world, but he must also rain written languages too, and a power to read them, beside. And then the readers, if they were read, would want to know how the book grew to be a book, the revelation how revealed. And there was no way but to begin, here and there, with natures most open, most susceptible, gathering in their several seeings and testimonies, and bodying for holy truth the word they have received. If a Bible could be gotten up mechanically, as showers are gotten up in the chambers of the sky, it might be justly concluded that all men ought to have it. But it has first to be incarnated, so to speak, and wrought into humanity, much as Christ was, and so revealed through humanity; for the fact is that all such kind of truths must be enunciated in persons; even as the truths of astronomy require to be enunciated in orbs and orbits. And then, forever after, the truth has to be lived over and acted out, by a kind of reincarnation in good men's lives, in order to have its meaning. There must be a ministry of love and character going with it; graces to shine, patience to suffer, sacrifices, labors, prayers, ordinances and rites of worship, and assemblies kindled by their glow, else the book is dead, or too nearly so, both for want of meaning and of evidence. And so you perceive that Bibles could not be made faster than men are good enough to have revelations made through them; and could not be multiplied or disseminated faster or farther than the graces of love and sacrifice, and the patiently enduring and bravely daring enterprises are quickened, that shall carry them abroad and preach them. Bibles therefore can not outgrow or outrun the church. And God is not to blame for this. However much they are wanted, they can not, in the nature of things, out-travel the grace they nourish. If it takes a million of years to get them published in this way everywhere, then it must take a million of years. Enough that Christ began to speed them on, at once, by his word, saying—"Behold the fields already white to the harvest." And again that he gave it for his parting charge—"Go ye into all the world and preach the gospel to every creature." Long ages ago, God was ready, going before his people, wanting to be revealed in every soul's knowledge. O ye long-delaying ages, linger no more. Gird us with salvation, Lord, for the dear Bible's sake, that we may give it speedily to every hungry, darkened soul on earth!

But here another and third lesson meets us; viz., that we are not to push the dissemination of this gospel by any false argument that dishonors God. Tell us not that every idolater, every man ignorant of Christ must perish—does everlastingly perish. Why should we push ourselves to this work of gospeling the world, by putting it on God, that he has given no possibility of life to so many millions of immortal creatures, reserving them all unto wrath, just because they were born into a lot of darkness? Rather let us tell what God is doing always for them, how nigh he is to them, how tenderly he works in them, what possibilities he opens for them, and how certainly he sometimes gains them to his love. Let it be enough that their disadvantages are so great; that they are humbled to a point so low by their idols, rotted into falsehood, buried in lust and shame, made crafty, perfidious, cruel and wretched in society; not finding how to interpret their own longings in religion, when such longings rise, or to climb up out of the thraldom in which they lie. Then, as we are so gloriously privileged, what shall we do but give them our privilege, and have it as argument enough that if we do it not, we show how very little our privilege has done for us.

Meantime, fourthly, let us have it as one of our most sacred duties to the Bible, not to use it, so as to shut ourselves and all that have it, away from God's immediate revelation by it. The external, verbal revelation is not given to be a substitute for the internal and immediate, but to be a guide into that. We are to find God after all by an immediate knowledge ourselves, just as all the outside saints have found him, only with an immense help in the Bible, which they had not. We are not to know God simply as reading the book, and getting notions or distillations of dogma and catechism from it in our head, living thus on a mere second-hand knowledge. That is making a fence of the book, requiring us to get all light from it, and not from God. No, the Bible is received only when it is spiritually discerned; that is when it brings us in where God is, to know him by our faith and love, and have him in a first-hand knowledge, even as Abraham had, or Job, or Jethro, or Cornelius. And then when the unbelievers about us complain that God is so far off, wondering why he does not show himself to his children, if he exists, by signs and wonders that can not be doubted, we shall not have made their difficulty just what it is ourselves, by setting up the Bible as the sum and last limit of knowledge, and not as a helper to find it. If we desire to know Boston, the map of the way will not show it, but will only take us thither, and let us get the knowledge for ourselves. The Bible in like manner tells us how others found Him, that we may find Him also. We do not know God in simply knowing their work. We only know him by an immediate knowledge, even as they did. If we use the book only for the notions, or the second-hand knowledge it gives us, we even make a barrier of it, and put God further away. The right use of it will not give us notions about God, but God himself. It will make God nigh, and make it felt that he is nigh, both to ourselves and to others, present to knowledge, pressing into knowledge in all human breasts.

It is a most sad thing, my friends, that many of you, not in the way of religion, so little conceive the nearness of God to you. You know the Bible, and what may be known about God as reported in it, still nothing appears to be concluded; you are not established in any thing, but filled with questions only, and put groping. The Bible, after all, leaves God a practically hidden subject, and you turn away from it, wondering still where God is, and why he does not somehow show himself. Little do you conceive how very nigh he is, and how he is pressing in, through the Bible, through nature, everywhere and always, to be known by you, and by every human creature in the world. It is with you here and with all men, as it is with certain valleys in our great country, where the soil is underlaid with vast stores of water, pressing upward to get vent, and the people have nothing required to set fountains spouting at their doors, but simply to bore a passage through the crust of earth, and let the waters up. Just so all created mind is underlaid with the knowledge of God, having oracles set in its secret depths, so that whosoever will let the everlasting love and presence force itself in, or up, will have an immediate and pure, an original and free knowledge: a living water that will freshen its life, and slake its thirst forever. He gives you his revelation without, only that he may be thus revealed within. He loves to be known, publishes himself in all things visible, speaks in all things audible, fills all height and depth with his presence, besets you behind and before by his counsel, and there is no soul living that he does not breathe in by his Spirit. All souls are his children, yours among the number. As he came to Job, and Cyrus, and Cornelius, so he will to you, if only you are sufficiently opened to him by your prayers and alms, and works of faith to let him in. Having one revelation of Christ in your hand, you will have another in your heart. You will grow into a full, original, clear beholding, not needing that any man teach you, having that anointing that teacheth all things. This is your privilege—would that you could see it—in this light of God to live, and in its ever brightening splendor to die.

In closing this subject let us not forget to cast a

glance forward to the future life, in which all righteous souls are to be gathered. Many of them will belong to the class of inside saints, some to the class of outside saints; the former will have known Christ all their lives long, and been fashioned by his new creating gospel and character; the latter will now meet him perhaps for the first time, and will salute him in blissful discovery, as the unknown friend they had always with them, and the conscious helper of their life. When therefore, my brethren, you lift your song of praise to the Lamb, some of these will be able to tell you more of his worth, it may be, by their want of him, and their struggles after God without him, than you by all you have gotten from him. To meet and commune with these outside saints, outside no longer—how blessed will it be? And what a beautiful variety will they give to the general brotherhood! They are brothers whom you did not know, but you embrace them even the more tenderly, and hold them in the dearest honor. Thus grandly now is the Master's word fulfilled—"Other sheep I have which are not of this fold; them also I must bring, and they shall hear my voice, and there shall be one fold and one shepherd."

XIX.

FREE TO AMUSEMENTS, AND TOO FREE TO WANT THEM.

"If any of them that believe not bid you to a feast, and ye be disposed to go, whatever is set before you eat, asking no question for conscience' sake."—1 *Cor.* 10: 27.

THESE feasts to which the Corinthian disciples are invited, are sometimes rated by the apostle himself as "banquetings and abominable idolatries." Though probably the feasts thus designated were the great religious festivals, which were often mere orgies of lust—celebrated of course, not by invitation, but at times of stated recurrence. The feasts to which he is referring here appear to be only ordinary entertainments or feasts of invitation; though even at these the guest will not seldom encounter many disgusting excesses and laxities of behavior—a fact which even makes it somewhat remarkable, that a disciplinarian as positive and faithful as our great apostle, does not forbid the acceptance of such invitations.

I discover two points included in the advice he gives, neither of which stands out on the face of his words, but they only need to be named to be distinctly seen. The first is that down upon the low plane of mere ethical observance, he does not think it incumbent on him, as a teacher of the gospel, to enforce any Puritanically close terms of restrictive morality. It is not for him to legislate over such questions. In this field the disciples must have their own liberty, and be responsible for their own judgments and the right understanding of their own liabilities. So far the world's law is also theirs, and he will not undertake at all to settle the casuistries occurring under it. And to set them on a yet manlier footing of liberty, he shoves restriction still further away by telling them, when they accept such an invitation, to go with a free mind, hampered by no foolish scruples that will make them an annoyance, both to the host and the company.

So far then he sets them free—free that is in the exercise of their own responsible judgment, clear of any mere scruples not intelligent. But we have scarcely noted the position given them under this liberty, when we begin to see that he is thinking of a second, higher kind of liberty for them, which, in his own view, makes the other quite insignificant. Thus he drops in, as it were in undertone, at the middle of his sentence, this very brief but very significant clause—"and ye be disposed to go"—putting, I conceive, a partly sad cadence in his words, as if saying inwardly, I trust not many will be so disposed; for the dear love of God, in the glorious liberty of our discipleship, ought to be a liberty too full, and sweet, and positive, and blessed, to allow any such hankering after questionable pleasures and light-minded gaieties.

In that we are free, and in this more free; too free to want the other kind of freedom, or care anything for it. Which distinction thus developed I now propose to use, in its application to another, but not very different subject; viz., *the true law and right use of amusements.* I think we can see that the apostle would speak on this question, precisely as he does of mingling in the entertainments and festivities of the unbelievers. Indeed the two matters are too nearly one to be easily distinguished in their reasons and governing principles. Entertainments are amusements, and amusements entertainments. We begin then—

I. *At the free;* taking up the question of amusements as a question of ethics, or common morality; which, in all the discussions I have seen, is taken to cover the whole ground of the subject; as if it were the only matter to settle our opinion of what is right under the world's law—what is proper, becoming, and safe. And here it is that the apostle begins, though he has other and higher points to raise, we shall see, in a different key. In this view, or in this plane of ethics, it is not to be judged a sin, he says, if you go to the entertainments where you are invited. It may be, or it may not, and of that you must every man judge for yourselves, in your own freedom, at your own responsibility. If you want the exhilaration, there is nothing morally wrong in exhilaration. If you want the festive play, such play is forbidden by no common principle of life. But it is incumbent on you, if you go, that you go to be one with the company. To go half condemning yourself in what you allow, to go packed full of little timid scruples, abstaining, questioning, and making yourself an annoyance to the company, is even a christian impropriety or absurdity planned for beforehand. Undertaking to enjoy the occasion you must not churlishly mar the enjoyment, by looking askance and timidly on every thing done. You must not be asking whether this thing or that, which is innocent in itself, has been flavored by some form of incantation; whether this or that article of food has been seasoned from a cup partly offered in libation. Be not there as a man tied up in scruples, but as a man rather who is free, and knows how to enjoy the innocent hilarities of the occasion. If you speak of duty, this is your duty, else it was your duty not to be there. You are not there to be higgling at questions of casuistry about things innocent in themselves.

Taking now this ground, we have a broad, just, platform charter for all manner of amusements not licentious, or corrupt, or indulged beyond the limits of temperate use. And it would be well if certain over-rigid disciples, and teachers of religion, much honored in the former times, had been able to allow and justify this kind of freedom. Such were always asking questions for conscience' sake, about things that are really innocent in every thing but abuse or excess; and gave in this manner an air of austerity to religion that was only forbidding and repulsive; creating reactions also for infidelity or the total rejection of religion itself, that have been growing more and more detrimental in their effect. Happily some of our most forward and capable teachers now are pressing a revision of the whole matter, and cutting loose detentions of scruple, in reference to a great part of the amusements that in times past were put in embargo. They take up the question of amusements as a question of morality, and bring out their decisions in the plane of ethical adjustment. And the general conclusion is that of the apostle—be free, only be responsible for all excesses and abuses. Do not reduce religion to the grade of a police arrangement, and make it a law of restriction upon the world's innocent pleasures. It can not afford to hold a position so odious, and withal so nearly false; for there is no sound principle of ethics that makes it a wrong, or a sin, to indulge in plays and games of amusement, save when they are carried beyond amusement, and made instruments of vice, or vicious indulgence; when of course they are wrong, even as feeding itself may be. Why strain a principle of restriction till it breaks, and lets out the waters of sin to sweep it clean away, and all sound virtue with it? Draw out terms of detention just where detention is wanted, and not a long way back, to make sure of allowing no possible danger. Why, there is danger in food—must we therefore keep it off by starvation, or must we set limits on it by the right use of our liberty?

There is, I grant, no kind of amusement that may not be the beginning of some vicious excess. But if we are to cut off every thing which has a danger in it, and may easily run itself into excess, we shall have almost nothing left. There is a possible intemperance even in the use of water. Dress has this danger. Study has it. There is no kind of business that may not easily rush itself into some infatuation, or finally some course of fraud that blasts the character. Political life—who that goes into it, with however good intentions, does not put himself in fearfully critical momentum towards bad associations, and selfish combinations that are corrupt? Even religion may hurry itself into excesses of fanaticism, that rapidly burn out character. Every thing in short requires self-regulative prudence. Innocent in itself, it can be, and very often is, a gate that opens towards excess. The true thing to be said is—all these things are free. Refuse them not, but have a guard against their perils. We can not refuse every thing that has perils in it, for then we should stand back from every thing. Take amusements under the same law; not to be mastered by them, but to master them, and be just so much further advanced in all high manly virtues

Sometimes a distinction is attempted between recretions and amusements. But as all recreations are in some sense amusements, and all amusements recreative in the same manner, the distinction is of no great value. The distinction between athletic sports and amusements holds good partially, because of the gymnastic effects obtained by one, and not by the other. Boating, fishing, hunting, bowling, base ball, and the like, have a certain value as modes of athletic exercise, and yet there is not one of them that may not be connected with gaming or some other kind of license. Let every man have his liberty in them, detained by no foolish and weak scruples, and then let him be responsible to himself, for such kind of practice in them as belongs to a pure, well kept life. Let him not be afraid to enjoy himself in them, or be tormented by foolish misgivings, as if it must be wrong to have such pleasures. Ask no questions for conscience' sake till the confines of just use are reached.

The same is to be said of dancing. If there be lewd dances, whether round or square, as we certainly know there are, these are for nobody. Masquerade balls are contrived possibilities of license, and belong to high society only when it runs low. Late hours of dancing, in crowded assemblies, heated by exhilarating bowls, are both morally and physically bad, and the true discretion is to avoid what takes away discretion. But dancing itself is beautiful movement, and may well be a recreation wholly innocent and pure. Music is the chime of motion, and motion in the beat of music touches a fine, deep law of the creation. And if there be exhilaration in it, why should there not be, when the rhythm of the world prepares it?

Billiards have been largely connected, and now are, with the vices of drink and gambling. The public tables of cities are commonly infested by this danger. But as private tables multiply, the perils of the game are much less felt, and many are inquiring whether any other indoor amusement can be found that is less exceptionable in itself, or has more to commend it. Men and women and invalids can have the game together, and it is not in any sense a game of chance. It provides a mild, gently athletic exercise. It trains an exact eye, and an exact hand, and a close computation of the combinations of causes, all of which are gifts of great value. It is only a little more fascinating than it should be, and is likely to occupy time that should be given to other things. The same too may be said less emphatically of croquet, which is only a kind of out-door billiards. It has, too, just as little inherent connection with gaming. Must we add that when billiards are practiced at public tables, and the defeated party takes the expense by forfeit, with perhaps another forfeit in cigars and wine, there is a double peril incurred, both of gaming and of a drinking habit. All such dangers are factitious as regards the play itself, and will less and less appear when it is an accepted pastime, and is set in its proper place.

Games of chance, like cards, and dominoes, and backgammon, have a certain recreative value, but no value as exercise. They are objected to by many because they are games of chance; and, to a certain extent, with reason; for if any young person gets absorbed in that kind of game, so far as to have the habit of his mind cast by it, he is just so far incapacitated for the wise conduct of life. Who can be weaker or more nearly a fool, than a man who goes into life looking for luck in every thing, expecting to get on by luck and seeing really no other hope. Still there is a certain diversion in seeing, for an hour, how chances go, and even a kind of instruction beside; for a great many things in the world are turned, as far as our human perception goes, by what to us are chances. The sound rule here appears to be, that no one should be so much in these weaker games, as to be addled by them, and forget that carving out his way by stout endeavor, and a keen perceptive judgment of causes, is the true manly wisdom. He may play with chances enough to see how they go, but if he worships them as a devotee, and lives in their thin atmosphere, he will be as nearly nobody as he can be and be a man. Sometimes it is urged for these lighter games that they make society. Rather say substitute society; for that is their worst objection. To shuffle, and cut, and deal, and throw the dice, are exactly not society, but when over indulged are just the way to keep it off, and make an empty-headed play of the fingers, the only accomplishment learned or possible to be enjoyed. Conversation, humor, social and intellectual vivacity, get no place to grow at these tables, where the parties wink and do not speak, and where the glow is kindled by the chances; not by the souls engaged.

The opera is a kind of amusement that is furnished by one of the finest of the fine arts. It is music floating in sentiment, or sentiment dramatized in music. It is very nearly as good as a good concert, and scarcely more objectionable—only it can be, and sometimes is, a great deal worse. Be it as it may, a man who finds no atmosphere but this to live in, no food but this soft luxury to enjoy, will turn out finally to be a man wholly steeped in sentimentalities, having no great purposes and manly energies left.

The theater is or ought to be the most robust of all amusements not athletic, but in its common associations, it is worst and really lowest of all. To take it in this day and find amusement in it requires a man some way down the scale of pure sensibility already; otherwise the atmosphere will have a smell of disgust. Were a true redemption possible, it might teach great lessons of virtue and character, and be even more and better than amusement. If sometime a man asserts his liberty in going, he will yet much better keep his liberty in staying away.

So far we go in tracing the right of amusements viewed in the plane of morality, or moral casuistry. Considering the question on its mere ethical grounds, we find no law against amusements, but only against their excesses and abuses. As Paul said to the Corinthians so we say, be free; make up no mere scheme of legal, self-restrictive, or ascetic virtue. Ask no questions for conscience' sake, such as badger and worry the soul's liberty. Christianity is no dog Cerberus barking at the gates of festivity, and galling the neck of all innocent pleasures. Least of all does it contrive to force a new chapter into the code of morals, that was not in it before, and can not be maintained by its accepted principles.

If now some of you should be surprised and alarmed,

by the exposition thus far made,—the same which is now being offered by many, as a complete exposition of the whole subject—there is yet another and very different exposition to be added, which is even the distinctly christian part of it. As we have asserted the free, so we now go on—

II. To assert *the more free.* Thus the apostle, when he slides in his subjunctive clause—" and ye be disposed to go"—does it, we may see, regretfully and with a feeling sadly overcast. He understands that many of the best beloved, godliest, and freest of the brotherhood will not be disposed to go, could not in fact be so disposed. They are in so great liberty that their inclination itself is quite taken away, and he wishes, how tenderly, it were so with all—as alas, he knows it is not. Did he want himself to go to those feasts of the unbelievers? Could he think with desire of having a good time there and being greatly refreshed by the hilarities of the guests? And why not? We can not imagine such a thing, and why not? Because his great and gloriously Christed soul is too full, and ranging in a plane of joy too high, to think of finding a pleasure in such trifling gaieties. They are chaff, only chaff, to him. So when he says—" and ye be disposed to go," he well understands that there are some who will not be disposed. Kept back by no ascetic scruples, or legal restrictions binding their consciences, they will be kept back by their very fullness and freedom and the uplifting sense of Christ which ennobles their life. They are free in a sense to do it, but they are also more free, too free to have any disposition that way. Their tastes are too high, their inclinations too transcendently pure, and the gale of the spirit raises them into a divine liberty that is itself the crowning state of life. The mere hilarities of feasting are too coarse and tumultuous to suit the key of their feeling, and will only be disturbances of their peace. They are able to come down now and then it may be, and touch the plane of nature in ways of playfulness; but it will not be to launch themselves on tides of high excitement, and be floated clean away, but only to freshen a little the natural zest of things, and keep off the moroseness of a too rigid and total separation from the socialities and playtimes of the world.

Our question of amusements then appears to be very nearly settled by the tenor of the distinctively christian life itself. The christian in so far as he is a christian, is not down upon the footing of a mere ethical practice, asking what he may do, and what he is restricted from doing, under the legal sanctions of morality. That kind of motivity is very much gone by. He has come out even from under the ten commandments—mostly negative and restrictive—into the love-law which unites him to God and his neighbor. And here, out of his mere liberty in love, he will do more and better things than all codes of ethics and moral law commandments require of him. He is so united to God himself, through Christ and the Spirit, that he has all duty in him by a free inspiration. For where the spirit of the Lord is, there is liberty. He acts now from the full, not from the empty; having inclinations outrunning mere duties, and doing all things, so to speak, by the overplus of joy. He is not shriveled in scruple, but full-orbed in love; and if he asks, at all, what is duty to be done, it is not what is duty by the moral code, under its legal motivities, but only what is due to the supreme affection that has united him to God and His Son. So that when you come to him offering some kind of amusement, he does not fall back straightway on his conscience, asking whether he may have it, or trying whether he can tease the reluctant monitor into acquiescence,—he does nothing in that way of legal exaction—but he says more likely to the offered amusement, "No, I do not want it;" or, in the apostle's word, "I am not disposed" that way. And this he does without debate of privilege, and without any argument of constraint; he must even constrain himself not to say it. Others looking on may judge that he is under they know not what scruples, and is making himself unhappy by not daring to claim their enjoyments, but it is they that are in the absurdity, not he. He is only too free in his great, nobly divine pleasures, to find any thing but loss and meagre littleness in theirs. Their world is not his world, and he has renounced their world, not because he must, which they probably think, but because he has gotten by it and above it.

And here is the reason, I conceive, why we keep on debating this question as we do, in the footing of the mere moralities. The people of the world bring it always to that standard, and do not imagine that christian souls can bring it to any other. And even they, when taken off from so many amusements by the new inspirations of their life, do not see quite likely that, being a question of practice, it need not therefore be a question of mere ethical morality; and so they let it be debated for them on the same old footing. Whereas what they now call duty is a wholly different matter; viz., what is due to their new footing of liberty and unity with God. And it turns out by a similar mistake, that graciously enlightened teachers themselves, are all the while debating the question of amusements, even for christian people, as if it were a question only of good morals. If they accurately understand where christian souls really are, and how, in their divine ranges of liberty, they are lifted into other dispositions and higher kinds of enjoyment, they would put the question of amusements in a very different way. It is not the question whether we are bound thus and thus, in terms of morality, and so obliged to abstain; but whether, as our new and nobler life impels, we are not required, in full fidelity, to pay it honor, and keep its nobler tastes unmarred by descending to that which they have so far left behind them.

It may be well to put the question in a different way, which yet will not be really different except in the form. It comes to us every hour, that men who are deeply immersed in some great work, or cause, have no care for any thing else, least of all for any thing that appears to be trivial. Indeed almost any thing is like to seem trivial, which is not in the line of their engagement, even though it has far greater consequence. Any thing which has become the supreme end of life, sinks the significance of every thing else. In the pursuit of gain, if we speak of nothing higher, they will look upon amusements how commonly as mere nonsense, and will sometimes even forget the feeding of their bodies. How then will it be when a christian man has become thoroughly engulfed in the work and cause of his Master? It is now his passion. He wants nothing else. He only wants to love it more, and do more for it, and, compared with this, every thing is trivial; he has no taste for the gaieties of mere natural pleasure. Christian people are set off thus, in a sense, from the amusements other people delight in, by the stress of their own new love, and the heavenly engagements into which it brings them. Of course, on mere ethical grounds, they have a right to do just what every body has, to claim all the justifiable amusements, and go as far in them as moral safety may allow, but to claim that right, they must descend a long way into the spirit, as into the law, of the world, and be really of it themselves. These things we say are innocent, but they are not innocent to them, because they bring down a spirit lifted far above into better affinities, and nobler ranges of good.

Here open accordingly some very deep lessons for christian souls, that must not be lost. Being not simply free, as all men are, to have their amusements, they should also be more free, free enough not to want them; or to want them, at least, only in some very qualified and partial way.

A young christian, for example, goes to his pastor and says, "There is going to be a masquerade party, or it may be a great game supper and dancing party, where many of my friends are to be, and I am invited; will it be wrong for me to go?" "No, not wrong, the answer must be, as far as the mere question of morality is concerned. But I am none the less sorry to see that you want to be there. It shows that you have either lost ground, or that you have not gotten as far forward as I hoped in your christian life. You certainly might be close enough to your Saviour not to be disposed to go, deep enough in the conscious joy and serenity of your love to be totally indisposed to go. But you seem not to have reached this height. Go then, if you will, but understand exactly what it signifies. To be restrained, or kept back, by mere scruple, at the legal point of morality, will do you no good. And if I should raise a scruple for you here, and you still should go, it would only put you in a struggle with your conscience, and set you on contriving moral arguments of defense, for what is only spiritual defeat, or defection. If you are disposed to go, it is better for you to go understanding what it means, and have nothing else to think of."

And what shall we say of the many christian people so called, who are always putting the question of amusements on trial, under the test arguments of common morality? Where is the harm, they ask, of this or that? Where is the principle? What is the law that condemns it? Is it not better in these innocent matters to be free? Yes, and is it not better yet to be more free?—to be living in ranges of illumination so clear and full, and in holy liberty so high, that no such hankering after the little driblets and titillations of pleasures called amusements, will be felt? God's true saints below, even like the saints above, should be a great way in advance of any such unsaintly kinds of privilege.

Others again who do not mean to claim any such privilege, as for themselves, have much to say of doing what they can for their young people, and the green age of society, in preparing festivities and pleasures, such as will keep off the impression that religion is an austere matter, having only frowns to bestow on the common amenities of life. But no such impression of austerity is ever given, I feel bound to say, when religion is so lived as to be an atmosphere of joy and true liberty. Here is no austerity, or the look of it, but there is a glow, an ever-bright content and hopefulness, a jubilant, all-loving sympathy, which keeps every thing fresh and sweet as the morning. Of course there should be gentle unbendings, and moderate connivings at play, such as will suffice to show that no morbid, self-restrictive, legally distempered conscientiousness makes a bondage of duty. All mere niggard scruples, and rigidities of scrupulosity, must be evidently far away. And they will, in fact, be farther away from all christian people, living as in joy, than from any that make a point of catering for amusements, when living in evident dearth and dryness. What are these dry, dreary people doing, some will ask, but contriving how to moisten a little the aridities they live in?

Besides, we need not be greatly concerned lest the green age, down upon the plain of nature, will not find as many festivities and ways of hilarity as are really wanted, even if christian friends should not be making up card parties, and dancing parties, and private theatricals for them. Why, there is no trip-hammer beat, that keeps up a louder and more constant noise, than the advertising racket of our newspapers; telling, every night and morning, what new shows and budgets of fun are ready to be opened—circuses, rope-dances, feats of magic, troupes of colored minstrelsy, menageries, learned birds and pigs, automaton players, gift-concerts, operas, public balls, theaters, anniversary dinners, and I know not what beside. Our very brain is put a-whirling, if we try to just keep track of the diversions promised. Many of these things are innocent enough in themselves, some of them instructive, but we have altogether too much of them. And too much of innocent amusement is not innocent, but even morally bad, another name for dissipation itself. Hence in this view the very last thing any christian person, woman or man, need concern himself about, just now, is the contriving of diversions to relieve the austerity of religion. It may be that we sometimes take on a hard, dry, God-forsaken look in the religion we have; alas! I fear it is true, but O if we had more, if we had enough to live in it and by it, there would be no so glad faces, or winning graces of life, as our liberty in the Spirit would show. The very atmosphere of such is fresh and bright and free as the day dawn. They live above scruple, they do nothing by constraint, they go beaming where they go. Every one sees that they have the deepest satisfactions, and are most completely alive of all people that live. They will bend sometimes to indulgences, which the churlish miscalled saints, living under scruple or ascetic law, condemn, but it will be evident that they rather yield to them in amiable deference to others, than want them for themselves. Or if they do it now and then, as in deference to their own natural instinct of play, it will seem that they are only freer because they are full, and not that they are craving such allowance because they are empty. It is hardly necessary to say, that they will not be averted, even by their liberty itself, from any festivities or games that are athletic, or belong to the gymnastics of bodily exercise. They are human and have human bodies; and it is not supposable that the joys of the spirit should make them neglectful of the joys of health, and the full-toned vigor of the body. Even the Spirit of the Lord, we are told, does not withhold his quickening touch from mortal bodies.

But must we not, some very conscientious disciples will ask, be faithful to put a frown upon these pleasures in the lower plane of morality? must we not declare them to be wrong and raise a testimony against them? That is about the worst thing a true christian can do. They are not wrong in themselves. It is you that have gone above them and their law, not they that have come up into conflict with you. The opposition between you and them is without any real contrariety of principle; you being swayed by religious inspirations and they by rules of ethics legally applied. And there is nothing you can do against religion more hurtful, than to make it the foe of all innocent enjoyments, in the reach of such as have not the higher resources of religion.

It only remains to notice certain interpellations by which one or another will think our conclusions may be turned. Thus it will be suggested by some who mean to be disciples, but are living in a key so low as to be over fond of amusements, that the class who are not disposed to go with them, must be christians of a superlative order, such as all who are to be saved need not of course be. They certainly are superlative in the comparison suggested; but whether they are better christians than they need be, or than all ought to be, is a difficult and rather delicate question. Whoever is contriving, by how little faith or how little grace, and with how large interspersing of of gaiety and worldly pleasure, he may make his title to salvation good, is engaged in a very critical experiment. He is trying how to be a christian without being at all a saintly person; how to love God enough, without loving him enough to be taken away from his lighter pleasures; and he really thinks that aiming low enough to be a little of a christian, he still may just hit the target on the lower edge. Perhaps he will, but is he sure of it? And if he really is, what miserable economy is it to be so little in the love of God and the joys of a glorious devotion, that he can be just empty enough to want his deficit made up by amusements? If that will answer, a very mean soul, certainly, can be saved.

Another class, not christian and never pretending to be, are out upon such kind of people as get to be miserably over-good, and can not take the fun of life as it comes. They do not want such christians. It makes them angry to see them, set aloof by what they call their piety, from even innocent amusements and pleasures. "If any thing can make us infidels to the end of the chapter, it is to see how all human pleasures turn sour under the look of these people." Well, it may be that God has not undertaken to make people good to order, after your particular style, and whether your style or his is better, he will certainly take his own. But will it make you an infidel to see human beings, naturally just as fond of pleasure, and every way as selfish as you, so thoroughly given to works of mercy and sacrifice, so fascinated by God's pure charities, so deep in the abysses of his love, that they have not a sigh, or a want, for the dear gaieties you live in? I can hardly believe it. On the contrary, it seems to me that such a fact should convince you, if any thing can, that what has so wonderfully exalted them will equally exalt you. Surely it must needs make a very great difference in the soul's outlook on every thing, whether it has God revealed within, or is living without God. Might it not make as great difference in yours? Therefore when you say that you do not want such christians, might not all your impressions be different, if only you knew what they so perfectly know, in their better plane of life? There certainly should not be any thing odious in a life whose quality is grounded in the simple love of God.

Well, it comes back then, after all, a larger number in more various shades of character will say, to this; that all christian people are restricted and put under bonds not to allow themselves any liberties of amusement. And since we all alike are put in obligation to be christian, what is the conclusion we arrive at, but that we are all under the same restrictions, shut up to all the austerities of religion that we just now thought were to be escaped? That is no fair conclusion, or in fact any conclusion at all. Doubtless every nominally christian man is bound to be thoroughly christian. And so is every unbeliever, every really unchristian man. But take it as we may, our being bound thus universally to the choice of Christ, does not any way touch the matter of the amusements; for who ever comes to Christ as a disciple, is never cut off from these because he is under requirement to that effect, he only drops them out because he does not want them, and is turned away from them by his new born liberty itself.

Here then, my friends, in this high plane of royal liberty, it is our privilege and calling to live. Worldly minds, minds faintly christian, if such are possible, can hardly imagine, rushing as they do in their emptiness after all kinds of pleasurable diversion, to fill up the void of their feeling, what supreme fullness of life is here vouchsafed us. They even look askance upon our gospel, as if it were proposing to shorten their privilege, and cut off the few endurable things they are able to find in the world. Unspeakable delusion!—would that they could see it. No, my friends. The real purpose of our gospel is to set us clear of all restrictions whatever that work legally, and bring us out to reign with God in God's own liberty. It says, "all things are yours," and permits us to live in that broad wealth which consists in universal possession. Nothing is farther off and deeper down below it, than that we are now to be set in scruple, and careful debate, about what social pleasures and diversions are permitted, and what forbidden us. Permitted or forbidden, we shall not want them, or go after them, because they are chaff to us; and we only let our gospel down below itself, when we assume that any thing can be settled for Christ in that plane of argument. We have meat to eat which is better. We sit in the heavenly places, having it ever as our prime distinction there, that we would rather suffer with our Master, than be feasted without him, and would even willingly die to behold his face.

XX.

THE MILITARY DISCIPLINE.

"Thou therefore endure hardness, as a good soldier of Jesus Christ. No man that warreth entangleth himself with the affairs of this life, that he may please him that hath chosen him to be a soldier."—2 *Tim.* 2: 3–4.

The Christian life is often illustrated, as here, by some comparison or figure derived from military life. Sometimes the comparison is general; as when the whole struggle is called a warfare. Sometimes the particular point of the comparison turns on the matter of persistency; as in the resisting unto blood. Sometimes on the matter of courage; as when the righteous are declared to wax valiant in fight. Sometimes on the precision of stroke and parry in close combat with evil; as when one fights in a cavalry charge—not uncertainly, or as beating the air. In the passage from which I now propose to speak, the point of the comparison is different—it relates to the stringent and exact discipline of the military service; the total separation of the soldier from his own private affairs, and the absolute subjection of his body and life to the hardships of the camp, and the will of his commander.

The life of a soldier is the hardest, roughest, most exactly restricted life to which a human being is ever subjected, and it is well understood, as a first maxim of military science, that it must be so. It makes no difference, therefore, whether it be a volunteer enlistment or a forced levy; no matter whether it be the army of a free state or of a despotism; it is well understood that it must, in either case, be subjected to the same stern military discipline.

The general-in-chief, in the first place, must have no questions of his own about the policy or righteousness of the war. He belongs to the state just as the cannon do, and he must go exactly where he is sent, to fight the war prescribed. His subordinate officers, in all grades, must be as implicitly subject to him as he to the civil power, and the soldier must be subject to them in the same manner. The army is, in fact, to be a variously compounded, closely compacted machine, whose wheels and limbs of motion are men—the bodies and minds of men. They are to move with an exactly timed and exactly measured step, all as one. They are to be wheeled up into the cannon's mouth of the enemy, just as they are wheeled about in a parade exercise, having no more question of danger, or of self-preservation, than if they were made of the same material as the truck-machines of their cannon. They are to wade through swamps and rivers, at the word of command; to sleep on the ground, if need be, without shelter; to live on the coarsest, saltest fare; and when it is required, on half allowance of that; to keep their sentry-walk in the rain, just as it is set; or, if they must, to stiffen there in the winter's cold, sooner than leave the beat assigned. If they have a home and children, it is to be nothing, as long as they are in the field. If they have lands that want their care and culture, harvests waiting to be reaped, property and debts that require their attention, these are nothing—no man that warreth entangleth himself with the affairs of this life, that he may please him that hath chosen him to be a soldier. If his superior in command is tyrannical and harsh, he must choke his resentments and not vent his impatience in words of complaint; for that alone, if permitted, would loosen the fiber of order and discipline. When a victory is gained, it must be enough that his leader is applauded. Or if some other subordinate, less deserving than himself, is commended for promotion, he must take it as the fortune of war and be silent. Nay he must even have a certain soldierly pride in not whimpering or complaining of any thing. In a word, he must endure hardness as a good soldier; for it is the manner of a soldier to endure every thing, bear every privation, without a murmur of discontent; to eat what is given him, march when the surgeon decides that he is well, whether he can stand or not; melt or freeze, leave his body on the plain, or give it to fill a ditch before the enemy's ramparts, just as the cause or word of command requires. This too, neither in a way of dogged self-compulsion, nor of timid and slavish subjection. It must be done with appetite and ardor;

for the true ideal of the military discipline is not reached or realized, and the army is not set in the true fighting order, till what is called an *esprit du corps* is formed, such that individuals forget themselves in the spirit, and pride, and fire, of the common body and their common cause. It is to be as if the cause were beating time like a march, in their hearts, and the tramp that measures their step, were but emphasizing the common purpose of assault and the common confidence of victory. In this army spirit, or enthusiasm, which consummates the drill and discipline, every thing is done with freedom, because the individual consciousness is burned up, so to speak, in the common fire of the camp, or campaign. The soldier cares no more for himself. He lives in his commander, and the brave monster called an army, that his commander has organized. Or sometimes it will be true as just now it is with us, that, apart from any power of drill, a grand enthusiasm for his country and its laws has taken possession of the soldier, and so far sunk his individuality, that he throws in ease, and home, and children, and life itself, caring nothing for the sacrifice, and scarcely remembering his particular, infinitesimal self any longer. And this, in some form, is the condition of all true military power. Having lost this fire of the camp, the army is said to be "demoralized." Having never found it, the army will be only as an army of sheep going to the slaughter.

Now the apostle, as we have seen, conceives the christian calling and service, under the analogies of the camp and a military soldierhood; and I have drawn out this brief picture of the military order and organization, that we may trace the lesson he gives us, in some of the great points of correspondence, where the analogies are most instructive and impressive.

It is not conceived of course that the christian disciple, enrolled in his Master's service, is to encounter all the bad points which give so hard a look to military life. He perfectly knows that he is not thrust forward in a bad cause, or a cause of which he has any the least doubt. He knows beforehand, too, that his cause is sure of victory; not perhaps of immediate victory, not of any such victory possibly as insures against temporary defeat, and even long ages of losing experience and discouraging warfare. Still he has this one point given him to fasten his courage, which is given, never, to a contesting army; viz., that his cause is absolutely sure of victory at the last. It is a great point also of distinction, that no injustice is going to be done him. Nothing will ever be required of him that violates his own personal convictions, or breaks down the integrity of his judgments. He will suffer wrong by no fraud, or prejudice, or partiality, of his superior commander, but will be estimated always exactly according to his own soldierly merit and his faithful prowess in the field. His fellow men or fellow disciples may not do him justice, but may even put dishonor on him where he is to be most truly honored. Still he will only be the more highly estimated by his great leader, that he stands fast when beset by so much of hostility and detraction around him, doing just the service which others most decry and hold in least esteem.

Abating now so many points of wrong, or unrighteous severity in the conditions of army service—for God has never any unjust or over severe terms to lay upon his servants—there is yet a very strongly marked similarity between that service and the christian discipline. His enrollment for such discipline includes the totality even of the man. He is to keep nothing back, but to put in home, house, worldly property and business, and even life itself. He engages to endure hardness as a good soldier, and even more absolutely than any army soldier not to entangle himself with the affairs of this life. He takes a kind of military oath, in fact, to follow his Master, and do his perfect will; to renounce all delicacy and self-indulgence, to endure privation, to not shrink from distress and torment, and even to witness a true confession by the martyr's fires. No ties of kindred or country are to detain him from going where he is sent, or doing what he is commanded. And what is wholly peculiar to his kind of warfare, he is to fight alone, when called to it, and maintain his charge even against the world. In the service of arms soldiers go to the charge, or the contest together, under one or generally several commanders; but the soldier of Christ stands out often by himself, in solitary warfare, where he is to win his victory for God and truth alone. More generally he will have multitudes enlisted with him, and the great army of believers will be set in the drill with him and he with them, all to be responsible, in a degree, for each other. They are all to have their appointed places and times, and come into the close fixed order of a compact system. They must take every man his part under the great leader, throwing nothing over upon others which is given them to do, and they must take the peril of it as being kindled for it, in the glorious, common passion of the common cause. Patience, endurance, courage, fidelity and even a kind of celestial impassivity, must be set in their otherwise inconstant, misgiving, self-indulgent nature. And the only tonic force equal to this must be found in devotion to the Master, carried to the pitch of soldierhood in his cause. The service they are in will often be hard, a drill of duty and observance dreadfully irksome to the flesh, but as soon as they find how to put every thing into it, and have gotten all their thoughts, feelings, fancies, wishes, enlisted for the war, and all private liberties and caprices of will subjected to the camp order of the mind, even the hardness itself will become a kind of buoyancy and celestial aspiration.

Now this representation of the christian life, by means of the military, is one that is rich in spiritual instruction, as regards a great many points of principal significance. Some of those I will now undertake to present.

I begin with the particular matter suggested by the apostle; viz., the putting off or excision of the world, as an interruptive and disqualifying power. We get weary of hearing so much said against the world, so many cautions set against it, so many renunciations and denunciations piled up to fence it away. Why such a fear, a jealousy so wearisome, of the world? Is it a bad world? Has God made some mistake in the constitution of it? Is there not something ascetic, something a little superstitious, and to speak plainly, something a little unrespectable in this world-renouncing way? And when we insist on the unworldly character of all true disciples, and hold up such as examples of a specially standard character, what is it, they ask, but a milksop that we make our ideal man? Do we then put this same judgment down upon the soldier, taken away, as he is, from all his affairs and affections; his property, his home, his business and business-custom; forbidden now to use a finger for his private and personal interests, or even to let his family at home have place enough in him, to so much as slacken his feeling in the duties of the camp? But why is this? why is he allowed no more to have any world, or any thing but a body in drill, and a mind set for endurance? Is he thus unworlded to take the mettle out of him? Does it in fact make a poltroon of him or mere broth of a man, as we just now heard of the unworldly Christian? Does not every military commander know that, letting his men go home once a month, and come back with their heads full of family and business cares, unmans them practically, for the time, and so far incapacitates them for any brave, tough-handed service. The only way to make great soldiership, as he well understands, is to take his men completely out of the home world, and have them circumscribed and shut in by drill, as being mortgaged in body and life for their country. Trained to flinch at nothing and suffer any thing, he makes them first impassive, and so, brave. And under this same law it is that all christian disciples are required to strip for the war, throwing off all their detentions, all the seductions of business, property, pleasure and affection. All such matters must now drop into secondary places, for the understanding is, that no one gets the great heart, or becomes in any sense a hero, till his very life is drunk up in his commander, and his supreme care to please him that hath chosen him to be a soldier. Instead of being weakened by the stern renunciations of his unworldly discipline, it is precisely this which gives him all robustness and heroic fire in his calling. In just this drill too have all God's mightiest witnesses been trained.

Consider next how the military discipline raises spirit and high impulse by a training under authority, exact and absolute. In which we see, that going by authority and being always kept under Christ's positive command, is not a way, as some might think, of diminishing our personal vigor, and reducing our pitch in the manly parts of conduct. Be it so that we have it put upon us by Christ, as the perpetual charge of our life, to keep his commandments. And then let the question come, how we are going to preserve any real personality, without having, in some large degree, our own way? Can any thing save us from a total incapacity, when we are required to be acting, moment by moment, under authority? Does it then reduce the soldiers and all the subordinate commanders of an army to mere cyphers, when they are required to march, and wheel, and lift every foot, and set every muscle, by the word of authority; when even the music is commandment, and to feed, and sleep, and not sleep are by requirement? Why, the service rightly maintained invigorates every manly quality rather; for they are in a great cause, moving with great emphasis, having thus great thoughts ranging in them and, it may be, great inspirations. Not many of them ever had as great before, or ever will have again. And all these powers are the more wholesome, that they come in as commandment; for it is one of the grandest functional superiorities in man, that he can be commanded as the animals can not; that his nature is not a block but a drum, reverberative, grandly, to whatever highest thing is sounded. So that, after all, and say what we will of our own personal free arbitrament, the grandest things that ever come into us are commanded in. We even get more volume by what is commanded us, than by all that we do. Authority, authority, God's all dominant, supreme authority, is our noblest educator; for more than all things else it wakens up our life, and impregnates our sentiment with all that is most heroically true and good. Our human nature is most blest and exalted in its homages; and no soul is so miserably unblest as one that never had any. To be governed, it is true, is sometimes nothing different from being thrust down, but to be governed for a cause, or an idea, is to be graded up in pitch and not down. When our soldiers return from their campaign, how often is it remarked of one or another, that his good-for-nothingness is somehow taken away, and that his very gait is manlier; as if he were a man squared up by command, and the new-felt possibility of consequence to his country. And so when the soldiers of Christ throng in after their great campaign is over, what will be more surely discovered in them, than their everlasting ennoblement in Christ's great will and commandment. And yet not that so much by what he commands, as by the reverberative sense of being under a command so high.

Another lesson even more instructive. How often is it imagined, by outside beholders, or felt by slack-minded, self-indulgent disciples, that the military stringency of the christian life is a condition of bondage. The disciple puts his liberty in mortgage, it is thought, and is never any more to be free. The very conception of a life so bitterly scathed and cut away by self-renunciation, is wearisome, ungenial, and repulsive—is there not some conception of a good life more generous in the style of it, and such as better accords with the liberality of the christian salvation? Since Christ has made us free, why not stand fast in our liberty? Yes, but how are we going to stand fast in liberty, when liberty itself is standing fast in nothing, keeping no fixed terms at all? Why, it is even the chief matter of the military drill and the stringent closeness of it, that by no other means can the liberties of impulse and inspired momentum be raised. The cause is nothing till the camp begets a soul for it, and the camp is disciplined for that end. And the understanding is, in every qualified commander, that he never gets the free, great spirit into his men, till he gets them solidified in drill, under his peremptory word. He must train their every motion, if possible, to be commanded by him. And if at any time the discipline gets relaxed or broken down, then the army, as he well understands, will be demoralized, because no common impulse takes them longer, and no grand martial fire is possible to be kindled in their inspirations. They are no more held in hand closely enough by the discipline, to put them in impulse and the swing of liberty. Their cause, however good, inspires them no longer. Just so the christian body is prepared for the exaltations of liberty, by consenting, every one, to the exact discipline of a soldier. Keeping the walk of Christ, as he would the beat of a sentinel, obeying under mandate, taking the rule of duty in exact observance, inquiring always what God lays it upon him to do, what place to fill, what sacrifices to make, what hardness to endure—coming under the yoke thus to learn, he does indeed learn, and finds it a yoke most easy; nay, even freedom itself. Just accordingly as he sinks himself in the steadiness and completeness of his obedience, he mounts into liberty. Here courage springs, and all the free-born sentiments of inspiration break into play.

This matter of liberty is, alas! how little understood, even by those who most harangue the people and the political assemblages concerning it. Liberty is not the being let alone, or allowed to have every thing our own way. If it were, the wild beasts would be more advanced in it than all states and peoples. No, there is no proper liberty but under rule, and in the sense of rule. It holds high sisterhood with law, nay it is twin-born with law itself. Even our existence droops and drags a chain, if it can not touch some principled way of order, to be ennobled by it. There is, in fact, no bondage so dreadfully sterile as vagabondage; that which strays and straggles where it will, and finds no hand of discipline ever laid upon it. It is in a slavery most dreadful because it has no significance to itself. Hence it is that the strictness and stiffness of the army discipline, that which puts the soldier under guard because he does not set his eye by command, or comes on parade with an untied shoe—hence it is, I say, that in such condensation of discipline, the army breaks into liberty, rushing even upon death itself. It does not grope along the roads and fences vagabond-wise, but it bounds over all barriers by the word that is in it; blazing like a fire-tempest in the faces of the enemy. Self-consideration is gone out, the word and the cause are all that is left.

This is liberty, and spiritual liberty is close akin. It is being in such drill under Christ's commandments, that it has no longer any thought of cost or consequences. It goes by no constraint but only by inclination, and the more strictly it has learned to obey, the more exactly, tenderly conscientious, it has become; if it is not slavish in its exactness, but is caring only to please him that hath chosen it to be his soldier, the more gloriously free it will be. There will not be a galling thing in the service; even the self-denials, if there be any, will be free. The discipline looks hard, I confess, when regarded from afar and externally — even an apostle calls it enduring hardness— and yet the stringency of it makes it the spring of liberty. No such liberty, no real liberty at all of the spirit, could be made by any smoother and more relaxed process. There is a kind of strictness, I grant, which can well enough be pitied; viz., the strictness of cowardly scruple and fear, but when the man is full up with his law, commanding himself in it, all such expenditure of pity may be saved. That man "walks at liberty because he keeps God's precepts," and he keeps them not as tugging up anxiously after them, but as a military body-guard set for their defense. Plainly enough there is no bondage here.

Let us also take another lesson from the military

discipline, finding in it how to put a more genial look on our crosses and required self-denials. Ungenial and repulsive as the law of the camp may be, there is no such thing in it as enduring hardness for hardness' sake, no peremptory commandment for commandment's sake. Such kind of discipline would not be training, but extirpation rather. And yet how many of us christian disciples fall into notions of christian self-denial that include exactly this mistake. As if it were a proper christian thing to be always scoring, and stripping, and mortifying ourselves. How shall we ever be true soldiers, if we do not make a hard time of it? how shall we resist unto blood if we do not make a fight, and press hard enough to bleed in it? Thus how many who really wanted to be soldiers have retired into cells, renouncing family comfort and love; or renouncing marriage; or renouncing shoes; or renouncing even their consciences—taking spiritual directors, by implicit obedience to whose ghastly dictations they may kill out even their private will and judgment, and all deepest convictions even of their personality. All which is just as good and no better than the discipline of an army kept up, not to make an army, but to unmake the men. No such army discipline was ever heard of. Alas that we should have it in the church, and that not merely in the ascetic schools of the monks, but in a presence more subtle and scarcely less desolating among our Protestant peoples. What is self-denial as we most frequently think it, but a practice of self-deprivation? And then having made our mistake, we either put ourselves to it, making life a desert, and calling it our piety; or we only make a feint of compliance, and drop into a piety more stunted, because it is confessedly wanting in the chief thing. It is very much as if the soldier, instead of throwing life and home, and every thing most dear, upon the service of his country, were put to the drill for stripping them away, no matter for the country. That would be rank military oppression, and not any army discipline at all. Let us not think much of the christian soldierhood, endured by the poor monks, in the dismal abnegations of their so called self-denial; as little of their groans of bondage and sorrow, shut in by the walls, where as prisoners of God, they have spent their weary blighted lives; but let us find instead how dear and free a thing self-sacrifice may be, when it takes away our self-seeking, and brings us out in a life of uncalculating devotion to our Master's name and cause. The truth is, my friends, that our human nature is made to go a great deal more heroically than some of us think; and our soldiers in the field, thank God, are just now making the discovery. O what worlds-full of great feeling are given us, if only we can die into the causes of the worlds! We make the soul a vastly more prosy affair than it is, imagining that self-privation will starve it into goodness, and penances do the work of repentances. Why if the fires of patriotic impulse can help our sons and fathers in the field to rejoice in so great sacrifice for their country, what pain can there be to us in our painstakings, what loss in our losses, when the love of God and of his Son is truly kindled in us?

Let us also note for another lesson, opposite to this, that the military discipline has as little direct concern to beget happiness, as it has to compel self-abnegation. There is so great peace and sweetness of enjoyment, in the genuinely christian state and calling, that such as are highest and most advanced in it, are in danger of being too much occupied with what may be called the pious luxury of their experience. Probably they do not call it by that name themselves; but being consciously exalted above measure in it, they conceive their joy to be itself a kind of self-certifying oracle and witness in their hearts. They speak of it often, they magnify it over abundantly it may be, and fall into a strain of elysianizing; as if that were the unquestionable test of the highest and best way of life. Hence their great endeavor, the main object of their search, is to find how their delicious rhapsody began, and how others also may be wafted into it. If we call them soldiers, which perhaps they are in a sense, and if only fit occasion were given, would show themselves to be, still they are, so far and just now, soldiers not in armor, but lying on some sunny bank, and celebrating there, in free discourse, the pleasures, nay the peace, of their warfare; also in free chorals, the fervors and inspiring confidences of their cause.

Probably they have it not in thought, just now, to be enduring hardness, or in fact that they are under any call of soldierhood. The elysian property of their feeling is just now their principal concern; and it may be a very considerable danger of their largely blessed, half ecstatic state, that they will run to dissipation in it, and die out by and by, into a state of dryness and exhaustion they will not like to confess. It is never altogether safe for such as we, to be simply happy, and that may be the reason why the best and solidest of us never are. See how it was with the great apostle, "fourteen years ago." He was caught up into the third heaven, he knew not whither, and scarcely any better who he was—in the body or out of the body—thrilled of course with unwonted, unspeakable delights; but having been up among God's roses, he came back with a thorn! And that thorn, as we can see, was the life of him. Without it, pervaded all through with the perfume of his joy, he was no more any soldier at all, and scarcely a man. But having a Satan to buffet him inside in attacks on his infirmities, he began to glory and be glad in a more sublime fashion, having now the power of Christ resting consciously on him. That now was a grandly mortal style of joy; for there was a roughness or obstructive element in it. He is not a soldier now, sunning himself at his ease on the bank of the river, but he is in his fighting trim, girded in high liberty for the onset commanded. We must not think, my brethren, that the crown or decisive test of our experience is that we are happy—a most pleasant thing it is if we are—but as certainly as our fight is not over, we must look for hardness to be endured, and woe be to us if we do not find it.

There is yet one point of this military analogy, where in fact it is scarcely any proper analogy at all, but a kind of universal law, running through all kinds of mortal endeavor, secular, moral, mental, and spiritual; viz., that whatever we get, we must somehow fight for it. What begins in the conflicts of tribes and empires runs down through all kinds of experience. We have to fight the soil by labor, and conquer from it our bread. We get knowledge and mental discipline, by a long, unflinching, steady battle. We build by scoring timber, burning clay, and hewing rock. We build states by scoring constitutions, baking laws in the fires of opinion, and squaring down magistrates for their places by the cutting edges of our votes. And so we go fighting on through every thing, and most certainly of all, in religion. It is waging war, though it be for the Prince of Peace. Fighting a good fight, is the only way to finish the course, and the crown of glory comes in no where, save at the end. And so much impressed with this fact is our great and truly most heroic apostle, that he occupies a good part of one whole chapter in naming off and, as it were, showing how to put on the whole armor of God—girdle, breast-plate, shoes, shield, helmet, and sword—

and he even conceives that Christ is our captain leading us on. Then follows another apostle who, making his appeal to seven successively named churches, puts them to their task each one, by the promise, so many times repeated—"To him that overcometh,"—"to him that overcometh." And then passing up through, into worlds above the world, he beholds the victors coming in with palms in their hands, and these, he cries aloud, "are they which come out of great tribulation;" and of other victors if possible more highly ennobled — "they loved not their lives unto the death." And so, in one view, it is only battle we are waging here all the time. We open the gate of the kingdom by great throes often, such as make us bleed. Our life is the battle in the cause of God, and God is going finally to emerge in the full honors of his own most proper and glorious title, THE LORD OF HOSTS.

To realize, my brethren, a conception so truly sublime is, I fear, not possible for some of us, living in our present key. We are, many of us, living daintily, I fear, and half theoretically. We have no persecutions, and we settle into very dainty notions and habits. There is a want of rugged vigor and muscle in us. The ring of true metal is wanting. To please him that hath chosen us to be soldiers is not so much our thought, as that he will somehow find a way to please us. O that God would give us back once more some heroes in godliness, such as lived in the old time now gone by. Or better, far better, that he would gird us all to be total, and strong, and steadfast, in the cause of our Master—clear every one of entanglement; sturdy, and stiff, and simple, and right; refusing all the softer methods of the self-enjoying luxury, and having it as calling enough, to be in the complete war discipline, as well as the complete liberty, of eternal obedience to God.

In tracing this analogy between the christian and the military discipline, I have not said any thing of a matter that is even painful to be named, the case and question of desertion. By what state reasons and conditions of absolute necessity it is put down as the greatest of all crimes, and punished with inevitable execution, we do not require to be informed, and the heartrending and truly shocking scenes that make up the after-breakfast horror of the camps are alas! too familiar. The parallel I will not trace. Are the religious state reasons less decided? the mischiefs of christian desertion less demoralizing? the grand necessity here less imperative? Fellow soldiers and comrades, I can not look down this gulf; for the bottom of it is I know not where. But this I know; that, if you do not deny Christ, he will not deny you, and that if you serve him in such devotion as to make a cheerful and glad service, you will never be stolen away from his cause, by any most seductive bait of treason.

XXI.

THE CORONATION OF THE LAMB.

"The throne of God and of the Lamb."—*Rev.* 22: 1.

Regarding here the mere grammar of the words, we have a partnership deity presented. Though perhaps the English version, speaking not of the throne of God and the Lamb simply, but of the throne of God and *of* the Lamb, gives a more plural cast to the words than it need. However this may be, no difficulty is created; for since person, when applied as in grammar to God, is only a finite figure, derived from our human personality, a plurality of persons may represent him as truly as one, and perhaps even a great deal more truly, because more adequately. It is indeed a fault of any single name, or symbol for God, that it presents him too easily, in a too definitely bounded figure. Nothing, in free use, will save his dimensions, which does not leave us to behold him in a maze, by that to be magnified. And if three persons, or more, are employed to create the maze, we have nothing to complain of, provided both the dimensions and the personality are practically saved.

But the matter I have now in hand is not the plurality encountered, but the name; to do, in this really supreme article of the gospel story, what a late able writer has undertaken for the Progress of Doctrine in the New Testament—showing how a lamb becomes the Lamb; a very humble, common name, the highest of all proper names; climbing up through long reaches of history, into the throne itself of God. I propose, in other words, *to trace the ascending progress, issued in the final coronation, of the Lamb.*

The ascending stages of this progress we shall best discover if we glance at the scripture record of the story. The word *lamb* begins of course at the creature, and the creature required, first of all, to be created, having just the qualities of innocence, inoffensiveness, incapacity of resentment and ill-nature, ready submissiveness to wrong, necessary to the intended meaning, and the finally sacred uses, of the word. Lambs of nature were first stage symbols. for the due unfolding of the Lamb of religion.

Then follows, we may see, a process in which artificial meanings are woven into and about the words and images provided, by the religious uses of sacrifice; for God is now to be displayed in the dear passivities of sacrifice. Thus the sinning man—Abel for example—wants a liturgy for his repentance, one that shall both move and express the tenderest contritions, the sweetest hopes and confidences of reconciliation. Spontaneously therefore, as some think, or more probably by a special appointment of God, he chooses this most passive, most unsinning, unoffending creature, and says—"Be this for me," offering it in fire, as the appeal of his faith and his prayer of reconciliation. Used for ages in this manner, the lamb becomes a kind of sacred image, and the blood of the lamb an accepted symbol of reconciliation, or forgiving mercy.

By and by, after many centuries have passed, Abraham is put on acting a strange scene of sacrifice in the offering up of his son; wherein he is to be carried through incidents and a story and a struggle of loss, that will be the analagon, or type of another, still more mysterious sacrifice, where God provides another, holier lamb himself. And the story ends in fact in a strange, enigmatic, yet apparently forehinting utterance—"God will provide himself a lamb"—words that reached farther than he could even understand himself, to be sometime fulfilled in the offering of the cross, as the consummate fact of sacrifice.

Next we come upon another more advanced stage in the process. For when the Lord is going through Egypt in judgment it is ordered, for the comfort of his people, that the blood of a lamb, now become a sacred element and type of God's all-sparing mercy, shall be sprinkled on the lintel of their doors; beholding which the destroying angel shall pass by and spare. Hence that blood of the lamb is called the token of the Lord's passover. And so the passover observance was continued for ages after, till it subsided, as being evangelically fulfilled in the Lamb of the cross, and the christian supper. And the Providential correspondence of the two is curiously noted in the fact, that as no bone of the passover-lamb was allowed to be broken, so the cross should break no bone of its victim.

Next we trace another stage of advance, in that strangest and, humanly speaking, most unaccountable of all scriptures, the Messianic picture of a mighty suffering some one, in the 52d and 53d chapters of Isaiah. The prophet has no name for him, breaking directly into his picture and saying, as for God—"Behold my servant," able only to present the nameless great one by his own wondrous figure itself. If he is a mortal, there was never any such mortal conceived or heard of before. The unbelieving critics have never been able to make out the picture. What being is he, they have asked in vain, who, inverting all the ordinary modes of judgment, is "to sprinkle many nations," and "be exalted and extolled and be very high," and "see his seed and prolong his days;" because he is "brought as a lamb to the slaughter," and "hath poured out his soul unto death;" because "he has made intercession for the transgressors;" because "he is despised and rejected of men," "wounded for our transgressions, bruised for our iniquities;" because in short he is the lamb "on whom God has laid the iniquity of us all?" There stands the picture on the page of prophecy—who shall ever be seen to answer it? Centuries come and go, but the lamb that is to be, struggles all this time in the womb of Providence—expected and not seen, yet waiting always for the birth.

At last the fullness of time is come; when a strange new prophet appears, announcing the kingdom of God now at hand. And he breaks out suddenly at his preaching and baptism by the Jordan, as a particular unknown man is seen approaching to claim the baptism, in the strangely worded salutation—"Behold the Lamb of God that taketh away the sin of the world." Now at last the advances and preparations of so many ages are ended, the Lamb of God is come. Only what conceivable impulse, if not the direct impulse of the Spirit of God, could have opened the prophet's mouth in this strangely-worded salutation? And who is he that he should bear this appellation? That will be known some three years hence more perfectly. When this wonderful, only spotless being of the world, after having breathed purity and love on it for so long a time, goes to his cross in dumb submission to his enemies, and dies there staining the fatal post with his blood, having yet no bone of his passover-body broken, we begin to catch some first intimation of the prophet's meaning, when he declares—"he is brought as a lamb to the slaughter," also of the New Testament prophet in his strange salutation—"Behold the Lamb of God." And then what does he himself do, three years after, when he encounters the two disciples going back, heavy-hearted, into the country, but open to them all the ancient scripture, showing out of it how certainly Christ ought to suffer, and so to be the Lamb of prophecy. And what does he give them to see, in this manner, but that all sacrifice and passover are now fulfilled forever in his divine passion?

Then, passing on a stage farther, we are completely certified and cleared in our impressions, by the discovery that, at this same Lamb and passover blood, all apostolic preaching begins. God's new gospel of life is the revelation of the Lamb. For this, says Philip to the eunuch, is the prophet's "lamb that was dumb before his shearers." And this, says Peter, is "the precious blood of Christ as of a lamb without blemish and without spot." And this again is Paul's "propitiation," "reconciliation," Christ "made sin," to bear it clean away, and in fact his whole book of Hebrews beside.

Then once more the progress of idea and doctrine that has been advancing stage by stage, from Abel's day of sacrifice onward, and is now published, far and wide, by its apostles as a gospel of salvation for mankind, culminates, in full discovery, at its true last point, in the scripture book that, for that reason, is called the Revelation of Jesus Christ. No matter whether these openings of heaven to John reveal scenes of worship literally transacted there, about the throne, or only visional images and machineries beheld above, that represent so many chapters of future world-history coming to pass below; no matter whether the last two chapters open the real paradise of God above, or only prefigure a regenerated moral paradise on earth. Still in all these visions, whether read in one way or the other, the Lamb of God is seen to be now in the ascendant, receiving his divine honors, surrounded representatively at least, and so far truly, by innumerable hosts offering their homage, wielding also, as in rule, a majestic and complete Providence that regulates the world's affairs, and makes it now his kingdom. And the result appears at last in what may rightly be called the coronation of the Lamb. Where, emerging from his subject, bleeding state, he ascends to his rightful dominion, and is entered into his glory. He now is God, as before he was the Lamb, and the more completely God, that he is God more gloriously known for the addition thus made. Three times over in a very short space the two words God and Lamb occur together, as if to be henceforth forever joined in like ascriptions. First no other temple is wanted, "for the Lord God Almighty and the Lamb are the temple thereof." Secondly no other light is wanted; for "the glory of God lightens it, and the Lamb is the light thereof." And last of all, thirdly, "the pure river of the water of life," the river of universal healing, is seen "proceeding out of the throne of God and of the Lamb." At this point the sublime progression of the Lamb is ended, for it can go no farther.

We behold him now enthroned everlastingly, at the summit of all order, majesty, dominion, truth and worship; as truly God as God, and God more truly and sufficiently God, that his image is complete in the glorious addition of the Lamb. The grand acclaim and coronation hymn is lifted by multitudes and nations without number, and by the angels round about the throne—ten thousand times ten thousand and thousands of thousands—"Worthy is the Lamb that was slain." And the word goes under the earth, and, as it were telegraphically, under the sea, filling all masses and spaces of the creation—"Blessing, and honor, and glory, and power, be unto him that sitteth upon the throne, and unto the Lamb forever and ever."

Of course it will not be understood when we trace, in this manner, the stages by which the Lamb ascends to his throne, that he is actually promoted to another grade of being. The real exaltation is to be in us, or in the raising and filling out of our ideas. For the long-drawn, visibly predestinated progress we trace in the outward history, is a progress for our sake, and not a progress in God. And the object of it is, to help our ascent towards the full and practically true conception of God—God as he has been forever, and will forever be. The real coronation, after all, is not complete till it is completed in us, in our thought, in our advanced apprehensions of God, as a character centralized, in some sense, in the sensibilities of his lambhood. This advance in our thought—this new God-sense, I go on accordingly to show will contain, especially, these three very important factors.

1. The received impression that God is a being morally passible; capable, that is, of a suffering proportionate to his goodness.

2. Also that his nature itself is relational constitutionally to both sin and redemption.

3. That he is most powerful, does his greatest and most difficult things, by his freeness to suffering.

On these three points, I conceive, our thought is moving and to move. Taking the point first named, what does it signify, that God has now the Lamb throned with him, but that He is now to be more and more distinctly conceived as a susceptible being; to be great, not as being absolute, or an infinite force, not as being impassive—a rock, a sea, a storm, a fire—but as having great sentiments, sympathies and sensibilities. Nothing has been so difficult for men as to think of God in this manner. The human soul is overborne, at first and for long ages, by the statural dimensions of God; filling up his idea with mere quantities; putting omnipotence in the foreground, and making him a grand positivity of force; adding omniscience, or absolutely intuitive knowledge, adding also will, purpose, arbitrary predestination, supralapsarian decrees; exalting justice, not as right or rectitude, but as the fearful attribute of redress, that backs up laws regarded mainly as rescripts of will in God, and not as principles. And just here, in fact, is the reason why the Lambhood nature of God was so late to be revealed, emerging, as it were, a completed fact, in the very last chapters of the Revelation. The dynamic notions of God had covered the whole ground of his attributes, and there was no room, no capacity for any the least conception of him, as a being able to endure an enemy, and suffer even burdens of sorrow for his sake. So calls out the prophet in his wonderful chapter of the Messiah Lamb just referred to—"Who hath believed our report, and to whom is the arm of the Lord revealed"—who, that is, in this coarse age, can even take the sense of my story? Why it shows a tender plant wilting in a dry ground. There is no high look in him. He is not a green bay-tree, nor a fire, nor a storm. The story comes too soon for us, and what can we do but hide our faces from him? And we of this late year ANNO MUNDI could not any better apprehend the matter of God's passibility if it had not been inwoven or interthreaded with external story, by the suffering Lamb. Slowly and very gradually the sense of some such thing is taken. But I hardly dare guess how many centuries longer it will take, for even our theologians to conceive God in the greatness of his feeling, and the depth of his sacrifice, without putting forward trains of argument that begin at his omnipotence, and all-sufficient absolutism, and the gross bulk matter of his infinity. He has always been at work to mend this defect in us; protesting by his prophets, in the matter of his sensibilities, that he is "hurt," "offended," "weary," "was grieved forty years," that "in the affliction of his people he was afflicted, and bear and carry them all the days of old." All this in words to little or no effect; but now he shows us in the Lamb, as the crowning fact of revelation, that he is a God in moral sensibility—able to suffer wrong, bear enemies, gentle himself to violence, reigning thus in what is none the less a kingdom, that it is the kingdom and patience of Jesus. All this we see, as distinctly as we can see human feeling in a human person; and still we do not actually see it, when we look on it with our eyes. A great part even of our christian theologians do not believe that God is any way passible or can be. Only the human nature suffers, they argue, that alone can feel the touch of a sorrow. Furthermore if God is passible, what is left, they ask, of his greatness? And yet moral greatness, without great feeling, great moral passibility, is even absurd; for a morally great and perfect being is, by supposition, a being in great sensibility; the more easily wounded because of his sensibility. And what is compassion but a kind of passibility? What is long suffering but a way of suffering? And the loving of the unlovely, is there not a pain struggling also in that? Is not purity quick to be disgusted? tenderness to be wounded? righteousness to be stirred with displeasure? Instead therefore of being set aloof from suffering because of his moral greatness, God is in a liability of suffering just according to his greatness. Physical suffering is of course excluded by the fact of his infinite sufficiency, but that is a matter quite insignificant for him, compared with his moral suffering.

Under such conceptions of God we of course approach the great matter of atonement, in a wholly different predisposition. We shall look for something that belongs to the Lamb, something in the nature of suffering patience, and sorrow. If he prepares a new footing of forgiveness, it will not be by what he enters into the legal, or politically legal and dynamic factors of government. He will not square off the law and level up the dues of transgression under the law—but he will simply turn a crisis in feeling. The very problem is, in great part, to bring out the everlasting Lamb element in God's nature, so that he may be the saving power of a new worship. A God who is mainly supreme will, or absolute force, having his greatness largely in his quantities, will really have no place for the Lamb as integral in his nature. He will therefore be conceived chiefly as the grand avenger, standing for the satisfaction of his justice, and requiring to have it taken even from the innocent, if it is to be released in the guilty. If he is to forgive, the law-score must be made up in the same manner, and the penal dues of the law exactly paid, the curse of it, without a peradventure, suffered. Which forgiveness, pledged and praised as free, is really no forgiveness, but is only a release passed under the squaring-up principle, and simply signifies that the books are made even, leaving nothing to forgive. No such freezing scheme of legality appears when the Lamb is conceived, as from within God's nature, tenderly bearing his enemy, and so making good the proof that whatever may be due to his polity, he is not hampered by it, but is able to forgive without pay. Even as I forgive my adversary or enemy, when I can make cost for him, and suffer bitter loss for his sake—unable to perfectly smooth the recoil of my nature from his wrong, and make clean work of my forgiveness, save, as by such cost endured, I am effectually propitiated towards him. So also we conceive the propitiation of God; for the Lamb is not other than God, outside of God, suffering before God, but he is with God most internally, necessary to the very balance of his perfections, even as he is with God in his throne. What we call grace, forgiveness, mercy, is not something elaborated after God is God, by transactional work before him, but it is what belongs to his inmost nature set forth and revealed to us by the Lamb, in joint supremacy.

We come now to the second point above stated, as involved in the coronation of the Lamb; viz., the conviction to be more and more distinctly felt, that God's nature itself is relational to both sin and redemption. Dealing only with dynamic factors in God's nature, that is with what belongs to his mere stature and capacity, imposing doubts of sin are crowded on us. God, we say, being omnipotent, can prevent all sin; since then he does not, he must prefer to have it —hence our convictions of blame are only illusions. Sin is misdirection therefore, circumstance, an evil planted in the seed, that is going to be good in the fruit. But our God, as we see in the Lamb, is not all force, he does more than to just swing the hammer of his will and purpose; he can suffer, he can bear the contradictions of evil, he can win a cause by triumph in a sorrow—could from eternity do it. For there stands in the throne as it had been a Lamb slain from the foundation of the world; and this Lamb-creator could create in self-sacrificing patience, just as he redeems in the same. Thus he wanted, for love's sake, moral natures about him, and could even bear any thing to bring them out perfected in their true good and glory. Their sin—for sin they assuredly would—would hurt him all through; but he is one who, for so dear an object can bear to be disgusted, and displeased, and burdened with sorrowing concern. Therefore sin could be, and we do it as in God's warm bosom, that can so far let us sting its suffering benignities. It is not the run of causes, not bad-going circumstance, no flour of the gods which their millstone of necessity grinds. The Lamb could suffer it, and for it; therefore it could be and is. As sin is relational to the Lamb afterward, so the Lamb was relational to sin beforehand. We are not going therefore to pitch our tent and stay in the desert of the All, where nothing answers to nothing, save as one kind of sophism answers to another, but we shall begin to have it as a discovery most dear, that so much of what is greatest in God is relational to sin. Instead of doubting so ingeniously whether sin is sin, we shall even begin to look upon our Lamb, standing in the world's throne, with his scars and blood-stains on him, and we shall find a grandly philosophic cheer in believing our sin, as we did not in denying it.

Sometimes we begin to imagine that the sense of

sin is likely, as things are just now going, to quite die out. No, the Lamb is in the throne, and it is impossible henceforth, that a God unrelational to sin, or a Fate unbeneficently relational, should ever be accepted by the settled faith of the world. If our faith, as we have it, is not regularly progressive, the same is true of many rivers running toward the sea ; they run backward in long circuits often, still they are even running towards it when running away from it, and are sure to reach it at last. Let us have no concern for this matter. We shall never get by the sense of sin, till the Lamb in the throne becomes a lost idea. Simply to think the supreme eminence there of the Lamb is to look on him we have pierced, and see him rising higher and yet higher, age upon age, and feel the arrows that were hid in his sorrows growing even more pungently sharp in our guilty sensibility. All the more resistless too will be the stabs of bad conviction, that they are meant to be salutary, and are in fact the surgery of a faithful healing power.

We are also shown by this revelation of the Lamb in the throne, and shall more and more distinctly see, that the nature of God is, in like manner, relational to redemption. The two points, in fact, go together and are verified by the same evidence. But while sin is not any work of God or of the Lamb, we are continually calling Christ's life and death his work, or his work of salvation. And we often put such operative force into the language, that one might think it a wholly perfunctory matter that we speak of—an undertaking or enterprise accomplished. It is true, I admit, that the Scriptures speak of Christ's engagement as a work; he also himself calls it his work; but it is only so far a work as it needs must be, to bring out a character and a feeling. It does not create the character or the feeling, it only gives them to us as they were in God before. He opened a way of forgiveness, as we often say, but the opening is to us and not to God. He was just as truly a forgiving God before. That is, it was in him and always before had been, to smooth out his heart in forgiveness to enemies, by making cost for them, and enduring them in the patience of sacrifice. The bleeding Lamb was in his nature before he bled on Calvary. His very being and character were relational to redemption, before they were related to our redemption. It is not for one moment to be imagined that Christ the Lamb has somehow softened God and made him better. He came down from God as the Lamb that was slain from the foundation of the world, and the gospel he gave us is called the everlasting gospel, because it has been everlastingly in God, and will everlastingly be. It does not simply mean that God is able, and always had been, to put himself on terms of benevolence with us. He is on such terms originally, with all beings of all worlds, and even with the animals. The free forgiveness of sin implies a great deal more than any such well meaning disposition. For in every moral nature most righteous, and partly because it is righteous, there is a certain recoil from the bad, a certain moral anger that does not cease because he says the word "forgive." Well-willing, or benevolence, signifies nothing in the matter; there must be sorrow, suffering, bleeding endured; something that makes cost on the passive side of the nature. Then, and not till then, the true forgiveness comes; a blessed and clean reconciliation, thinking no more of just letting the culprit go, but rejoicing in the fact that it has gained a brother. And this is what we mean when we speak of propitiation. We mean that God's nature is so far relational to redemption, that his glorious passibilities are bleeding always into the bosom of evil. There is a fixed necessity of blood, and he has the everlasting fountain of it in his Lambhood. So that condemnation for evil, or sin, is not a whit more sure to follow than forgiveness, sweetened by self-propitiation.

It was proposed to show, thirdly, that having the Lamb now in the throne, it will be more and more clear to men's thoughts that God's most difficult and really most potent acts of administration are from the tenderly enduring capacity of his goodness, represented by the Lamb. The richness and patience of his feeling nature, in one word his dispositions, are the all-dominating powers of his reign. What he is in the Lamb—determines what he is and does universally.

Thus if you look in upon the stock-powers of his mind and character, you will be very soon convinced that his dispositions are the first matter with him, just as they are with us. From them every thing proceeds. The Lambhood of his dispositions will subordinate every other function. His counsel, wisdom, plans, cosmical order, purpose, will-force and creative fiat begin at his dispositions, and not his dispositions at them; for what could they do in preparing dispositions that by supposition are not? Always, in all rational beings, the dispositions are first, and the actings afterward. The Lambhood nature therefore in God dominates all other nature in Him beside. What we have been calling the dynamic factors of His being, which in fact the philosophers commonly take to be the whole of it, are only purveyors and executive servitors to the dispositions. And all they do will be done to further the ends and fulfill the mandates of the dispositions. So that, looking in upon the glorious realm of attributes and powers in God's internal armory, we may not scruple to say, that even there the Government is on the shoulder of the Lamb. And if it be something for God to rule the world, it can not be less for the Lamb to bear like sway in God.

A second illustration of the supreme potency of the Lamb, or of God as represented by his painstaking love and sacrifice, may be discovered in the fact that he is able to love the bad; that is to love directly across moral distinctions, and even in spite of all deserts of character. He can love the cruel, the blasphemers of his name, the mean, the filthy, the disgusting. It is true that by his gracious help we ourselves can be raised up to the same high level with him in this prerogative of his Lambhood. But it is not the teaching or conceived honor of the world. Outside of the gospel, it is universally assumed that love is related to loveliness, and that loveliness is the qualifying base, or quickening cause of love, save that in what is called natural affection the love is purely instinctive and goes by necessity. But in proper voluntary love, what man or teacher of morality ever imagined the possibility of loving the bad, and even of loving them into love and the goodness of a new-born life? And is there any greater stretch of power conceivable than that? Let any mightiest soul of mankind, who is not in the way of sacrifice with Christ, try what he can do in loving the bad?

Observe again also that the Lamb assumes to go through souls with a lustral and transforming power, from his passion. Therefore behold, behold the Lamb of God that taketh away the sin of the world. He undertakes, in this manner, by the quickening force of his cross, to beget them, as it were, anew, and be the new creator of their life. All this by the depth of his feeling and the sovereignty, so to speak, of his sacrifice. And who is there that, without him, will undertake, in any such way, to new character the race, or even a single man. What other power of gods or men can cope with such a problem? Doubtless a man may be managed correctively, in a way of partial improvement, by his fellow man, but to be transformed regeneratively, and have the sin taken out of his fiber, who will do that? Yet in Christ there is a godly or rather lambly sorrow, tender as the dews of the morning, and liquidly vital as they; there is a bleeding out of God's own sensibility on the rock no mortal persuasions could melt, which is his inevitably dissolving baptism, and from out of this our repentances run clear, even as the brooks run out from their springs. And so, with a meaning how deep, how grandly triumphant we chant our confession—"For the blood of Christ cleanseth us from all sin."

And again it is a singular and mightily impressive demonstration for the Lamb, that he goes into causes, retributive causes, incorporated in the system of nature itself, and turns them off from their victims. The grace does not stop at nature, as if here was a barrier impassable, but it undertakes boldly, instead, to so far stop even the wages of sin itself. But it does not call on the dynamic forces of God to intervene, and shake off by a fiat the retributive laws and causes that have fastened their grapple on the man, but it infuses gently into him or into his faith, that personal, supernatural, life-giving spirit, that will go through his disordered members, and touch, as it were solvently, all the secret bonds and propagative chains of causes by which he is held, and is otherwise so to be holden forever. It does not require force in such a case to break the chains of causes; any drop of the blood of the Lamb, any tenderest touch, that is, of God's sorrowing life and feeling is enough. Why the very joints of the rocks—did they not burst open when the blood of the Lamb fell on their faces? And when that Lambly power gets entered into any bosom of transgression, what shall we see but that all the retributive laws of all the worlds, crowding in, can no longer hold him fast, or keep him back from his liberty.

We make another very wide and very impressive stage of advance in our apprehensions of the essential supremacy of the Lamb, when we discover that our notions of the governmental order of the world, or what we call Providence, are becoming, and will hereafter seem to be, more and more graciously mitigated. Having now the Lamb in the throne, we are to have no more a merely punitive and dry absolutism; our Providence will be a true Lamb-Providence. I mean by this a complete world-government working in the interest, fulfilling the counsel, and dispensing even judgment, in the feeling of the Lamb. We shall remember his word when he went up—"All power is given unto me, in heaven and in earth. Go ye therefore and teach all nations, and lo, I am with you always." We shall not look to see him bursting out in retribution suddenly, and hurrying on his judgments, as many in their feeble panic have been wont to do, but making gentle suit rather, and waiting as in pauses of sorrow. He will set all things civil and religious working together for his great kingdom's sake, as a being absolutely one in all; purifying churches by their dissensions, truths defiled by their corruptions, principles of order and liberty by great conspiracies and public wars, learning and science by the ravages they muster of unbelief and presumption; leading in and out thus the successive ages of history, to settle new problems and winnow clean away the chaff of society. His work is silent, and commonly shows no sign; the timepiece runs without any click of sound —but yet it runs! And when some great world-crisis comes, in earthquake, or storm, or fire, we know that only a seal of the everlasting, seven-sealed book of Providence is going now to be opened for a new chapter, and that Christ hath prevailed to open the book himself. And we hear the four-and-twenty elders round about the throne crying—"worthy art thou to take the book and open the seals thereof, for thou wast slain, and hast redeemed us to God by thy blood." It is only redemption now that carries on the counsel of Providence, and opens the seals thereof. John's book of Revelation becomes, in this manner, a book of Providence all through, celebrating, as the crises arrive, all the overturnings of Christ's advancing empire, with successive hymns and acclamations; chanting everywhere the Lamb, the Lamb, the Lamb that was slain; sometimes, when public wrong is incorrigible and fierce, the wrath, and always the victory of the Lamb; closing off at the river that proceedeth out of the throne of God and the Lamb; and showing there installed and everlastingly established, a glorious and complete Lamb-Providence for the world.

Once more and briefly, I must carry up my subject a stage higher, and show you the world of the glorified crystallizing and crystallized, in the all-dominating sway of the Lamb. The everlasting, universal kingdom reigns by him—"Of whom the whole family in heaven and earth is named." It is not in the dynamics of God's nature, the will, the counsel, the operative work and purpose, that the kingdom is organized, save as these are first organized under his blessed dispositions; we nowise give the true account, till we say, "to make all men see what is the fellowship of the mystery, which, from the beginning of the world, hath been hid in God, who created all things by Jesus Christ." There he is in the throne where he fitly belongs—"That at the name of Jesus every knee should bow—of things in heaven, and things in earth, and things under the earth. And that every tongue should confess that Jesus Christ is Lord to the glory of God the Father." Therefore, "Blessing, and honor, and glory, and power, be with him that sitteth upon the throne, and unto the Lamb forever and ever."

There comes out now, my friends, in the closing of this great subject, a question which I have not so much as named, though it has all along been urgently propounding itself; viz., what of the deity of Christ? Is he the Lamb in the throne, or is he not? And if he is not, what of Christianity? For one, I really do not know. In this article of Lambhood, and the coronation state which reveals it, I behold the major-part and supreme glory of deity; and without this major-part I really do not see much in God to attract me. I do not very much want a God whose endowments and quantities, such as human thought and philosophy muster, are the principal sum of his nature. But I want a God relational to my sin and my redemption, a God whose sensibilities and self-renouncing passibilities are the containing causes of his dispositions, and the determining causes, in that manner, of his character and counsel. Such is the God our scriptures offer us, and the story of the Lamb ended off, by the crowning of the Lamb, is really the dearest and grandest of all the divine evidences; and when we distinguish this most tender and sufficiently authorized pledge of forgiveness in the throne, where God, as being the Lamb, hangs out his flag of sorrow, calling us back, we shall want, I think, no other evidence of his deity than what we have in our feeling.

XXII.

OUR RELATIONS TO CHRIST IN THE FUTURE LIFE.

"And when all things shall be subdued unto him, then shall the Son also be subject unto him that put all things under him, that God may be all in all."—1 *Cor.* 15 : 28.

THAT Christ is to be in some sense eternal, and the eternal joy of all believers, we can not willingly doubt. Or if any one may turn this rather singularly marked passage of scripture, in a way to make it signify his being sometime merged in God, so as to be no longer discoverable, whether in his person, or in his kingdom, we may easily set the declaration of Christ himself over against it—"And if I go and prepare a place for you, I will come again and receive you unto myself, that where I am there ye may be also." A full hundred other passages equally explicit might be added from the gospels and the epistles, all affirming it as a principal distinction of the heavenly felicity, that Christ is eternally present in it, giving recognitions of his friendship, and permitting free approach to his person. A very great part of them indeed are also from Paul, and it is no wise probable that what he says in one is to contradict and overturn all he teaches in the others. There is no way then, as we may see at a glance, but to seek some intermediate and modified construction of his one passage, that will accommodate the faith declared in so many others, of a future felicity, constituted by the presence of Christ with and among his people. In doing which we raise the very important, and, to all right living in the gospel hope, grandly practical question,—

What kind of personal relation to Christ we are to hope for and hold, as our authorized and fixed expectation, for the future life?

I confess that I undertake this question partly for my own sake, hoping to be drawn by the deliberate treatment of it, towards conceptions more satisfactory and determinate. And if it should happen that this is the last sermon I am permitted to give, it will not be amiss that, for once, I have preached to myself. It may be too that others, who are waiting for the veil to be lifted, want the same kind of help that I thus confessedly seek on my own account.

Among those who hold the Trinity more lightly, or in a more nearly Sabellian way, as a dramatizing of God to serve the occasional uses of redemption, it is common to assume the discontinuance of it, when the uses of redemption no longer require it. Having completed the subjugation of evil, the Son is now to be subject himself, that God, who has put all things under him, may be all in all. God is thus reduced back to his complete normal unity. Trinity is gone, and the absolute One, the strictly Unitarian God, has the whole field to himself.

But there is a fatal want of depth in this conception. If there was a necessity of the Three to carry on the redemption of the world, as this partly Sabellian view supposes, it was not a necessity of sin, but of mind—finite mind, all finite mind; existing therefore *ab æterno in æternum.* Besides a further account of the matter is possible, showing that God's personality, and also his practical infinity are no otherwise maintainable, than by means of trinity. An impersonal God, such as pantheism offers, is a merely Infinite Thing, in which all our religious instincts are mocked; finding no attribute of rationality, or love, or moral consciousness, that permits dependence, or even the sense of a personal relation. We must therefore have, we say, a personal God; and we make issue for God under that word. He is either personal, we feel, or else he is naught.

And yet God is not a person—we are obliged to deny what we affirm in the word. He is only a person in the sense that he is a rock, or a sun, or a sea. He is not a literal rock, sun, sea, but only these in a figure. So he is no literal person, but an infinite substance, shadowed to our feeling in such qualities as belong to person, borrowing this finite figure from ourselves. If we understand ourselves, we only mean by the word, that his incomprehensible nature is such as to permit us a practically social relation. After all, his personality is best affirmed, only when he is represented as three persons. For if we call him one person, as in the supposed better philosophy of the Unitarian teaching, using and reiterating always that finite person-figure, it results in a gradual and inevitable sinking of God's magnitudes, till he falls into place in the pronouns of our grammar, as being virtually one of ourselves—working in our humanly personal methods of conjecture, computation, inference, reasoning by words, thinking one thought after another, willing in new determinations. We try to save ourselves from this collapse in idea, by adding on the epithet infinite as a magnifier; and it is as if God were only a man written large, without any thing added for enlargement; for if we call him an infinite person, the noun, person, is the only part of our designation that has any positive meaning, and the adjective, infinite, is merely a negative of boundary that indicates our purpose of enlargement, while adding nothing, as regards the divine quantities, to accomplish it. And just here we discover the real merit and value of trinity, in that it saves the just dimensions of God's attributes, without making an impersonal platitude of his infinity. As the grammatic one person for God is a finite figure, so are each of the three. They are, therefore, neither one nor three, a completely exact notation for God; but the three, when taken all together, do compose a large approximation, the best that human language permits. Set in personal relativity with each other and with us, they preserve and keep always in sight, the personal quality, or function; creating, at the same time, a maze for the mind, by the indefinable cross relations of three persons, such as practically infinite the conception of God's nature; which they do by raising a pitch of mystery that prevents any mental collapse into the always diminishing effect of a single person.

We help ourselves in the conceiving of space in a way strongly analogous. We call it infinite space, well knowing that we are weak on the adjective. We then take up three lines of direction, length, breadth, and height, and running them out till we are obliged to stop—for we can not make them more than finite—we give them as our notations of infinite space. And yet the lines are not space at all, they are only instrumentations by which we conceive it. In much the same way, we conceive the infinite personality of God, by three persons, all grammatically finite. They are instrumentations inherently necessary to all finite mind, and, being necessary, God can never be thought of in any world without them, so as to save the full effect of his personality, and the proximately full impression of his greatness. They are just as necessary for the due conceiving of God, as the three lines were just now seen to be for the conceiving of space.

If now it should occur to some one that our trinity is grounded thus in ourselves—that is in our finite want—and belongs in no sense possibly to God; and if it should be demanded, since three finite persons, or images of such, are wanted to preserve the magnitudes of God, why not six, or sixty? it may fairly be answered; first, that too great a number would produce distraction, landing us in all the vices and weaknesses of polytheism. Probably three persons come about as near producing distraction as it may be advisable to go; creating a maze that, being carried farther, might fatally unsettle the composure of our faith. Six lines of direction, or sixty, might do something to help out our conception of space, but the three just named will do more. But, secondly and more decisively, it may be answered, that there are reasons, or distinctions in God's own nature, as thought by us, answering exactly to our necessity as finite beings, which fix the number three to be the number of the persons. Thus, as we just now found three lines of direction, which may be called the categories of space, so there are three principal categories in the nature of God, which take up or contain, as far as finite thought is concerned, all that he is. Thus we may think God as the All-Father, the Original Base or Fontal Source, out of whom all things proceed and at whom all beginnings begin; also as the Word or Expression Principle, the All-Beautiful and ideally Perfect Form of God's Intelligence and Holiness—which Word is Son, as being the perpetually born image of the Father, when he thinks himself, and bodies himself to us—also as the Pervasive Spirit or Going-Through Principle, by which God moves and sovereignly Imbreathes in us and things—the Everlasting Waft of Deity. So we have, in these three categories, the composite material of God exhaustively conceived, as Father, Son and Holy Ghost. Nothing more can be added, which they will not take in. And these three categories we represent as persons. Which three are persons only in some undefinable way that puts them in practical relationship with us. They do not move transitionally in space. They neither forget nor remember but always absolutely know. They have no new thoughts and no personal development. They do not plan among facts, but in the everlasting possibilities back of facts. And yet they are so related to our moral and social nature, that we can be sure of an approach and an experimental realization. We call them persons, not knowing exactly what we affirm, and yet none the less confident that we are affirming what is somehow related to our inmost social life. Our image is imperfect, but it is as good as the grammar of human speech allows. Or if some one should suggest that for aught that appears our personal pronoun *they*, covering confessedly personalities we can not definitely conceive, but can only play into our socially religious nature, may after all be only neuter plurals, plurals of *it*, such as grammar endows with imputed personality when in fact they have none, it must be enough to answer, that by setting them,—the persons—in trinity, as one that is three and three that are one, we affirm a cross identity and coalescence that is not possible of any three things and can be only of persons. And in this view it is the particular merit of trinity, and is forever to be, that, as finite persons, we can steadily hold the personality of God, without reducing him at all to our measures; as we certainly should, if we thought him always as a single person.

We have now a great first point established; viz., that when the Son is spoken of as finally to be made subject, or so far discontinued as to let God be all in all, it can not be meant that the Son is to be taken away, or disappear, in any sense that modifies at all the fact of trinity. If God is to be all in all, it must be as trinity and not otherwise.

In adopting this conclusion I am properly required to make answer to an objection that may be raised; viz., that when the everlasting need and fact of trinity are thus asserted, there ought to be an appearance of trinity in the Old Testament, which is not there affirmed. Expositions are to be given hereafter from the Old Testament for a different purpose that will sufficiently answer this; I need only observe therefore here, that while the trinity is not formulized in the Old as it is in the New Testament, the material of it is all there, as visibly as if it were set forth in the New Testament formula itself. Furthermore, I will first add, what is even a curiously forward evidence, that Trinity breaks in fact on discovery, in the very first chapter of Genesis; and that too in a way the more striking, that there appears to be no thought, or intellectual consciousness of the fact. Making nothing of the fact that the very name God [*Elohim*] is plural, for we do not know what causes back of the word gave it the plural form, we have first the Fontal God, the Father, the God in first beginning "creating the heavens and the earth." Then we have the Movement or Waft-Power, the Spirit moving "upon the face of the waters," to beget form and order in the formless. And finally, coming to the creation of man, we have a deliberation that for some reason indicates, in figure, at least, a plural consciousness, saying, "Let us make man in our image and likeness." In which words "image and likeness" reference is had to the Everlasting Son who is the God-Moral humanly conceived, the image and type of all God is, in his possibilities of Beauty and Character. Finding trinity thus in the very first chapter of Revelation, we can not be required to look farther.

Going forward then into the future life, so much appears to be determined; that we shall there know God unalterably and forever as trinity—Father, Son, and Holy Ghost. The Son therefore, as discovered in trinity, is of course never to be merged, or passed out of sight, or in such a sense made subject. How then shall we understand the apostle when he testifies that the "Son" shall be subject or retired from the view? He is speaking plainly of the Son as incarnate, or externalized in the flesh, visible outwardly, in the man-form and known as the Son of Mary. He it is that, after having—as a king outwardly regnant,—put all things under his feet, is in turn to become subject also himself, that God may be all in all, and the machineries hitherto conspicuous be forever taken back as before the advent.

The only objection I perceive to this construction is, that the word Son here appears to be used in connection with the word Father—"delivered up the kingdom to God even the Father,"—"then shall the Son also"—as if it were intended to say that the Son as in trinity is to give place to the Father as in trinity, and he to be henceforth sole deity. But there is a two-fold relationship of Father and Son appearing and reappearing constantly; viz., that of the Father to the incarnate Son and that of the Father to the pre-incarnate Son; that which gives him earthly Fatherhood and that which gives him celestial, ante-mundane Fatherhood. The apostle was not careful here to put a guard for the saving of the eternal Sonship, because he did not imagine the need of saving that, any more than of saving deity itself. He was only thinking of the mortal Sonship, and giving us to see the essentially temporal date of its continuance.

Trinity then as he conceives will remain, but the mortal Sonship, the man, will disappear and be no more visible. And let us not too hastily recoil from this. It may be that we have been promising ourselves a felicity in the future world, made up almost wholly of the fact, that we shall be with Christ in his humanly personal form, and have used this hope to feed our longings, quite apart from all higher relations to his Eternal Sonship. There are multitudes who mean to be, and really think they are, supereminently Christian people, whose piety is but a kind of caressing of themselves before Jesus the man, or a canting, or caressing repetition they practice on his name. Their word is Jesus, always Jesus, never the Christ; and if they can see Jesus in the world to come, they do not specially look for any thing more. Heaven is fully made up, to their low type of expectation, if they can but apprehend the man and be with him. Sometimes it is not difficult to see that the piousness enjoyed in their cantillation of the name Jesus is really idol worship. It is hardly necessary to say that in such a use of the ever dear name, they put a virtual fraud on the gospel. The gospel hangs, for all its operative value and spiritual consequence to the world, on the fact that Jesus is the Christ, the man-form used as vehicle for the eternal Word and Lord. Religion reaches after God, and God is Trinity, and all the gospel does, or can do, by the name and human person of Jesus, is to bring us in and up to a God, who is eternally above that name.

Our relations to Christ, then, in the future life, are to be relations to God in Christ, and never to the Jesus in Christ. They center in the triune deity, and specially in the Eternal Word or Son, who is represented more specially, for a time, in the person of Jesus. But when that which is perfect is come, that which is in part will be taken away. Christ will remain, because the Eternal Son is in him, but the Jesus, the human part, will be made subject, or taken away, because all that he could do for us in the revelation of God is done.

There is, I know, a much less questionable conception of our gospel which has its blessedness in Jesus, because it meets God in him, and is specially drawn to his humanity, because it even finds the fullness of

God bowed low in his person. This so far is genuine gospel. And it would not be strange, if a disciple thus wonted in God, should imagine that the joy of his faith is conditioned forever, by the human person at whose ministry or from whose love it began. What then is the future glory, he will ask, if it does not bring him in, where he can see the very man of the cross? 'All my expectation stretches hitherward,' he may say—fabulating visit and vision to express his grief—'I cross over to be with him, I press in eagerly to behold him, but I can not find him. I grope along the dusky streets of gold, asking where the Son of Man is to be seen, and they tell me that he is made subject, and is no more to be visible. Whereupon I sit down baffled, and sick, and even spilling some sad tears on the pavement; groaning inwardly that my heaven turns out to be a poor illusion, a confidence of beholding the man, who yet in fact is nowhere. Dreary and forever dry world this, where the chief among ten thousand, he in whom I learned to seek all good and find all dearest peace, is gone out forever and lost!' Ah! but you shortly catch a note that is music indeed, a strain that has been a long time wonted in your heart—"Worthy is the Lamb,"—"The Lamb that was slain,"—"for thou hast redeemed us to God by thy blood." And who is this but him that you seek? Surely he is somehow here, and this is somehow he. You missed him, perchance, because you were looking too low down, out of the range of deity, to find him; whereas now you find him throned in God, hymned in God, as the everlasting Son of the Father—and yet he is somehow Son of Mary still, even as he is the Lamb that was slain. Whereupon, as you think farther, you begin to see, that the humanly mortal, the humble and poor Christ, dusted with sore foot travel, as on his way up from Galilee, is in fact the everlasting Son, as in Trinity, and took his mortal guise only for a day, that he might prove his gentle condescensions and draw us in the level of brotherhood. And then, ascending to the Father, and the glory that he had with him before the world was, you have it as your liberty to possess him still as charactered in his mortality, to hail him as the Lamb, or behold him as the mortal brother, and see in fact the whole Christ-feeling in him, such as he was to you when he was with you below.

Our conclusion then is that the pre-incarnate Son of the Father is the incarnate Son of Man; the same that was made flesh and dwelt with men, bore his mortal poverty, wept his mortal tears, and died, for men, to be the propitiation for their sins. Only he is now made subject; which means that he returns into God where he belongs and is duly glorified. How else should it be with him? Of course he would not stay incarnate forever. He is not here as being mortgaged forever to humiliation. He came into his mortal work that he might be made subject when his work is done; which being made subject only means that he is entered back into God and the ascendancy that belongs to Him as the all in all. And lest he should seem in this reëxaltation to be lifted quite above us, and lest we should seem to have lost the lowly one we learned to love so tenderly, and now remember as having been so nearly evened with him in his lot, how grandly will it comfort us to know that he is now, and is forever to be just what he was historically; that as he was the Lamb of God, so now he is all that in the throne; that as being in the form of God he took the form of a servant, so now he is a servant in the form of God; bowing all his honors sweetly down to let us see our Christ centered everlastingly in Trinity itself. Back there under that veil is the Son of Mary, the Child of her Manger, the Healer that came about on foot, and slept uncovered by the roads and on the mountains, he that was bowed to suffering, he that could be hated and die—all this he is above, as charactered for us by what he was here below; nowise exalted above it, but rather by it, forever. Gone by as the Jesus, also as the Christ under time, he is yet the Eternal Son forever Christed by his mortal story; so that we behold him eternized as our Christ, and hear him saying as it were out of his humanity—"I am Alpha and Omega, the beginning and the ending which is and which was and which is to come." It is as if the Christ we loved were visible in all his dear humanities, though Trinity alone is left.

At this point we reach what may be called the outline conception of the subject. But to make it more clear, and settle the relation of it more definitely to certain current ideas, I undertake to controvert and correct our current ideas in two particular points, where they seem to obstruct any such conception of the view already stated, and forbid us to rest in it, as one of the finalities, or true Last Things.

1. We have it as a commonly accepted article of doctrine, that the incarnate person includes a human soul, and by this human soul, contriving what is to become of it, all our perplexities in the question of our future relations to Christ are created. That, as being incarnate, he has "two natures and one person," is agreed by us all; but when we come to analyze the human-nature part, as the teachers began to do some centuries later, finding it composed of "a true body and a reasonable soul"—that is of a proper human body and a proper human soul or spirit—there is more room for doubt. I do not here deny that there was a proper man-soul involved in the incarnation, or incarnate person—I carefully abstain from doing it—but I do most peremptorily deny that any one can show it. Doubtless there are inferences enough that may be drawn to make it a most logically irrefragable conclusion. Is he not distinctly called a man many times over? and what is a man without a soul? He also prays, he acquires knowledge, he moves about in space as omnipresence does not, he suffers and by suffering is made perfect, and, to sum up all, he makes advances mentally in the ways of a strictly human development—represented therefore as growing in wis-

dom and character, like all other human children—what then is left us but the conclusion, as by necessary logic, that he had a proper human soul included in his person? Accordingly we have, I know not how many sermons showing the complete humanity from the complete and distinctly observable human development. The argument goes to the mark easily, and we really suppose that every thing is established. But the moment we cross over to the other shore the tables are turned, and we find that about the toughest matter we have there on hand is, to find where the man-soul of Jesus is to go, and what is to become of it. We began before we crossed over, to observe that our "two natures and one person" had been running us into two natures making two persons, and we also had some twinges of suspicion that our very exposition of the development assumed the fact, not of a finite human nature only, but of a finite human person to be thus developed; for a mere human nature, observe, included under the "one person" of the first orthodoxy, and dominated by the supreme consciousness of that one person, will signify as little to itself, as any floating speck does in the tide-swing of the sea; and then what liberty is there as a condition of development? Accordingly now, in its second-life state, this man-soul becomes a most unreducible, nondescript being that allows no classification.

First, that the eternal Son of God, having his place in God as trinity, is to be duplicated forever in a Sonship out of trinity, we can not imagine; for what then is to become of this second outside Sonship? Next we can not more easily imagine that, as being the Eternal Son, he has taken up the man-soul of the incarnation to be forever component in his divine nature; for in that case, from and after the incarnation, God would be a different substance, a conception wholly inadmissible—no such codicil to the divine nature belongs to the New Testament. What then next if the man-soul, taken up, be disengaged from the incarnate person and become a proper man, a Jesus visible forever by himself? If so there is certainly no very special felicity to come of being with him. After all we have said of his development, he can have no specially supereminent character. He has lived in shadow all his thirty years, under the all-swaying will of the one superdominant person. He has not done a work, or thought a thought, or loved, or willed, or suffered, or conquered a temptation, on his own account, in the right of his own free agency. Had he been chloroformed and laid by these thirty-three years, he would be as far on in all that constitutes character.

We go back now from this excursion across the river, and reëxamine our argument for the man-soul from its supposed development. And here we discover that our logical inferences were all at fault, in the fact that the incarnate person is an abnormal person, and for aught that appears, wholly out of range, for any sort of argument we are master of. We might as well reason out the fire of the burning bush by the inference that it can not be fire, because it does not burn; or the wine of Cana by showing that, having come out of the water, it must have been in the water before. All arguments in the categories of the ordinary are but idle play, when applied thus to the extraordinary. The facts of the development do indeed prove development in some sense; but the real question still is left—whether the incarnate Son of God himself was not that soul or nature that was developed? That he became the germ, the born infant, the child, the boy, the youth, the man, and finally the ascended and glorified Son of the Father, passing on *gradatim,* and up through, taking and making all the history himself is not a whit more difficult than the fact of incarnation itself—infinite in finite. And do not the scriptures very nearly assert this conception? As when they declare—"And the Word was made flesh," we understand them to say that the Word itself became the ensouling principle, the man of the incarnate person. So when Christ calls himself the bread that came down from heaven, adding—"the bread that I will give him is my flesh, which I will give for the life of the world," he is evidently thinking only of his own divinely conscious person, and the body by which he gets connection with the world. Nothing is farther off than to imagine that he is thinking here of a man-soul lurking under the flesh that is not it, nor himself. Again also, when the apostle says—"For since by man came death, by man came also the resurrection of the dead;" he does not mean of course that a certain human soul or nature in Christ raises the dead, but that he himself in his divine order and life does it—he is the man. So again when he says—"For as by one man's disobedience many were made sinners, so by the obedience of one, [i. e., one man,] many were made righteous," he has no thought of saying that the obedience of the man-soul person was able to impart righteousness, but only that the incarnate Lord is able, as being himself the man. And yet again, once more, he tells exactly who this man, so potently working is—"the second man is the Lord from heaven." In which he comes as near saying that the man of the incarnate person is the Lord himself, as he well could. All these declarations I cite, not to prove that there is no human soul in the person of Christ, but to show how little accountable the scriptures are for the common assumption made of it. It is an incumbrance that we reason out for ourselves, by inferences from facts totally abnormal; an elephant that we capture, and after that can no way find what to do with it.

It further remains to say, as regards the particular matter now in hand, that the scriptures give us, in the positive, conceptions of God as related to man, and of man as related to God, such as very nearly supersede all these difficulties respecting Christ hereafter, and open a fair possibility of being practically with him as subsisting in trinity. Thus, if we take what is said, several times over, of our being made in the image of God, and of Christ being incarnate in the same, an inference runs backward, as we may see, that God is in our image, and also in Christ's image, and Christ and we in the same image; whence also it follows that, before creation and before incarnation, God himself was somehow, or in some sense, Man. He had, that is, an anthropoidal nature, which anthropoidal nature is a kind of Divine Man-Form or Word, by which he thinks himself, incarnates himself, and types himself in his creations. And thus it is that the Jehovah angel, and all the mysterious visitors called angels, take the man-form in their appearing, whether in fact physically bodied or not. Thus Daniel saw in vision a celestial Son of Man not incarnate—"behold one like the Son of Man came with the clouds of heaven, and came to the Ancient of days," [the Father] and had given him, as he came near, "dominion and glory, and a kingdom." Again he represents Nebuchadnezzar as looking down into the fiery furnace, where he had cast the three bold confessors, and crying out in astonishment, "Lo, I see four men loose, walking in the midst of the fire, and the form of the fourth is like the Son of God." And this same notion of the Son of God as being in the form of God, and so a Man, travels down, we see, through the New Testament—"Who being in the form of God, thought it not robbery to be equal with God. But made himself of no reputation, and took upon him the form of a servant, and was made in the likeness of men."

Now in this brief retrospect of the scripture ideas

and methods, we discover, as plainly as need be, that when the Son was to be incarnate, it was not necessary for him to take up a tiny man-soul, not before existing, always to be unused and without character of its own—humanity was in the type of his own everlasting person before. He must needs begin his incarnation at the germ state of our nature; for he could not otherwise be incarnate as in history; he would only break in casually, as an apparition or epiphany, to break out again when he pleases and be gone. But he wanted to be integral in the race, and live himself into record with us, even as Aristides, or Socrates, or Antoninus. So he took the germ-life and its tiny possibilities just as all men do, and in that life, as if limited in a sense by age, and size, and experience, he expected to grow, or unfold *gradatim* into all the stages of wisdom, and power, and progressive manhood. "For though he were a Son [Son of God] yet learned he obedience by the things which he suffered, and being made perfect—graduated into full divinity—he became the author of eternal salvation unto all them that obey him." We are not inside of this development, we can not reason it, or imagine it, for it is abnormal. We only conceive that the Son of God himself is the subject of it, and that we have no more reason to suppose a man-soul joined with him in it, and possibly eternized in him after he has passed the grade of a man's development, than we have to suppose the germ-life, the infancy, the child, the boy, the young man eternized, when the advances made in years leave them behind.

Our being then with Christ in the future life, begins at being with the Son of God in trinity. Nay it both begins and ends with that; for if, in our miseducated ways of thought, we seem about to miss, in that manner, being at all with the personal manhood, in whose conscious friendship it was our hope to be joined, we discover the Man, even the God-Man everlastingly present, integrally present, in trinity before either we or the world began to be. Furthermore we may also discover that the matter which most distinguishes the fact of his reascension to the Father, is not that he is gone up as a human-nature soul to be glorified, and to set us in the faith of an everlasting companionship with him, but that being himself the Eternal Man brought low, he has gone up to be glorified again, as he prayed himself—"And now, O Father, glorify thou me, with thine *own self,* with the glory that I had with thee before the world was." And what hope can be as inspiring and reassuring to us as that Christ has gone up thus to be the Son of God, and has lost nothing, left nothing behind, because of his humiliations. We must not ask to have the story end off in dejection, and to see the man sit weeping still and forever in his sorrows. We want exactly what is given us to see, the due enthronement of his sacrifice, showing him exalted forever to the throne of God and of the Lamb. Only in that word Lamb, regal as it is now become, there is a flavor of tenderness and loving patience that gathers up all the memories of the cross, and flavors by them even the divine greatness itself. Such is God, as the great Lamb-history paints him. Ask we then for the man? the man of the cross? this is he; not another Son of God better than the trinity affords, but the very same that was before, more lovingly conceived, in that he has brought himself down low to us, wading deep in our sorrows, and tasting even death for us and our sins.

2. The other point to be considered and corrected is more simple, and may be dispatched more briefly. Thus it is an impression of many that we are to be with Christ, in the sense of beholding him with our eyes. But it can not be imagined that we are to behold God, whether in three persons, or one, in this manner. The only beholding conceivable is that of faith. And there is a talent of faith in our human nature, that is much taller and closer to the infinite, than some of our wise unbelievers have commonly dared to conceive. It does not report things for knowledge, or cognitive perception, at some nervous center, as in the five senses; and does not work below with them, ranging always in the same field of matter and external fact, but it strikes out into a wider and wholly different, where things invisible and above sense have their own other-world. God, and truth, and right, and love, and the eternal invisible heaven, report themselves to this faith-talent when it is offered in congenial trust, and it is as if the general overhead or whole sky of the mind were quickened with a sense above sense, wide enough to

let in their evidence. It glimmers at no point, as when the five senses take in their knowledge, but it is the whole consciousness opened believingly to God, and the grand supersensible realities of religion. And so firmly pronounced is the conviction of the realities beheld by faith, that not even the realities of the senses are more strongly, often not as strongly, held. God, "the unknowable" as he is called, will sometimes utter himself in the knowledge thus of a believing consciousness, more indubitably than a rock or a mountain seen by the eyes. Faith beholds more piercingly than they, looks farther in, sweeps a larger horizon.

Besides, there is an impossibility, as regards making a heaven about Christ in terms of sight, which many have not considered. All sight objects are, by supposition, under conditions of space. They spread, they have measures of extension, and the seers themselves must have room. Christ therefore can be had by the eyes, in the future life, only as being at some point of space, and having his beholders round him in space. Seeing, observe, implies just this, else we do not know what we mean by it. How then can we ever be with him, where he is? how get near enough to him, one in a million, once in an age, to so much as look upon him? Instead therefore of trying how to sharpen our apprehensions of Christ by making it a case for sight, we had better, far better, sharpen our ideas of faith, and learn its amazing capacity. O what revelations of Christ come to us even here—greater by a thousand times than the mere eye-beholders of the Son of Mary ever saw, when he walked the earth. How much greater then are to come, when the vision of our faith is purged, as it will be. Ah, if we could stop our singing "When faith and hope shall cease," and begin to sing "now abideth faith, hope, charity, these three," into what more glorious, more inspiriting atmosphere should we be lifted! And God forbid our ever passing to any other world where faith, the grandest of all human powers, has nothing any more to do. Indeed what are we here for, when the matter is sounded to the bottom, but to get our inward visualities unsealed for the all-perceiving, illimitable faith-sense discovery of God and his kingdom.

Observe also this remarkable fact concerning faith, that it always sees the invisible in forms contributed by the visible; that is by what has before been seen, remembered, felt and wonted in experience. Thus it is how often that persons just born into the new life are taken by the conviction that they have actually seen Christ; which is true, in the sense that he has come into their consciousness, though not in the sense that they have seen him with their eyes. Faith has no draperies of its own, but is seeing its objects always in images borrowed from sense and memory. Thus beholding the state of the blessed, it imagines it to be a kind of sky-state and calls it heaven—adding gardens, and rivers, and gold, and gems, and a city that came down from God, even the new Jerusalem. And so when the Eternal Son, as in trinity, is beheld by faith he will be reclothed out of his earthly story, and it will even be as if there was a doubling back on the sight of his humanity. I do not say that our faith-perception will see the prints in his hands, or the scars on his brow, but we shall have him in the types of our memory, and think of him as the man of sorrows, the Lamb that bore our sins, the buffeted, the crucified. So that our being with him will be a beholding leveled eternally to our feeling, and a gloriously fresh partici-pation allowed us in the flavors of his humanly divine society.

Let me now add in closing, what I am thoroughly aware of, that I have not been trying to set this great world of the future in fascinating colors, or to engage you in the pursuit of it, by fresher and more glowing attractions. I have not been preaching it, but engineering for it rather; I have not shrunk from letting it be a difficult subject. And my reason for it is, the painfully fixed conviction of our being so far at loose ends in our conceptions, that steadiness of aim in the heavenly calling is scarcely at all permitted us. As to condition, circumstance, sceneries, and surroundings, we are indeterminate of course. But it should not be so, in our conceptions of Christ himself and his relations to us. For if we are striving after him and to be with him in a mixture of contrary and impossible ideas, or to think of him in a kaleidoscopic play of figures that put us at cross purposes continually in regard to his person, and to God and trinity as related thereto, we are rather distracted and baffled than helped by the inspirations of our hope itself. Hence to persons of intelligence and thoughtfulness, there is a random look of undiscerning declamation in what is said of the great future, that costs them, in the loss of their respect, more damage than we often know. There ought to be a possibility of salvation for sensible people. But there hardly can be, if we leave the great subject of Christ's future under vague, impossible, or even contrary conditions. I have been trying to initiate a more fixed conception of it; speaking in the conviction that there is no other, in which the Christian disciple can better afford to dig even whole years, if he can fitly master it. In no other field will his advances yield him greater returns of strength. In this study he will have his religious ideas concentrated more and more about Christ. He will discover a new glory in Christ, and conquer a new stability centered everlastingly in him. He will think of his friends who have already crossed the river, and will seem to be apprehending a little what they have now apprehended, O how distinctly! and to be with Christ—who is now become his clear possibility and steady North Star light—he will hold himself to the mark and make sure progress onward.